EATING FROM
THE CHERRY TREE

by

Vivien Ella Walden

A Memoir Of Sexual Epiphany

AUTHOR'S NOTE

Some names and events have been altered to protect people's privacy and for the sake of the story.

Dreaming that you see a cherry,
indicates that you are to find love.

To dream that you eat cherries,
predicts that you have damages ahead or that you
will be involved in intrigue and competition.

To dream of unripe cherries, is a sign of
problems ahead.

To dream that you picked cherries, predicts
that you have profits ahead, joy and happiness
in the family will also come.

A cherry blossom is a sign of hopes realised.

The cherry blossom symbolism is a very
significant symbol of power, typically it
represents a feminine beauty and sexuality
and often holds an idea of power or
feminine dominance.

CONTENTS

ACKNOWLEDGMENTS

*To all those present and past who have had my back and
supported me along the way*

and to the many that have paid the price.

PREFACE

"Good sex is the ultimate life experience. An orgasm felt deep inside that can be held on to until your quivering body and brain explode is an art in itself. Does this ultimate pleasure have a price? Of course, but doesn't everyone in some way pay it?

There are lessons that I have learnt that I have a need to share. Of how it is possible to descend into the abyss of sexual exploitation and emerge smelling of roses.

Reliving the truth has proved harder than I had thought, the flood of imagery amazing. I am swamped by visions, swept away and catapulted backwards into memories of childlike innocence. Did I delve into things I shouldn't have as a child? – Indeed I did.

Images of a complex girl have emerged, who ran from her heritage, bared her perfectly formed derriere and partied with the elite and famous. Gangsters, politicians, film stars, musicians and artists, they all knew of her industry, it was not unlike theirs. Being a stripper, call girl, hooker, or madam, you have to know how to dance to the music, be a good actress, stand up to the toughest, deal with the law and paint your own picture for all to see.

Entering into a life of 'commercial sex', be it on the stage, a brothel or bedroom, the most important skills are learning the art of negotiation, self-esteem, and knowing how to seduce a man completely, keeping him intrigued, before and after the clothes come off.

Every woman has different roles to play in pleasuring a man. But the 'working girl' who is skilled in her art is the one to be held on a pedestal. For she is the one who makes it possible to keep those home fires burning."

1

Chapter 1

The Ticking Clock

'We are of such stuff that dreams are made of.'

'Your face lights up when I come into the room.' Until he told me this I hadn't been aware that the smile that grabbed him was any different to how I greeted other men when they stepped into the reception of my Gentlemen's Club. The confidence that exuded from him was typical of most handsome men who called for services of pleasure. An awareness that it was always them doing us the favour, rather than the other way round. The truth was with all men, handsome or not, there was an overwhelming need to escape the normality of life.

The welcoming smile that drew his attention was staged practised. There was no real thought or feeling behind it and my smile remained constant as I took his money and that of the friend with whom he had arrived.

Pouring them a welcome drink, I had no desire to alter my expression, which lay firmly fixed as he requested the 'dirtiest' girls available, at the same time taking a phone call from his wife while eyeing the selection of beautiful bodies in front of him. Not one girl but two were required to fill his needs and while words of endearment like 'sweetie,' 'darling' and 'I love you' dripped from his unfaithful mouth towards the little wife at home, he at the same time beckoned each girl to come and rub up close to him while he took pleasure in sampling the firmness of their breasts and the softness between their legs.

The sight of the clock on the wall reminded me that these two lustful likely lads, who held an incredible sense of entitlement, were the last to take a trip up the stairs to fantasy land and get those bed springs squeaking. The working day was nearly over. It was past midnight and another hour would pass before I could leave this life and enter my other – less intriguing, less dramatic, less thrilling, perhaps, but what I now craved for.

Why do men commit adultery? He didn't seem to be a neglected husband, not with the amount of 'sweetie', darling' and 'love you' that flowed from his mouth. But, not to put too fine a point on it, if you are not having the sex that your man wants then someone else is. And as I sat alone in the room, wishing the clock's minutes to tick by, I took the time to think about the answers to two questions, the first one often asked of me, the second I am sure often discussed among those who thought they knew the answer.

Why do men commit adultery? The answer is simple: 'Because they are animals'. Society suppresses that guise, wishes to go against it and tries its damnedest to encourage monogamy. It ain't going to happen ladies! The male 'animal' will always want to pass on his sperm to as many willing females as possible. It's a natural need to prove their dominance. Once you realise this fact and accept it you are on the winning side and can easily whip your man down to size. Adultery is a 'playful game' and what's good for the goose is good for the gander, right?

Secondly, how come a sweet little Jewish girl, brought up in the hub of her religion by caring, devoted parents came to this style of life? How did it start and what triggered it? I hadn't so much forgotten as couldn't bring myself to remember or admit to myself why. Over time the reasons had faded into the mist. Other things became more important.

Whether I could remember the reasons or not was immaterial, the truth could have filled a handkerchief, soaking wet in my hands. And the sooner the question was answered and accepted the quicker I could dry my eyes of the memory.

If only my mother had told me I was pretty, something every little girl needs to hear, perhaps then the actress would have emerged and the acting stage she had chosen for me would have been trodden with confidence. Instead, I took to a different stage where my curves grabbed attention and where I would gain the acclaim and admiration I yearned for – from men that are so good at giving it.

'What nationality are you?' I would often be asked.

'I'm Jewish.'

It felt hard to wrap my mouth around the word 'Jewish'. It hardly seemed true anymore. Now with time and a need to learn more about my 'Jewishness', I had discovered the Talmud has an obsession with sex. Amazingly, it has to be the only religious text in the world to discuss and compare the penis size of its most venerated sages. I had become intrigued to discover a text of the highest respect was filled with an adulation for sex.

My thoughts were abruptly interrupted by, 'Hello, I need a word with you madam.' It wasn't so much what he said, but the way he said it, and with those words came a dreaded thought that it was going to be a long, drawn out night. I guessed right, I had an irate customer with deep concerns.

'I asked for deep throat oral but she shook her head and replied with 'sorry beiby I caon no do'. Unbelievable, I've coughed up 50 quid more than I usually pay to see this girl and she's treated me like some stinking tramp!' Whether this was a fair assessment by this man of leisure was anyone's guess. It was obvious the Brazilian beauty with her seductive accent had made her feelings clear and felt no reason to offer a rebuttal. I had always had the reputation of saying what I mean and meaning what I say, that was undisputed. Eliana, with all her Brazilian pizzazz, didn't possess that characteristic.

My thoughts had to be put on hold for a while, the clock on the wall would go on ticking, it now made no difference. Taking hold of my senses I took a good look at her accuser; his ego had been bruised, not to mention his self-esteem being shot to shit. The situation had to be handled very delicately. He needed to be built up, reassured, his self-esteem elevated. Comforting him would be easy, all I had to do was discretely mention the only reason for her refusal. It could only be that maybe the generous size of his penis would be too much for her to take. This did the trick and his ego immediately resurrected. Slipping my arm in his and guiding him towards the bar and offering him a refreshing drink, I placed the menu in his hand. 'Have you not checked the menu?' I sweetly asked. 'Take a look, there is bound to be something there to whet your appetite.' The menu was very different from a restaurant menu. 'Starters' consisted of foreplay activities, 'Main Course' consisted of different varieties of sex. All explained in great detail so there was no doubt what your choice would consist of.

With that he read the menu like he was studying for a degree. 'What is this here, 'hot and cold French'?'

'This is an oral technique,' I explained, 'where liquids of different temperatures are put on her mouth to stimulate the oral experience for you, would you like to experience it?' His reply was immediate – yes of course he would! 'Do you wish to have different company?'

Again his reply was immediate. 'Oh no, if all is good with Eliana, I am happy.' All was good and off he strutted up the stairs, apologising on his way to the Brazilian beauty who knew the hot and cold French experience would have to be sizzlingly good.

Pouring a well-deserved vodka and tonic with lots of ice I joined the remainder of my girls in the dressing room. I was greeted with anxious faces waiting for me to give the go ahead for them to change into their day wear and leave for home. 'Look at the time boss, how do you not lose it with arseholes like him!' They had checked the clock and it was indeed well past closing time.

My reply was simply said: 'What gift do you think a good madam has that separates them from the others?' Gaining their attention I continued. 'It's the gift of anticipation, and I'm a good madam, I'm better than good, I'm the best, I'm the perfect madam. I know how hungry they are and I help them choose the food from the menu. I know when they are tired and a bed will be shared with the right girl. I know when they are on edge after a hard working day – I know it before they do.' With that award winning explanation a look of respect appeared on their faces; hugs and kisses followed as I gave permission for them to get ready for home.

Returning to the bar for another well-deserved drink, a toast from a well-oiled business man greeted me. 'To my favourite madam who has helped to make my day feel good.'

My hard working day was nearly complete. 'I'll drink to that,' I said, and I did. He would return home to his unaware woman fulfilled and content, and I would be happy knowing I had helped him commit adultery for the good of all concerned.

When the last kiss goodbye was given I could see in their eyes and hear in their voices that they regarded me fondly, and that was 'thank you' enough. Pulling out of the car park I gazed into my rear view mirror, there were my girls hugging together, making their way to the taxi cabs that were patiently waiting for them. My thoughts were, I felt thankful that I had the opportunity to know them. They ran me through every emotion from cheers to tears, and had worn their way into my heart. These grown up women could transform themselves into helpless children with the blink of an eye.

My drive home seemed to take forever; I was so consumed in thought I didn't remember passing familiar places along the way. It was as if the car was driving itself, confident in the knowledge that it would get me home safely. I had taken my thoughts back in time recalling my childhood and the life I had chosen. How it started, what triggered it.

Chapter 2

The Family Affair

'Show me a child at the age of seven and I will show you the adult.'

'Mummy, did I have a pretty nose as a baby?'

'All babies have a pretty nose.'

'No, I mean me. Did I have a pretty nose?'

'What's pretty, anyway? Blow your nose and it will go smaller.'

Falling down the front door steps was a blessing in disguise. I was seven years old and, while looking up at my mother who was hanging out of the bedroom window waving me goodbye, I missed the step and went crashing down on to the gravel path.

School was out and in came the neighbours and a very anxious auntie, who stood looking at me in amazement, the shock on her face leaving me in no doubt as to how bad I looked. I couldn't tell – no mirror was allowed near my face.

Rather than hurrying me off for medical attention, however, mother waited till father arrived home from work. 'Why haven't you taken her to the doctor's surgery?' he demanded, his eyes bulging with anger, and within a couple of minutes, he and I were on our way. The nose, that wasn't in particularly good shape before, was certainly out of shape now. Thankfully, my sweet father insisted on it being reset. I have had a few broken bones over the years, but this one was one I was thankful for.

My Jewish childhood was probably the same as many others: I had caring parents.

My father was a tall and slender man with a striking face, big hazel eyes and black, slicked-back hair who loved football and horse racing, was athletic, mild-mannered and loving – a deep thinker with a sweet nature. Ask me what I remember about him and it has to be his wonderful singing voice and his merry whistling that used to fill our home every day.

My mother was a little over 5 feet tall and attractive, with black, dyed hair, bright blue eyes and a curvaceous figure. She adored the movies and before her marriage had cultivated her looks to resemble the Hollywood 30s film star Ginger Rogers, and everything about her was 'Hollywood'. From the beginning she had stars in her eyes about her only child, her daughter. My nights were spent sleeping with tight rags in my hair to create a Shirley Temple look the following morning. Did the pain matter? No, but the result did. Her sewing machine would be ringing in my ears all night, as she set about producing the prettiest of dresses for me to parade in. She had the stage set for me from the very beginning.

Both my parents worked in the clothing industry, hunched over sewing machines for long hours, to take home their hard-earned wages. This was a trade that had been passed down through generations of Jews, starting with the first immigrants escaping the controls of the Tsar in Russia. They arrived off a train at Victoria Station in Manchester, weather-beaten and exhausted from their long journey, to walk the long road up to Cheetham Hill, then called Hightown, and settled among others who had suffered the same fate. This was the road my grandparents took and settled in and where, eventually, my parents met.

In Russia, Jews who received an education in anything other than Hebrew were few and far between. Both my paternal grandparents only ever spoke Hebrew or Yiddish and it was down to my father, as the elder son, to take care of their needs and act as their translator. My grandfather never worked as such. Instead, he took to the road with horse and wagon, playing his own written music on the piano to Jewish communities near and far. My grandmother was a subdued, kind-natured woman, who made the best chopped liver in the world. She would jump to attention whenever my grandfather needed her to attend to his constant demands. I used to be frightened of his barking voice and cling to my father's coat tails when visiting on a Saturday, the Sabbath.

Father's sister was ostracised from the family home. Rumour had it that when much younger she dyed her hair blonde, to pretend she wasn't Jewish, and that she enjoyed the company of men who were German sympathisers. It was many years later that, through my grandmother's ill health, she was allowed back into the family fold, although my grandfather never once looked her way to acknowledge her. She was, though, obviously intelligent, being Bamber Gascoigne's assistant in the early TV productions of *University Challenge*.

My father's younger brother was an extremely handsome man, who like Dick Whittington, headed towards the bright lights of London with all he possessed on his back, to find his fortune.

I never knew my mother's parents. Grandmother had been run over by a bus as she was crossing Bury New Road, Salford, and died instantly from the impact. My mother was 11 years old, not a good time to lose a parent.

My maternal grandfather didn't take long to find a replacement wife through an arranged marriage. The wicked stepmother, who my mother thought was the devil in disguise, starved her and her siblings of both food and affection. Her blood son meanwhile, was pampered and fed with delicacies of which his stepsisters could only dream.

The starvation diet led to desperate acts. In the depths of their hunger one day, my mother and her youngest sister Stella were standing at the kitchen door, watching prunes boiling in a large pot on the stove and, unable to resist the temptation, Stella ran to grab enough of the sweet fruit from the boiling pot to fill their empty stomachs. However, hearing their dreaded step-mother's return, she stuffed them up her knicker leg. Years later, when repeating this story to me on one of my regular visits to her home, she showed me the scar that was still there on the top of her thigh.

Stella was later suspected of becoming a prostitute, taking to the streets after she fled from home, when life became too tough. My mother left to live with her eldest sister and her new husband at the first opportunity, the two remaining sisters married young and took off to the safety of their marital home. Poor Stella was left to fend for herself, until she found a much older man to marry and take care of her.

This was the close family unit in which I grew up.

Every Saturday, my father and I would take the long walk up to Pemberton Street, leaving my mother at home. There I would watch, as a next door neighbour was called in to light the gas lamps and close the curtains with a long wooden pole, left at the side of the door. These acts were forbidden in my grandparents' orthodox home until the Sabbath was over. Later, as I grew older, I became confused and a little amused with my grandfather – orthodox in every way, except for making his Saturday racing bets behind the closed curtains, a ritual that continued until his death.

My father had few religious beliefs, declaring before Alzheimer's got a hold of his brain near the end of his life, that the atrocities he had seen through the Second World War had stripped him of any. So I learned little of why the Sabbath candles were lit every Friday, an act my mother performed in haste, without any real understanding of it.

The relationship between my parents was warm and loving. Sex was never taboo, they would hug and kiss at any given opportunity and she would pass my way as she was sent giggling up the stairs towards the bedroom in her corset and stockings, followed in quick pursuit by her very needy husband. So I developed a good idea at a very young age what went on between adults and how my father managed to calm my mother down after a dispute – it was always sorted out in the bed. Being extra curious, I would crawl on hands and knees from my bedroom once I heard the bed springs squeaking, to take a peep at my father riding my mother's body. I got the picture right there and then.

My mother's love of stardom and Hollywood movie stars encouraged her desire for her only child to become musically and theatrically famous and life consisted of working her sewing machine to pay for ballet lessons, piano lessons, elocution lessons, drama lessons and skating lessons. I excelled at all but the skating lessons and piano lessons, so my mother's dreams began to be fulfilled in those early days.

My parents worked tirelessly to make a life for the three of us. They bought a garden terraced house at 22 Murray Street, Salford in 1948, wanting a place of their own, instead of renting a property. This was the aspiration of many Jewish families in the area, who strived to do the same. The long rows of back-to-back terraced houses led towards Great Clowes Street, where, nestled at the bottom within a park, was Grecian Street Junior School where I attended from nursery through to taking my exams for senior school.

Moving up from nursery to junior school, I was soon told the rules that had to be followed. My mother had no wish for me to take up friendships with any pupil who wasn't Jewish and any requests to the contrary were met with a harsh warning. These rules were fought against and never adhered to, until she reluctantly had to accept that, even at that young age, her daughter had a mind of her own.

Chapter 3

Childish Innocence and a Woman Called 'Nipples'

'There is a garden in every childhood, an enchanted place where colours are brighter, the air softer, and the morning more fragrant than ever again.'

Janice Rosen was my best friend at junior school. She was a tiny girl, with big brown eyes and curly short black hair. In nursery school, she was always crying for her mummy and sucking her two fingers to pacify herself. We lived virtually back to back, with only a narrow cobbled street separating her home from mine, so we would walk home from school together from a very early age. I remember that if she didn't find her mother, she would run up and down the street, screaming and frantically searching for her. At junior school, she turned into a loud-mouthed bully, quite a trouble maker, although never with me.

Janice came from mixed religion parents. Her father was Jewish and her mother Christian, so under my mother's strict rule of playing only with Jewish children, she was banished from our home. However, after a lot of pestering, I was very grudgingly allowed to play with her on the street.

We used to spend our time fantasising together, taking ourselves into a make-believe world that started with us each 'adopting' a baby from nearby neighbours who were their real mothers and pretending the tiny tots were ours. As we wheeled our prams up and down Murray Street and

14

Rock Street where we lived, fantasy became reality to such an extreme that the babies had fantasy fathers and, at the tender age of nine we simulated sex, lying next to each other in a field hidden away from the real world, school skirts adrift and knickers around our ankles, popping pens into our pussies, pretending we were being poked by our fantasy husbands.

Years later, recalling this pleasure, I realised it was the awakening of my promiscuity.

This little escapism stopped when we went to senior school and our lives parted. Never again was it spoken about – in fact never again did we speak at all.

My sex education was further advanced, thanks to our fascination with a prostitute, a voluptuous sexpot of a woman we called 'Nipples'. She was about 25 and used to entertain men in her living room in Great Clowes Street, Salford, a stone's throw from where we lived. Her curtains were never drawn, because I guess she thought the wall surrounding her garden gave her enough protection. One day while on an adventure, we climbed the wall and creeping closer to the window, there she was, dressed only in a mink coat which was open, showing her naked body, her huge nipples erect like ripe red cherries. They must have been two inches long – how I wanted to baby-suck those nipples!

One day we were spotted and chased by her male visitor, but while Janice managed to escape over the wall, I was not so lucky and was dragged down by my legs and marched into the living room. Nipples bent down in front of me, her breasts clearly in view and, after giving me a good telling off, she kissed me on the cheek and sent me packing, inviting me to visit again after school hours only through the front door in future.

I then made regular visits, but there was a rule. If, after ringing the doorbell twice there was no answer, I was to go away. It was a sign she was entertaining and I would know not to disturb her.

Nipples was what I can only describe as a truly elegant woman. Looking back, I realise she was a hooker who performed expertly on her bed in the arms of the most sophisticated men. Yet to me, she was what every young girl could wish for in an older sister: sweet natured, affectionate, fun-loving and, in many ways, a child herself. She educated me in make-up and fashion and enjoyed talking to me about 'the birds and the bees' with a form of sex education that was naturally explicit – handy because the subject was never talked about at home. I loved the smell of perfume in her room and the exotic underwear she would flaunt in front of me. I guess it thrilled her to have a young friend who so clearly adored her.

Nipples had the longest fingernails I have ever seen. Her hands, with their long, tapered fingers, were carefully moisturised, then held above her head for minutes at a time. She explained this helped the veins to disappear and kept her hands looking youthful. I wallowed in her form of education. Her red hair was kept low on her forehead, with a peak – an attractive and unusual style which must have caught the eye of many men. She shampooed it every morning, let it dry naturally, pin-curled, then brushed it out into a luscious flow of shiny locks. On the odd occasion I managed to skip round to visit her on a Sunday morning, I would find her either with her pin curls in, or brushing her hair, ready for church, being the good Catholic girl she was.

She must have been about five foot seven inches tall and more often than not I found her walking around bare-footed, displaying her pedicured and varnished toes. The only time she put heels on was when the mink coat was draped around her body. Her face was always pale and powdered, with arched eyebrows that seemed to be painted on. Her eyelashes were dark and lush, surrounded by perfectly painted eyeliner. Red lips completed her make-up.

She loved flamenco dancing and I was bewitched watching her. I loved it when she grabbed my hands and span me round, dancing, laughing and having fun.

On weekdays, I managed about half an hour's visit each day on my way home from school, as long as she was not expecting a visitor. I often managed to linger around an hour on a Sunday morning, if I got there early enough and there were no other plans made for me.

Our friendship came to an abrupt end one winter's day when, having arrived breathless after running to Nipples' house on my way from school and knowing I was short of time because I had to be at a piano lesson, my visit was rudely interrupted by loud knocks and pounding on the front door. As Nipples stood in the doorway, my deranged mother rushed forward and grabbed her by the hair, throwing her into the cold outside, minus her shoes and stockings, everything except that precious mink coat. Grabbing me by the hand, she charged me up the street and, as she thought, to the safety of our home.

I never visited, or spoke to Nipples again, but on rare occasions I would see her stepping into the passenger seat of a waiting car, and if she spotted me, she would give me the biggest smile.

Chapter 4

Academic Freedom

'I always like to know everything about my new friends and nothing about my old ones.'

Now began another era in my life, my transfer aged 11 to North Salford Girls' Senior School, where we were expected to wear white shirts, navy skirts, knickers and a tie, which in my case stayed mainly at the bottom of my satchel. You would recognise a rebel by the way she wore her uniform.

I had no choice in which school I went to, it was automatically allocated as the closest to where you lived. It was a mixed religion school, which once again made life difficult at first, having to face up to the toughest, just to get through the school gates. Being a Jewish girl I had to prove my worth, until the jibes stopped once they realised there was more about me than just being Jewish.

There were 26 girls in each class and the mistresses certainly had their work cut out, keeping us focused on the blackboard. St Trinian's was definitely our style, both in appearance and attitude to work, but I slipped easily into the school routine, made friends and enjoyed the mixture of characters I met. Almost immediately, I was put into a top form, for although I was not naturally an intelligent pupil, I possessed an excellent memory, which I put to good use when studying for exams. If there any subject that came naturally, it was English language and literature. I also showed promise in art, but hated religious studies, when the classes were segregated – Jews in one class, Anglicans and Catholics together in another. Unfortunately, the segregation highlighted the undercurrent of anti-Semitism that existed, but my reaction was to concentrate on the mood outside the classroom, rather than what was going on inside.

By the age of 12 I was no longer a virgin, at least I didn't think I was. I had found out by trial and error with no help from the biology teacher's lessons that just left me more confused than before. It was while kissing and exploring my boyfriend David's body that we attempted penetration, so my mother's wise words, 'Keep your virginity till you are married, Vivien, then your husband will not be able to throw your past up in your face,' had already gone out of the window. Sending me to an all-girls' school didn't work, either. North Salford Boys' School was just up the road.

Most evenings were spent when possible on street corners or the local youth club joining gaggles of girls strolling in their finery, hoops skirts, stockings and a flash of scarlet across their lips. Gangs of boys watching every move strolled by with their Vaseline-sculptured hair with a quiff at the front. All evening they criss-crossed, exchanging glances, flirting in numbers, sometimes pairing off for a snog in a secluded corner. For many it was the start of a mating ritual. From boyfriend to going steady and then getting married, clearly laid out were the steps for a dutiful daughter to begin in her teens and to have completed by her early twenties, some having got there earlier.

The loss of virginity should be the turning point in nearly every girl's life but for me it was quite uneventful. Garth at my ballet school was athletic in body and quite gorgeous. I was mesmerised. We kissed and cuddled, fingered and fondled after classes, on our way home, until the day arrived when we felt the need to take things further and I gladly put my mother's wish for purity before marriage to the back of my mind in the excitement of what was to come.

It was then that I realised David hadn't done his job properly. One day, when we had the weekend free while his parents were spending some time away from home, Garth took the opportunity of rushing me to his bed. There was no pain, just a warm sensation and a little release of blood as he entered me and it was there that I felt I had my first penetrative orgasm, which set me on the road for needing to experience more.

Back at school, I began to mix with the movers and shakers, following their style in fashion. Two of these girls – Lynn and Caroline – were inseparable. They had been friends since junior school and while they lived close to each other in Salford, I was some distance away in Prestwich. They were both cocks of the class and although Lynn's head was never focused on lessons, except to make sarcastic remarks behind the teacher's back, she was clever. She kept her intelligence disguised behind a mask of mischief, but come exam day she always managed to gain top marks. Caroline had similar characteristics, but deep down she had intelligence enough to know that exam results were important and quietly took in all she was taught.

Lynn was the most rebellious girl in school and admired by us all. She had absolutely no interest in lessons, although if the Rolling Stones had been on the curriculum, she would have been top of the class. Her big blue eyes and thin face were framed by bleach-blonde hair, which was always heavily backcombed and if a strand was out of place, that girl never left her house.

The Rolling Stones were her main focus and Brian Jones was her idol. The classroom was agog with her claim to fame of how she managed to get invited into his bedroom when he was staying with the rest of the group at the Piccadilly Hotel in Manchester after a *Top of the Pops* recording. The story was that she found his room on the top floor after avoiding doormen and security staff.

Caroline was my closest friend at senior school and after a while I started a desire for her and I didn't know why. I had vaguely heard of lesbianism but would never have thought I had a leaning towards it, loving the scent of a boy so much. Caroline never returned feelings for me that way and probably never knew lesbians existed, so I guess she never took any notice of me brushing past her breasts and focusing on her full lips.

Her attachment to me came through a form of admiration when I stood up to bullies, especially for friends too weak to defend themselves. Through all this activity, my drama lessons continued, until I eventually won a scholarship offered by the Royal Academy of Dramatic Art (RADA). My drama exams were allowed to take place out of school but in school time, which created more tension in class. Why was I allowed to have the privilege of not attending classes, when the rest couldn't escape?

My inner actress was there already and the more I attained excellence by performing in front of great actors like Sir Michael Redgrave, gaining honours, the more I became noticed. All this clashed with the rebel inside me. In one way, I hated being separated from Caroline and my gang of friends, yet I also longed for stardom and the stage.

My school friends won. My rebellious nature had grown to such an extent that when I was offered a dream part in *Coronation Street*'s early productions, I refused to take up the opportunity, choosing instead to take on the crazy Swinging Sixties with relish.

Like millions of fans, I have grown up watching the popular TV soap opera and enjoyed the intricacies of the down-to-earth characters who walk the cobbled streets and enjoy a drink in the famous Rovers Return. How many budding actors and actresses have dreamed of a part in this award-winning saga? Yet at the age of 11 and looking much older than my years, I turned my back on being one of the first actresses to appear in the series.

From 1958 to 1962, I gained acting certificates at the London Academy of Music and Dramatic Art, based at the adult education centre in Manchester and also at the English Speaking Board, where Michael Redgrave was the president and where I gained honours in acting. It was my rendition of *'Anne of the Thousand Days'* that attracted attention. My exam report read: 'This was a most imaginative and spontaneous rendering' and somehow Margaret Morris, the casting director for the opening episode of *Coronation Street* who was determined that it should be filled with unknowns with natural Lancashire accents, was passed information about me. She contacted my drama teacher, Miss Sefton, who made arrangements for me to read lines for the role of wild child Lucille Hewitt.

This was 1960 and I had just started senior school. Lucille was 16 and came to *Coronation Street* in the third episode. Miss Sefton contacted my mother and I practised my lines with her until the day arrived for Margaret Morris to listen to my interpretation of the script, which I did with ease. The part was offered to me and when I turned it down, it was offered to Jenny Moss, who was 15. She was eventually sacked from the cast after establishing Lucille Hewitt as a main character. I believe that drink and drugs had come into her life and although the production team tried their best to work with her, it finally became impossible and Lucille said farewell to the soap in the 1970s. Jenny Moss died in 2006, after many years of battling booze. I guess the wild child Lucille was the right part for both of us.

Do I have regrets that I stepped back from fame and fortune? No, I am still alive.

Knowing my prowess with boys, Caroline turned to me one day for advice and guidance. She was going on a date and was suspicious he would want to sample her delights.

Strangely enough, when she told me her date was from the boys' school nearby who every girl drooled over, I was jealous, not of her, but of him. I was surprised how naive she was, being outwardly one of the sexiest girls in our school and her request took me by surprise. 'Could you show me a little how to act and what to do?' she asked. How could I refuse?

It was winter and dark by 4pm, so when school opened its doors, we scurried off to her home. Her mother had not returned from work and we made use of the time alone. Not really knowing what was happening to her adolescent sexuality, she was submissive at first and I am sure expected something a little less realistic than I had in mind. 'Let me hold you the way he will hold you', I said, slipping my arm around her waist and the other around her shoulder, while planting a kiss on her lips, urging them open. 'No-one kisses with their mouth closed,' I said, and urged her to explore my mouth with her tongue, moving on to kiss her ears and neck, I felt her body shiver as goose bumps appeared on her skin.

'After kissing, you have to know how to caress and be caressed,' I continued, while lifting up my skirt to stroke myself. I would have loved to have been a boy with a penis to enter her, but all I had was a very hard cherry. While she was caught in the moment, I moved my mouth down and started sucking her nipples, while a free hand rubbed hard on her clitoris until, with a little squeal of excitement, she exploded.

Breathless, I looked up at her shocked face. She had been seduced by a love-crazed schoolgirl. The truth though, as much as she never admitted it, I know she enjoyed that moment. But instead of wanting more moments, she would tease me, recognising my infatuation.

For two years, I walked around like a puppy dog, adoring and desiring her.

The end of Caroline came with the end of school. It seems through my life, each chapter of it is never, or very rarely, continued with friends from the chapter of life before.

Chapter 5

Up on the Podium

'The truth is rarely pure and never simple.'

Jimmy Savile first came into my life when BBC1 launched a new weekly programme called *Top of the Pops* in 1964. I was a star-struck teenager and his world seemed impossibly glamorous. I was not to know the controversy that would infect his life and reputation 50 years later, after his death in October, 2011.

When I first knew Jimmy he lived in a flat at 301 Great Clowes Street, Salford, where he was often seen sitting on the steps, chatting to passers-by. Those who ventured indoors told of black walls and ceilings and a scruffy interior. He had a need of adulation even then and befriended a lap dog known as 'Ugly' Ray Teret who use to follow him around like a shadow. 'Ugly' adopted the same style and mannerisms of Jimmy while becoming his support DJ, chauffeur, girl procurer, and general dogsbody.

Great Clowes Street had featured in my life some years earlier, when I visited Nipples, who lived only a few doors away in the same large block of Victorian houses. The Clowes family had controlled the development of the area, allowing wealthy merchants to buy large plots in Higher Broughton to build a mix of impressive detached homes and rows of terraced houses. Residents were of the professional classes and several of those properties still stand today, including the ones where Nipples and Jimmy lived. In its time, it was a very prominent Jewish area, but towards the middle of the 20th century, many of the large houses were divided into flats, causing the area to become run down and neglected. Jimmy's rented home was one of them.

He later moved and bought 103 Ascot Court, Bury New Road, Higher Broughton, Salford, and was there from the very early 60s to when he quit some 10 years later, leaving its contents behind him – either because by this time he had amassed that much wealth, or because he had to leave in a hurry.

He kept his Rolls-Royce and a collection of Bubble cars that he would use for fun, in garages at

Ascot Court and nearby Epsom Mews, which is where Pat Phoenix, who played Elsie Tanner in *Coronation Street*, lived. They were new luxury flats and, when the weather was good, you would often find Jimmy sunbathing, stripped down to the briefest of shorts, his gold medallion and huge identity bracelet glinting brightly in the sun.

Celebrities used to call on him there. I recall once seeing Des O'Connor and Anita Harris enjoying the sunshine with him. Jimmy was always brash and brazen, with an ego as big as a barn door and, I guess, amassing a bank balance to match.

I got to know him further when my friends and I decided that a visit to his disco at the Assembly Rooms opposite his penthouse was much more important than school lessons. Jo, one of my close friends at school, used to join us on this venture. She was a sexually attractive, seductively cute young lady, quite doll-like, with an old-fashioned elegance that was unique. I envied her long, wavy, dark hair, with the darkest of eyes framed with thick long lashes.

Her choice of dress reflected the image she loved to portray, with frills and lace, sheer stockings and a flower at the side of her face. No matter what the fashion was, she favoured her own. Her style was provocative, displayed with child-like innocence, often wearing over-the-knee stockings, displaying a bare leg above. Quirky and unique, she attracted the attention of adoring males, drawn to her like bees to a honey pot and Jimmy didn't hesitate to make a beeline for her.

When she spoke, Jo had a childlike innocence in her voice, but behind that façade was a very sharp, ambitious girl.

All the disc jockeys who played the records at the Assembly Rooms needed adulation and as young girls we played innocently to their ego, riding high on the music and the moments. It was normal, it was the Swinging 60s. My favourite was never Jimmy, but another DJ riding high at the time, Dave Lee Travis. I used to thrill when I caught his eye and I would spend as much time as possible, in between restrictions at home, at the Whisky A Go-Go lighting up the dance floor, taking part in the singing competitions and revelling in the electric atmosphere that he created.

Jimmy was always surrounded by young girls, but Jo was his favourite. She was the one called into his flat, or his office at the dance hall, and who was generous with her body. She would then come to find us much later, with packs of cigarettes and those treasured tickets to *Top of the Pops*.

These tickets were like gold dust and saved us queuing at the disused church in Dickinson Road, Rusholme, which was home to the BBC studios where *Top of the Pops* was broadcast every Thursday from its first airing in 1964.

To us, this weird, outrageous character, whose breath stank of cigars, had star status and was a means to an end. We were totally star-struck. Okay, we were underage and anyone parting a blouse to feel a breast, or a touch up in between your legs would now be classed as behaving illegally, but we were eager volunteers and didn't have to be asked. It was part of the game of life then and, crazy as it sounds, we felt in a privileged position.

It must be said that it upsets me to hear now just how

far Jimmy took his sexual perversions. No child is born to suffer and it seems, sadly, that many did.

His attraction was always with himself. After all, he was the star of *Top of the Pops*. When he was up on the podium next to the main stage, he often called us up to join him. He wanted to get as many girls as possible on the podium with him, so we all clambered up, squeezed up tight and those within reach got a tweak to the bottom, or a close rub, accompanied by a cheeky comment. All the DJs, including David Jacobs, Pete Murray and Alan (Fluff) Freeman, called up as many girls as they could to make sure it looked crowded on camera.

My little gang of girls were well known at the studio and as we went in we had to put little heel covers over our stilettos and were given bottles of Coke, I suppose to keep the heat down and the energy up. Once inside, I would go round the back into the dressing rooms to chat with the bands. Whenever the Rolling Stones were performing, my friends and I would sit with Mick and Brian while they prepared for the show. The Stones were on the cusp of stardom. Conversation flowed easily, as though we were talking to the average guy on the street. They were all very friendly and it was easy to relax in their company as they answered our girlie questions. I found them to be the most accessible, especially as they were often the main attraction. I was mesmerised. The last time I managed to put myself in Mick's company at the *Top of the Pops* studio, I was strutting my stuff in a colourful striped and very short zipped-front mini dress which just covered my bottom. I finished my style off with black patent thigh-high boots that clung to my legs like second skin, with my auburn shoulder-length hair set as high as I could get it and adorned with glossy lipstick, I went in search of the man I wanted to be close up too. Mick was in a small crowded dressing room with the rest of the band and some other musicians, warming up and practising poses in the dressing room mirror, big hair, big lips, big crotch. He commented on my dress, playing around with the zip in fun. Just being near him for those few moments, it was obvious he was so very different and I was in the presence of someone who was going to reach great heights.

The studio was crammed and if you were a good dancer you were spotted and given tickets for the following week. This happened to me quite often. It was always a little chaotic and I guess today it would be thought very amateurish, the cameramen on huge trolleys, each accompanied by a man crawling on all fours, clearing the path by swinging his arms against our legs to move us aside, so they could continue filming the dancers. Many a shocked expression was visible among the audience when the show was broadcast but we were frequently unaware what was happening around our feet as we moved in rhythm to the music.

The programme focused on the Top Ten hit parade, so you knew in advance who you were about to be close to for the number one spot. The Beatles were rarely present, instead the producer displayed a huge picture board of them. This was always the position to get in front of to be guaranteed a spot on TV.

Many budding superstars who came to promote their music could credit their fame from performing on that small stage miming to their songs, the singing not being live at the time.

I have fond memories of a guy called Cecil, who was part of the production team. If we hadn't been able to get our precious tickets from Jimmy, we would stand in the queue with other eager teenagers, and if there was an audience shortage, Cecil would appear at the studio entrance and beckon me and whoever I was with inside. My talent for dance had paid off.

FOOTNOTE: Ray Teret, on the 11th December 2014, was sentenced to 25yrs imprisonment for the sexual abuse of underage girls in the 1960s-1970s.

Chapter 6

Caught Up in the Moment

'Open your eyes, look within, are you satisfied with the life you are living?' – Bob Marley

I left school just months after my 15th birthday, in the summer of 1964, and enrolled on a six-month secretarial course at a college in Manchester city centre. With my newly acquired shorthand and typing skills I got the first job I applied for, working as a personal assistant to a Jewish lawyer in a small solicitor's office. He was a fatherly, caring boss and the six old English pounds he paid me was regarded as a good wage.

The city centre office was handy for me to meet up with two girls I had befriended on the course, choosing the Cona Coffee Bar on Tib Lane, at the corner of Albert Square to indulge in our girly gossip. It was here that we spent lunchtimes and most evenings, tumbling down the stairs into the long, narrow room, to find a booth to sit and chat. The jukebox played constantly, as long as money continued to be fed into it. It was home for all the Mods and if you had a love of music, from Joan Baez to Motown and blues, or arts and fashion, everything was there to listen to, watch, or talk about. This was the place to hang out.

The bar was crammed with tall stools and had a double coffee-making machine. Gus, the grey-haired owner, and his assistants, Judith and Martin, kept us supplied with coffee, served in cups the size of soup bowls, accompanied by giant burgers.

It was at the Cona that I became friendly with a young Asian drama student called Krishna Banji, who was in his early 20s. We talked enthusiastically about acting, the talent which was ultimately to make his fame and fortune. Krish was to become Sir Ben Kingsley.

Young Krishna had an infectious personality, with the biggest brown eyes and a mop of black hair and, although small in height he was big in presence. He never made an attempt to explain his Jewish heritage, but all his friends were Jewish, and some of them happened to know me, too. We were brought up in the same area of Salford and although my parents had moved up to bettering themselves in Prestwich, he was still living in Pendleton in the heart of Salford where he also went to college.

We had no physical chemistry but lots of common interests, discovered as we sat around the booths of the Cona among mutual friends. Krish told me of his amateur theatrical work and his dreams of acting greatness. We were similar in character. He spent his days in this imaginary bubble of fame, like he was truly famous, before he had actually trod the boards. This was a feeling I understood. I had experienced that same bubble. He felt like he was a curiosity to others. Every play or movie he saw, he became enraptured with the lead character and in his theatre of dreams, became that person. I knew those feelings too.

I discussed my acting ability and how I had stepped away from it because of the rebel inside not allowing me to go down that road. His reaction was that I didn't feel the need strong enough, or I would have stuck it out.

We always enjoyed our conversations when we met and ironically he took a bit part in Coronation Street in 1966, which proved a stepping stone to his career. It's amazing now to hear of his reputation of being pompous and pretentious, a man who keeps himself aloof from everyone and insists on being called 'Sir'. In those days, Ben was just a student called Krish, with a dream of acting greatness.

My entry into the world of clubbing started at the Cona and took me to darker places. I was sweet 16, a long way from saying I had never been kissed, but I hadn't touched drugs. That all changed when I moved into a different circle. Pretty soon, there was a choice for weekend entertainment. Black Bombers, Blueys and Dexedrine became the way of life and every Friday evening I made sure I got my supply for the Saturday all-nighter. I had an equal choice where to spend it – the Twisted Wheel, or Heaven & Hell, the Oasis or Jigsaw, perhaps the Jungfrau. Manchester was alive and kicking and the place for partying, in that magic era of Mods and Rockers, Vespa scooters, Mary Quant and Biba fashion.

While I have met a myriad of people, famous and infamous, my life's experiences have also included some darker episodes, suffering at the hands of predatory monsters. I have toyed with the dilemma of whether to include them in this book, one minute thinking maybe I should, then the next minute, maybe not. It is as simple for me to dismiss them today as it was all those years ago, as though they never happened, but here I am back at the chapter where they belong.

When does flirting and playfulness become exploitation and abuse? Answer: when you flirt and play with someone like Tony. We had met at the Cona Coffee Bar, along with other enthusiastic clubbers arranging their selection of amphetamines to get them where they needed to be – spaced out, talking nineteen to the dozen with a dry mouth that only bottles of Coke could cure and help to continue that wonderful high.

Tony was on the edge of the crowd I hung out with, but I paid him little attention until one Saturday afternoon when with little else to do I agreed to join him on a shopping trip to help choose a leather jacket he could wear for the Saturday rave. A short stop at his family home

33

followed to drop his jacket off and continue the day. I didn't see daylight until the following morning after managing to escape through his bedroom window to freedom. Thank God it was a ground floor flat as I dread to think of the outcome if it hadn't have been.

On entering the flat, he directed me immediately towards his room. 'Lie down on the bed,' he ordered, unbuckling his belt. 'Take everything off first, except for your panties and bra.' I remember nervously chewing my lip, with any objections I had falling on deaf ears. He was not for listening.

Following his orders I unbuttoned my blouse, my fingers shaking and my stomach churning. My trews didn't want to part for my unsure hands and at that point he reached over and with one quick motion tore them open and off.

'What do you want now?' I whispered, hardly able to control the throb in my throat.

'Go on, get down there,' he replied, tucking my hair behind my ears and pushing me on to the bed, spreading me flat on my back and ramming his penis with such a force into my mouth, then tearing off my bra and biting down hard on my nipples.

My screams were not of desire. I knew then, at that point looking at his twisted expression, that I was in for a battle to remain unharmed. I was a prisoner in his bedroom and had to follow his every command. I was aware enough to know there would be consequences if I didn't. The onslaught of his sex attack continued without a break all night and my shouting did nothing to disturb his family, who were obviously within earshot. I guess they must have heard it all before. Eventually, as he lay lifelessly asleep I managed to slip my clothes on and climb out through the bedroom window and run to safety. A tortuous experience of being raped and abused but I never disclosed the incident to anyone. I can't say I was scarred by the consequences, I just preferred to erase all thoughts from my memory and move on.

The second rape happened late one evening after leaving a disco with two of my girlfriends. Together we had accepted a lift home from some young guys who had spotted us leaving. I happened to be the last drop off and unfortunately suffered for it. The Transit van in which we were travelling came to an abrupt stop on a country lane and the three who had previously acted like gentlemen suddenly turned into animals as one by one they took control of my body, forcing me down on the back seat where I had been sitting and pumping me until they had no more to give.

When it was over they opened the rear door and set me free, driving off into the distance in haste. I mentioned the attack to my two girlfriends, but it was never taken any further and again I got on with the days ahead, without a further thought until now.

The third attack wasn't actually a rape but it could so easily have been. Thanks to the grace of God and my quick thinking I managed to escape from the one that could have ended my life.

It was early evening and I was in a hurry to get home after a long working day. Walking through the passageway that led to my parents' home, I was approached from behind. Sticking what felt like a knife in my back, he ordered me to get down on the grass verge. A strength came over me from somewhere and the words I managed to get out of my mouth possibly saved my life. 'Don't take me here, I live just at the end of the passage and there will be no-one at home.'

The words were uttered convincingly and with that he relaxed his hold and I fled like greased lightning without turning back to view my assailant. Knocking like a lunatic at the door, I threw myself into the hallway and my mother's arms. The police were called and a search of the area followed but to no avail. Unfortunately this monster was free to pursue his next victim. Once again I got over the experience and continued on my life's journey.

This proves there is a huge difference, not only in time but in attitude. Today all three experiences would have been reported to the police. They would have acted upon them and spread the word, which perhaps would have saved others from suffering the same fate. Then, it wasn't like that. Call it naivety, call it stupidity, it just didn't happen.

Back in my day to day life, I was exercising great skill juggling my day job with my nightlife. But there were the occasional misspent days when I would fake a cold or claim I wasn't feeling well, then skip out of the house after my mother had phoned my employer before she left for work. I wondered how he put up with me but somehow I managed to keep on acting through those parts of my life.

Sundays were spent recovering from Saturday all-nighters, and I would eventually find myself back home, coming down from the drugs I had taken the night before. Were my parents aware that my appetite had been fed this way as I sat at the dining table, unable to eat a bite? The subject was never discussed, so I guess not.

In those amazing hazy, crazy days of 1963, you could get up close to Mick Jagger at the Twisted Wheel and rub shoulders with R&B and soul artists of the calibre of Ike and Tina Turner, Ben E. King, The Yardbirds, The Kinks, Chuck Berry, Georgie Fame, Long John Baldry. The Rolling Stones knew they were treading the boards of the best venue to enhance their career. That's how artists promoted themselves in those days, on stage, live in the clubs.

Tommy was a Mod with attitude. He was the top dog of all the Mods and my man when I wanted him. At 26, he was 10 years my senior, a bad boy from the Wythenshawe estate. The fact that he was tough and bad added to his appeal, a rough diamond, who extended his roughness to the bedroom. Being tied up in his bed for rough sex was as addictive as feeling those weekend drugs running through my body.

Stones guitarist Brian Jones appeared on the scene when they were playing at The Oasis, a similar venue, but one that didn't have the electric atmosphere of The Twisted Wheel. He came in without Mick but with fellow band member Bill Wyman and took an immediate shine to my girlfriend. He made a pass at her and muttered something about her looking the image of his on-off girlfriend who it seemed had the same name. I was with Tommy, my boyfriend, and we didn't hesitate when we were invited back to Brian's hotel to enjoy some weed, music and laughs. She met Brian again, when asked to join him in London at a club where he was sessioning on stage with The Yardbirds. Her time with Brian was short but she had stories to tell of amazing moments in bed with him that other girls could only dream about. Quite an achievement, we thought, for a girl from Salford.

In 1965, The Stones were up there with The Beatles at the height of their fame. When in Manchester, Mick would go clubbing at Le Phonograph, a select private members club for over-21s. It was probably one of the only clubs he could be seen in without a fuss, the place to be for all visiting celebrities and also my new haunt. I had a new set of girlfriends to enjoy the fun. Even though we were nowhere near 21, there was never a problem with us being allowed in. We could always rely on guys who were members to see us safely through the door.

Once in, we were in our element, often being invited to sit in a booth where Jimmy Savile held court. We knew how to dress to impress and I guess we were fun to be around. Champagne was always on tap and the music and atmosphere great. Mick greeted us whenever he visited the club and was sweet enough to ask how we were. That's all it took to send shivers down my back and make my day.

All this hedonism came to an abrupt end when my parents decided emergency action was needed and that I needed stability with a nice Jewish boy. Enter Mike, many years my senior and a world away from my clubbing companions but with certain qualities I found myself liking. He was quite handsome, with a mass of dark curly hair and a hunky broad chest and a love of music, particularly Barbra Streisand, who I adored. What followed was not exactly an arranged marriage but a mother's desperate attempt to secure her daughter's future and find her lasting love with someone of her own religion.

To an extent, I got caught up in the moment, along with lots of other Jewish girls, who were falling head-first into marriage at the first opportunity. That's what my mother wanted for me but she knew without strong guidance I wouldn't be treading that road. It wasn't an easy project for her but she had noticed Mike's attention to me and decided he was the one.

He lived very near us, just down the road and round the corner, alone and obviously single. He was already heading towards his 30th birthday and, as we discovered, single after an engagement had fallen apart. He had amassed some wealth and his comfortable home was on a select, leafy road. His politeness appealed to my mother. Many a morning, he would stop as we were walking down the road to get the bus to work, open the passenger door of his car and offer us a lift. I found him a great convenience and took no real notice until one day I took a proper look at this guy behind the wheel. He was quite unusual for a professional guy, bohemian in style, tall and stocky, with a strong-featured face. I became quite interested.

Whenever I was still for long enough to hold a proper conversation with my mother, she always brought Mike's name into the conversation. Not that she was offering much help in pursuing the friendship, except for the use of the lounge, where she could indulge in providing cakes and cups of tea. Did I really need to go down this road?

In those days, inviting a young man into your parlour to sit on the sofa was an indication of serious things to come, so my mother hoped. In a moment of weakness, I allowed him access to me and quickly to my body, too. He fell into my pattern of life, which meant he had to give me freedom to do my own thing. My escapes were very rare but I managed it as often as I could as his attention to me was consuming. He bought me my first car and gave me a feeling of protectiveness, proving his tenderness time and time again.

The Jewish girls I had befriended already had engagement rings on their fingers and spent hours comparing the size of their solitaire diamonds. I in turn had fallen into the trap and was heading towards a fantasy dream of happiness, convincing myself that marriage to Mike was my destiny, to the delight of my mother. But lurking under the surface, I knew there was a problem and I was about to break his heart.

It was the sex that killed it for me. It was a farce, a joke. He was a poor lover and as much as I tried to fake an orgasm and bury my head in the sand, or under the bed sheets, it became a problem and one that would never be resolved.

Mike's problem was of the physical kind, he had a 'micro penis', a term I discovered much later in life. In fact, he hardly had a penis at all, the whole thing being the size of my little finger, when erect! So in less than a year, and tired of pretending, I made the decision to head towards another life.

It was a decision that left my parents devastated.

Chapter 7

Glimpse the Glamour of the Tease

'If I can be like you, just for one day, only you can show me. I don't know what to do and I don't know how to do it, if you will, show me how to be like you.'

My first sight of this hot and gorgeous 18-year-old was at a bar in Samuel Ogden Street, Manchester, called Mr Smith's. I had been invited to join two male solicitors from my office for lunch to celebrate their success in a court case and, as the champagne began to flow, there she was. Lexi Lee, the stripper, tall in her huge stiletto heels, with perfectly shaped legs that seemed to go on forever. One look and I was hooked on her image.

Lexi obviously knew how to make the best of her body. Her plump bottom, tiny waist and pert breasts, with perfect make-up, which included the longest black false eyelashes which stood out against her snow white complexion, emphasising her bright red lips, and red painted fingernails, the length of talons. Her wavy, long jet black hair was pinned up high with a large diamante clip. She was average in height, about five feet six inches, but preserved the impression of being taller, which I discovered once I got to know her. Those stilettos just didn't come off. Her unusual green and brown flecked cat-like eyes were one of her best features. She had great posture, maintained by constant exercise and a toned sculptured back which added to her appeal.

As I watched, I became entranced by Lexi's lunchtime

entertainment. She later told me she had no training in dance but it was clear she had mastered the art of the gestures and rituals of striptease. Her style was less bump and grind and more elegant gymnastic twists and turns. She was quite a contortionist and, unlike others, finished her routine completely nude. I learned this was allowed as long as you stood still as a statue, not moving a muscle.

Lexi used plenty of playful accessories in her act, from balloons to feather boas, but her most empowering signature tease was to make an entrance fully dressed, complete with hat, gloves and stilettos the height of stilts. There were many garments to prolong the act: stockings, suspenders, and several G-strings that gradually reduced in size and helped turn her strip into an erotic form, the dance and accessories being as important as the act of undressing itself.

She had poise, she was seductive and voluptuous, the picture of over-the-top glamour, sex sensational. Teasing her audience, she slowly pulled off her long black lace gloves and silk stockings, throwing them to the audience. Every man in the room wanted her body and some of the women too. When Lexi was expected on stage, the club was packed with excited voyeurs.

I fell in love with striptease, there and then, that first day, that lunchtime.

After her stage show, we invited Lexi to our table for a glass of champagne, sending a message via our waitress. She politely declined the drink but joined us briefly, long enough gain an invite to her home. It was the start of our long friendship.

At 17, I was exactly a year younger than Lexi, and at that tender age my body was in great shape, without the help of exercise. I had never considered myself to be a head turner in my early teens but now I had blossomed. I was the same height as Lexi but, unlike her, stilettos were not my favourite footwear until I took to the stage.

From top to toe I oozed the sex appeal that men desired. My shoulder-length hair was naturally dark, with glints of auburn, my oval face with high cheekbones, detracted from my slightly less-than-perfect nose. I had my father's eyes, big and oval, and great to emphasise with makeup. My lips were a big plus, too, naturally full and pouty. I had firm small breasts with pert nipples, a tiny waist and an amazing toned stomach that was the envy of many a girl. My plump, toned bottom was ideal to wiggle and I would strut my stuff on perfectly shaped legs. Finally, my hands, always an important item. They were long and slender, with immaculately manicured and polished nails. Lexi and I always regarded our hands as major assets and we took great care of them.

After this glimpse of the glamorous world of striptease, there was no holding me back. My dull office job paled in comparison and suddenly seemed pointless. I couldn't wait to join Lexi on the stage and entertain, there was no decision to be made.

I put a lot of thought into my tease routine. I wanted it to be glamorous entertainment without the use of balloons or big props, which could take the focus away from the fantasy of striptease. I intended to make it an art form which would last as long as I wanted it to, rather than a quick buck and move on. I had been blessed with an incredible body, destined to be admired, and I felt confident enough to let the world see it.

God made a woman's body to admire and appreciate, why hide it under clothing, when it can be admired in the flesh? Nothing beats a well-performed striptease and women who have it, should enjoy flaunting it. Being paid to please, what could be more thrilling?

Colin, Lexi's boyfriend and manager, was eager to introduce me to the club world, too, when he noticed how genuinely I was studying the art of striptease and practising my performance. It was made clear his job as my manager included taking care of my earnings and I was happy with that arrangement.

At first I practised at Lexi's home in a room she used as her strip boudoir. It was cluttered with her outfits, props and records, which I quickly made use of. I knew the style I was after and looked towards those vintage stars for inspiration, drawn by the look of Ava Gardner and Sophia Loren. I bought every magazine in which they were featured and tried to imitate their glamour. My transition had begun and there was no looking back.

I put my party days behind me and exercised, I gave up alcohol, ate like a rabbit and, from that day on, never dated the boy next door. I quit my job and sold my car to help pay for the cost of my costumes and everyday expenses. With the savings I had amassed, I was all set. Hello Miss Vivacious!

Over the weeks I worked on two routines created around the flexibility of my body. Those early ballet lessons spent stretching, developing poise and posture came into use and were about to pay off. I visited the club every Wednesday evening, the busiest strip night, to watch and learn. One of the keenest spectators was Jimmy Savile, who visited regularly with his entourage. He was amused to hear of my intention to appear on stage and he and his boys toasted my forthcoming striptease success.

As I watched the performers, it became obvious to me that stripping was an exercise in empowerment. I knew that when I finally took to the stage, I would present my body as on object of beauty, not just a sex symbol. If I was going to remove my clothes, I would do it with as much artistic appeal as possible.

For my performance I arranged to use the club's piano as my only prop, conveniently placed at the back of the stage. I wore a body-hugging black gown with a tight fishtail that started above the knee and was edged with a fur trim. Underneath was a boned basque, with padded bra cups to accentuate my cleavage. A G-string showed off my pert bottom and I wore black stockings with elaborate laced tops, and black stilettos with glittering soles, which added to the dramatic finale as I draped my body over the piano with my legs held high.

To strip, I first pulled off my lace gloves, raising them high above my head and swinging them round to the rhythm of the music, before throwing them to the side of the stage. Next, I released the fur stole, attached with sequinned press studded bands, again matching the beat of the music with each movement. This was also thrown aside.

The dress came off next, slowly unzipped with sharp movements which revealed a stocking top and naked thigh, before it was slipped gently down my body with my back to the audience, allowing them to see my bare bottom. As I wiggled sexily to and fro, the tight basque showed off the full extent of my voluptuous outline, with its 22-inch waist emphasising the curve of my hips. When the basque came off, all that remained were stockings and stilettos, which I removed with a kiss to the sparkling sole. Finally, I pulled my stockings down to the tips of my toes with slow suggestive movements before turning on my stomach, crossing and lifting my legs, bouncing up and down to the music in movements that simulated sex. Then as the lights dimmed I gave a wink to my mesmerised audience.

From the applause that greeted the end of my performance, I knew it had gone well and the weeks of practice had paid off. Looking across at the audience, I saw Jimmy Savile had nearly choked on his cigar and as I left the club, I felt elated, with a rush of excitement, mixed with a feeling of relief. I had achieved my goal, delighted that I had thrilled the audience and got through it unscathed.

The whole act took 10 minutes precisely, following the

club rule. Colin, thrilled with his new discovery, whisked me away. Not wanting me to linger, he aimed to retain the mystery of his new performer.

I was aware that I would be walking the stage at the best venue in the north of England. Mr Smiths was a cabaret club, casino and strip venue with an excellent reputation, a regular haunt for pop and rock stars of the era, who would end up there after their gig in the city. You could almost guarantee that you would be sharing the bar with famous faces. Owner Dougie Flood loved to feature top notch acts and when the club closed at two in the morning, he would be there to crack open a bottle of champagne with the stars and any selected guests allowed to remain inside.

Singing stars Dusty Springfield and PJ Proby, as well as comedians Dick Emery and Tommy Cooper, all entertained on the tiny stage. The music was mostly pop in the main room, while in the Drokiweeny room they played soul. The Bus Bar was a quiet place for a drink, with an adjoining casino. All the rooms were linked with corridors lit with ultraviolet lights and 1960s pop art adorned the walls.

The bouncer was a big burly guy, formerly a professional wrestler who very rarely had to use his skills. There were lunchtime strippers, and Wednesday night, the busiest night, amassed a loyal following, while Mr Smiths on Friday night led the way for weekend entertainment.

No-one ever knocked on a stripper's dressing room door, they just walked in. It seemed it didn't matter if you were in a state of undress, considering before long you would be baring your body to everyone in the audience, so what was there to hide?

A weekly stag night provided 'blue' comedians, with whom we frequently performed on stage, and when the lights went down and it was time for everyone to leave, I felt it amusing that most men crept out of the back door, while the women in the audience were totally unfazed.

I always regarded myself as more of a burlesque dancer than a stripper, although the element of 'tease' is key. It is the act of combining direct eye contact and body language to convey sexiness to the audience. In any event, taking my clothes off didn't give me a feeling of power, charming the audience did.

The main difference between a stripper and a burlesque performer in those days was that strippers made more money, and the only reason a stripper bared her body was to earn that money. Since the reappearance of burlesque in the 1990s, you now see young women who want to embrace their inner bombshell, attracting a wide range of audience who are bewitched with the art and in love with the 'tease'.

The arrival of porn on television killed off the strip clubs for some years. I am delighted to see it is back and more popular than ever.

Chapter 8

The Excitement of Release

The path to our destination is not always a straight one,
We go down the wrong road, we get lost, we turn back.
Maybe it doesn't matter which road we embark on.
Maybe what matters is that we embark.'

Manchester in the 1960s was like a big village, with a lively network of gossip. It was only a matter of time before my parents found out about my new lifestyle. I had already exposed myself to Auntie Stella, who came through my dressing room door at Mr Smith's one night in a whirl of excitement. Perhaps it was then that she realised we had the same verve for life. We were very alike and as loyal as I knew she was to me, I returned the favour, knowing she had been in a long, intimate relationship with her boss, unknown to my uncle. Quite often after that first meeting I would catch a glimpse of her either sharing cosy moments while dining in an intimate booth, or around the roulette table in the casino, and we became loyal soulmates knowing our secrets were safe with each other.

Still I had a nagging concern that somehow news of my stage debut would reach the ears of my parents, and I wanted to shield them from the shock of discovering the stage I had chosen for my career was for stripping on and not acting. Although I saw little difference in the two forms of art, I certainly knew my mother would have a different view and I didn't want to rub her nose in it.

I had sleepless nights worrying that Mike was active on the city club scene and would one night visit Mr Smith's and see me exhibiting myself. I had not left him in a good place mentally, being dumped from a great height, and so I was aware that he was not to be trusted to remain discreet.

Lexi in turn, had also had enough of the constraints put on her by Colin, and although she loved him, she yearned for freedom. It was a relief to discover that he cared for her enough to let her spread her wings. He was a clever guy to give her freedom, as the love she felt remained and he could keep in touch and look out for her from afar.

Our London future together took some weeks of planning. The right price and situation for our accommodation was vital, and through word of mouth we were recommended to try the Astor Court Hotel in Paddington. It was affordable and would provide us with a convenient base while we searched Soho for permanent living accommodation and our dream job.

Walking the streets of London was thrilling. It was home to nearly a hundred strip clubs and almost every doorway in Soho had little postcards advertising 'large chest for sale' or 'French lessons given'. How I love that French language!

After making enquiries with estate agents and asking around, we discovered 128 Meard Street, Soho, W1. What an address! It was a fine apartment in a period building in the heart of bustling Soho, nestled in a quiet leafy backwater, with the theatres on Shaftsbury Avenue and Leicester Square on the doorstep, all the shops and restaurants you could possibly desire within walking distance.

Lexi and I fell in love with it and, after paying three months' rent in advance, we moved in within two weeks.

The apartment had two huge bedrooms and was bright and spacious, with high, elaborately plastered ceilings and huge windows. It became our haven of peace and we made a rule to make sure it stayed that way. But first, we had to find work.

Raymond's Revue Bar was spectacular, fitted out in red velvet and gold rococo. You stepped in through a narrow doorway past glass display cabinets advertising tempting displays of exotic strippers, and a short walk along a plush carpet took you into the auditorium, with its elaborate stage framed by huge velvet curtains. The audience waited expectantly on upholstered layered seating for the show to begin.

In due course I was offered an audition and joined a group of similarly ambitious young women hoping to bag a place in this palace of fantasy. It was clear I would have to forget my Manchester experience and perform my most tantalising act. Star quality was needed to prove my worth as an entertainer.

With nothing but my petals and huge ostrich feathers to accompany me, I wowed the management with a ballet burlesque to classical music. It did the trick. I had landed a job at the best exotic show venue in town.

The days and weeks that followed were a blur of stage practice with a choreographer and dressmaker for costume fittings that were considered elaborate and daring. This was the Raymond Revue Bar and its standards were high.

At first I used the same dressmaker as the other girls but as I earned more, I could afford to find my own to create my personal illusion of erotica with which to stun my audience. Each show ran for a month, so while you were performing one routine, you had to practise for the next.

The rules governing nude performances were strict. We had to stand still as statues, while novelty acts used chimps and snakes, even a dolphin starred in a huge tank, trained to remove a girl's panties. This was showbiz like no other and seemed a world away from the much more amateur Manchester strip/burlesque scene.

There for the world to see was an illuminated sign declaring it to be a *World Centre of Erotic Entertainment*. It was clear I was working in a London landmark.

We girls knew it was the only venue in London that offered full-frontal on-stage nudity. It also paid top rates and if you became a stripper there, you were surrounded by the best in the business – excellent props, a stage filled with glitz and glamour, pure theatre, combining humour with eroticism. Revue girls were like family, helping each other and working hard to stay close. There was no bitchiness and lots of camaraderie. But it was all-consuming, desperately hard work and it took over my life. Once established, and as long as you kept audiences entertained, you were considered a part of the furniture, but you had to make sure you kept on top of your game.

Slackness was not tolerated, standards were high and it was run as a tight ship. Striptease was your life and there was no escaping a show, unless you were ill and unable to perform. Thankfully, I never took myself too seriously and never looked on it as permanent, knowing I would soon be tempted to move on. But it would be on my terms only.

A knock on my dressing room door at the Revue Bar one evening was my first introduction to Michael Klinger – a plump, cigar-chomping gentleman who reeked of success. I sensed a toughness, combined with enormous intelligence, and I was immediately drawn to him. Everyone knew he was an investor in the Soho Crompton Club and a hostess club called the Heaven and Hell.

He wanted to know how a nice Jewish girl came to strip in Soho. How did he know I was Jewish? The same way as I knew he was. A Jew knows another Jew immediately, even if you don't look it, you obviously are, as soon as you open your mouth to speak. Michael knew as soon as we exchanged words. Being Jewish and a burlesque stripper was rare in those days, and that night it was obvious by the way the conversation was flowing that he admired my spirit and found me, in his words, 'intriguing', a word that has been often used about me since.

He was curious to know more about me and I was eager to have more of his company, so I accepted his invitation to his dinner table. By his standards, I was a little wet behind the ears, but it was clear I had made an effort to increase my income and achieving it in the tough world of burlesque added to my appeal.

It wasn't the norm to join guests at their tables but he was different and I was quite amazed he wished to know more about me. His connections with the Soho gangster land were obvious by the respect he received from all who stopped to greet him. He had an uncanny memory for conversations we went on to have, and an eager enthusiasm to get to know my thoughts on many subjects. He asked each question only once, the answer registering in his brain as he formed a picture of me.

Michael was regarded as a ruthless businessman, with very few principles, sharp as a knife, a survivor who earned maximum profits in any deal he did. Money was his god. Yet, although he was as tough as hell in business, he had a soft side too, putting every effort into the success of his Gargoyle Club, which was strictly for Jewish girls and guys in their late teens to get together. Did I wish to go there? Of course not! He was the only type of company I needed.

The more I got to know him, the more I discovered what an amazing character he was. I considered we were in a relationship but it was never a word he used. He would have said 'caring friendship'.

I discovered he was a family man first before anything else but I admired that trait in him. He was loyal to his wife mentally, if not physically, and he obviously had a deep respect for her.

He lived in Belgravia, so quite a way from the streets of Soho, where our time together was spent in the clubs and bars. When he asked me where I would like to go, it was usually into the Surrey countryside, where we could relax unnoticed in a country pub, taking in the feel of the little villages.

I discovered that before he changed his life to become a cinema owner and later a film producer, Michael invented a machine that tested bombs without blowing them up. This had proved a major breakthrough in the war and, although he had a high-powered job in government, he didn't earn the amount of money he eventually acquired by having a Jewish head on his shoulders and a drive for success. From government to East End trader on the markets, to cinema and film, who wouldn't be fascinated?

Michael wasn't in good physical condition and sooner rather than later, I discovered he was boring in bed too. Variation away from the normal is necessary and can be so thrilling. However, he gave no real thought to my pleasure. Until I directed him that way, his desires came first. He loved me to strip slowly in front of him and then to slowly lower me on the bed like a prize piece of porcelain. He had a soft and tender way of kissing my mouth, eyes, neck and breasts and over my sensitive nipples that rose like erect cherries, responding to his licks and sucking, then down to my belly button and eventually reaching where I liked it best. I would instruct him while lying between my legs to eat me, but it didn't turn me on and the weight of his body couldn't allow me to encourage it to be mutual.

The truth is I guess Michael was my first experience of learning the ways of a prostitute, with plenty of moans and groans that came out of my mouth without feeling anything at all. I felt like I had a job to do and I did it well. In return I felt secure with him emotionally and physically, although I never felt at the time I was his only conquest and I didn't need to have that feeling. I was secure in a loving friendship.

His Heaven and Hell club was a well-known place to

hire ladies of the night. It was always busy, with many famous faces coming and going. I used to love the atmosphere and would visit towards the end of our friendship with friends male and female.

Lonely men paid pretty girls for conversation. Club links to organised crime never obviously reached its doors, unlike other venues, and it was here that I got to know the regular hostesses and learned how they tricked gullible men to pay large amounts of money for cheap drinks and, if the customers could afford to keep her in his company paying the bar bills till 3am, he could take her to his hotel or home for sex at a high price.

This was where I made my transition from stripper to hostess, as I realised what comfort I could gain knowing I could take off my panties, giving my body and being paid a lot of money for it.

Like any decision I took in life, I never took too long to think about it and so the move from being a paid stripper to a highly paid hostess was made shortly after my 21st birthday.

Chapter 9

21 – 'An Age To Remember'

'I've been 21 more times than I can remember!'

Turning 21 is a huge milestone for a young woman and many who take the step are still a kid at heart. As for me, I had taken the steps into adulthood quite some years before and so approached my birthday with no more enthusiasm than any other birthday. Perhaps I had grown up much too fast.

What also contributed to my lack of excitement were the long hours spent every day applying myself to performing to the best of my ability on stage. Any free time I spent with Lexi was a special time, especially our girly days where we would take ourselves off to Carnaby Street and Kensington High Street, browsing the boutiques. We shared a fetish for fashion and so it was that we took ourselves off to Biba Boutique on Kensington High Street, where we shopped to our hearts' content.

My 21st celebration was looming and a special outfit was on the cards, and where Lexi found the shortest, tightest hot pants and see-through blouse, my choice was a little less risqué. I settled for a mauve metallic mini dress that finished at the curve of my bottom. It came complete with matching panties. Co-ordinating metallic knee-high boots with a high platform, not unlike those worn today, fitted like a second skin around my legs. Our stage make-up was to become our evening make-up, being very dramatic with perfectly applied eye shadow and the thickest of false eyelashes. The look was completed with shiny lips for a perfect pout and lots of attention given to our hair to gloss it up and give it shine. It seems that those days of yesteryear are here with us again. We were two exhibitionists that loved to flaunt our curves on and off the stage.

Ronnie Scott's Jazz Club on Frith Street had been chosen for the occasion. I had discovered I was in love with traditional jazz and that when inside Scotties it was close enough to touch. There was no room for pretentious people, the rich and famous were often there. But there was no VIP treatment for any of them and no dress code either. Everyone listened and watched with adulation as jazz artistes sweated it out to hit that killer note. Everyone from Princess Margaret to the average working Joe swilling a pint of beer was rubbing shoulders and soaking up the atmosphere and when Scottie took to the stage and played his sax, he sent shivers down my spine. It was a feeling I experienced nearly 40 years later listening to musicians in Cuba. Enjoying those moments on my 21st birthday made it special and very different and I liked different with my men and music.

I had dressed to impress and intended to move into my 21st with gusto and by the time I eventually sat down at the table that Michael had arranged for my guests and I, making sure plenty of champagne was on tap, a huge bouquet had arrived from him, presented by a singing delivery boy. Very sweet, but there was no Michael to enjoy the evening with.

Ronnie Scott was on stage as master of ceremonies, cracking his jokes and introducing Matt Monroe and his band, who were the resident entertainment that week.

I already had sight of the man I wanted to spend my night with. He had spirited himself off the stage, perspiration glistening on his face, and noticing our table lit up with candles, flowers and presents, he came over, acknowledged everyone and wished me happy birthday. 'Oh please join us,' I blurted out, and after planting a kiss on my cheek, disappearing and returning refreshed, he sat next to me in the chair I had made sure was vacant for him. 'You were marvellous, simply marvellous,' I gushed. He had been playing his trumpet beautifully. I discovered when listening to his American drawl that he wasn't resident at Scott's but a session musician in Las Vegas and his time in England was soon to be over. Who cared about the future? The moment was now and this handsome guy was just what the doctor ordered.

Over the next few hours we easily slipped into conversation and as the evening rolled on I gestured to Lexi that I was about to make my exit and say goodbye to my guests. We continued into the night onto several night spots, popping in and out of each, then heading for a late night coffee shop. 'I better get you back before your girlfriend thinks I have kidnapped you.' Was he kidding? It was four o'clock in the morning and I had no intention of him leaving my side. I was happy, a little drunk and tired, but I wanted to wake up in the morning with him and kiss him goodbye. I needed no more than that.

He asked me if I was hungry and knowing I was, proceeded to order everything on the menu. Too much food, too much to drink and too tired for sex, but I wanted to end my birthday nestled in his arms and fall asleep just like that. He didn't take much persuasion, and after digesting all that food we made our way to my apartment and tiptoed into bed.

I had reached the stage of being completely fed up with the house rules and work rules. It was now time for change and change had to happen. When I woke later that morning, 21 and into a new year, entwined around his body while he was still asleep, I jumped into the bath then called out for Lexi but she was not at home. I then made a call to cancel my strip performance that evening, giving any excuse. I didn't care. Then I joined him back in bed where we spent most of the day and where I let my special guest entertain me.

The Flamingo Club on Wardour Street, with its R&B live music and heady atmosphere, was where Christine Keeler hung out years earlier and where events in her life had exploded into the Profumo Affair. It was also where Lexi and I decided to continue the birthday spirit some days after the event. We loved that club and would occasionally be tempted to move on from there and party. This night was no different. We eagerly accepted an invitation to an apartment where music continued, with lots of drugs in many forms available to get high on. The atmosphere was potent, with joints being passed around and white powder for anyone to snort. I regularly got high but not on anything other than booze and the odd joint. Not that I had any objection to anything stronger. Each to their own.

The drugs and booze relaxed everyone and before long frantic sexual activity was on the menu. There were tongues in my ears, my nipples and lips, fingers in my pussy, and the height of orgasm from penetration of a tongue or penis in my by now very wet vagina. Somehow Lexi had decided to lay her body next to me and all at once turned and pulled me close, covering my face and neck with kisses, her fingers lightly scratching my back as I lay, getting turned on and somewhat confused. I let my fingers stroke her lovely skin as she gently directed my face towards her breasts. 'Viv, how about kissing me just a little lower?' as she coaxed and guided me past her navel, shivering every time I touched a sensitive spot.

As I was about to get acquainted with her pussy, my attention was interrupted by the penis that was feeling stiff between the crack of my cheeks. Raising myself on my knees to take more advantage of his stiffness I turned to face him and take him between my breasts and leaning forward I ran my tongue along his shaft while he was trying desperately not to ejaculate, wriggling until he was able to bring his mouth to satisfy my swollen labia. Lexi meanwhile was ignoring any other advances and was totally focused on masturbating, while thoroughly enjoying watching and hearing my pleasure.

After four years of obviously wanting what others had, she brushed him aside, taking control of my body, frantically rubbing her clitoris on mine and riding my body like she had a penis.

A cannabis-cocaine mix can do the strangest things.

It was the last party and the last orgy we went to together, and it wasn't long before my sweet friend made her exit from London.

Was it the knowledge of our intimacy that made her mind up to return to Colin? She never said but I guessed she missed him and believed that was her only reason.

Chapter 10

Tricks of the Trade

'I believe that sex is the most beautiful, natural and wholesome thing that money can buy.' – Steve Martin

I was drawn to the Heaven and Hell club, with its name in lights, and I fell into the habit of visiting it, sitting at the bar for a drink and chatting to the girls as they arrived. They were as interested in me as I was in them, knowing that the boss and I had been intimately involved.

My regular companion was Louis, a milliner who made the most amazing extravagant headdresses for the stripping fraternity. He had become my close confidant and, as a bisexual with leanings more towards men than women, he was someone I could chat to in confidence.

Visually he was a work of art, vivid green eyes and dark hair tinged with the slightest of blonde highlights. He was striking and unusual, always immaculately turned out in the latest fashion trends which he uncannily knew suited him most. He was great company and, with Lexis's return to Manchester, he became my bosom buddy. Whenever work schedules allowed, I would join him to enjoy Soho's cafe society.

We first ventured into the Heaven and Hell after Louis had wined and dined me. We were eager to take on more of the late entertainment and I was curious to learn more about the hostess world and whether I possessed the ingredients to do it. It wasn't the kind of club that was likely to set you back a few hundred quid for a couple of hours' entertainment. The customers were there to seal business relationships, escape solitude and be treated like real men. The atmosphere was created with dark walls, mirrors, glittery band fixtures, and seductive lighting and, as I discovered, the emphasis was for the hostess to play, rather than work. They were expected to perform ritual tasks when company joined them – lighting cigarettes, ordering more drinks and pouring them into the waiting glasses of clients. Conversation was to be flirtatious, charged with an underlying eroticism. Sex was very much implied but not performed.

The first duty of a hostess was to make the client feel desirable, then to allow conversation to flow easily on to how much time spent in the company of this sensually charged woman would cost him. As I carefully stored all this knowledge, I was confident I possessed all the attributes to become a top hostess. But before my first paid encounter I had decided what I was willing to do and whether the money they were paying for their time could include a little extra fun for me.

I realised that the trick of the trade was to provide a client with your body and its sexual services but I decided to develop a routine which I could adapt. I would not just lie on my back and allow them to prod and poke me. I needed to stay in control all the time, even when I pretended not to, and I never intended to do anything I wasn't comfortable with. I would need to reinvent myself just for my clients and build a story around my name, changing it from Vivien to Yvonne – Yvonne Carla Rossi, my imaginative 'star' name. I even opened a bank account in that name, to be used exclusively for my venture into prostitution, for that was what I would be doing. I had no illusion about that. The thought of the money that would mount up in that name spurred me on. Wealthy in my own right, how wonderful was that?

The evening of my first venture into sex with a stranger

arrived at last. It was a scary prospect, but the thrill I felt stepping into that club that night was amazing. Mr S was quite famous in the TV world, although I didn't recognise him at first. I noticed his smile, displaying a brilliant set of teeth, as he leaned over the bar talking to the attractive barmaid, making her laugh. Whatever he was saying obviously did the trick, as she reacted with bursts of giggles. Her laughter was so loud you had to turn and notice who was entertaining her.

We caught each other's eye and as he lifted his glass in a gesture of 'cheers', I replied with mine. He excused himself from the barmaid and wandered over, asking in his dulcet tones if he could join me. *That's what I am here for*, I thought, but I quietly said, 'Yes.'

I drank the watered-down pink champagne, while he sipped his martini on the rocks. I liked his style but he wasn't there to impress me with anything except how deep his pockets were. I felt I had to treat this first part of the evening as though he was a hopeful lover and I let my imagination run away with me. It was the only way I could handle it, that first time. Knowing I had an understanding with the club that I couldn't leave till three o'clock in the morning we had many hours to enjoy each other's company. I discovered this made the rest of the evening easy, and by the time we were ready to depart, we had discussed everything down to the final detail, including what type of sex he liked, how long he wanted to spend with me and, of course, a little information, true or not, about his life.

If a client wished, he could pay the club for a hostess to leave early and this is what happened that first night, and then we were on our way. He told me he lived in St John's Wood, an affluent part of north London, and that he was employed by the BBC as a journalist. He could have been anyone. He agreed to come to my apartment. I knew I would be in control there, the pick of my music, my drinks, I could invite him to lay on my king-size bed, with its luxury ivory silk sheets, and fluffy towels bought from Harrods. No squeaks or creaks in the bedstead to put anyone off their stroke, condoms, lubes and tissues, and exotic oils easy to hand in the bedside drawers, the bedroom music set to play sweet-sounding melodies.

I had already learnt that money had to be spent before the fun began and my plan was to unfold a towel for him to lie on, so as not to risk any semen on the sheets, I knew my burlesque corsets and lingerie would heighten his sexual desire and harden his penis.

As we entered my apartment, I guided him towards the cosy lounge, turned on the music, and brought a bottle of chilled wine out of the kitchen fridge. We sat close and I let him kiss my chilled, wine-soaked lips gently, then let him undress me, slowly removing my black wet-look, figure-hugging dress by undoing the laces that ended with a tempting glimpse of my pert bottom. The dress slipped off, to reveal my black lace bra, matching suspenders, and tiny G-string.

Fishnet stockings were removed after he slipped off my stiletto shoes, sniffing the scent of my perfumed feet. As he admired my shapely body, I undressed him, offering him a shower and joining him in it. He seduced me there in a respectful manner, kissing my breasts and sucking my nipples, while his hands were soap-sudding my body. As we dried ourselves, I grabbed the bottle of wine and headed towards the bedroom, where I lay face down on the bed and asked him to start by giving me a relaxing massage. As he swept his oiled hands over my body, I turned over and sensed his pleasure, as I allowed him to open and spread my legs and massage around my bare pussy.

I trusted his touch, letting everything happen slowly, as I anticipated his progression of passion. He was selfless, not focusing on his own sexual needs, kissing under my arms and on my feet, hands, pussy and bottom, until he quietly asked if he could penetrate me. Emerging from a dream into reality, I quietly opened the bedside drawer and grabbed a condom, flipping it on to his oiled up erection. I had an orgasm before he did, which thrilled him, but when he exploded it was with a frantic pounding of my body and a loud roar.

What were my thoughts? The orgasm that I had enjoyed had cost him plenty of bucks and he had taken up two hours of my time. Another thought was how easily I could switch my mind to enjoying the experience, forgetting business and enjoying pleasure, followed quickly by another thought. I had forgotten to ask for payment up-front, something I would never do again.

Feeling powerful, feeling satisfied, feeling good about the cash, I rewarded myself with a facial, a therapeutic massage, a manicure and pedicure the following day. This working girl had to keep on top form, and I enjoyed the money knowing there was plenty more to come.

I would entertain men who had access to a disposable income, entrepreneurial instincts and the desire to be pleasured by a hot chick who knew all the tricks. Paying for it was their pleasure.

Chapter 11

The Seduction of the Steel Tips

'Everything in the world is about sex, except sex - sex is about power.'

The Gaslight Club in Mayfair and the Blue Angel Club on Little Portland Street were known for their intimate alcoves, the quality of the girls and the exceptional champagne, all at top prices. It was here that I next took up residence, alongside girls who were well-groomed and good conversationalists, who dressed in an array of long evening gowns.

You had not only to be appealing to the eye but also intelligent. The success of these clubs rode on the quality of the hostesses and there were ladies from all over the world. The interiors had a taste of the Victorian era, seductive and seducing with that touch of class.

The array of clientele that had the pleasure of my company varied as much as their sexual desires and the background from which they came. From an hour booking to an all-night stay over, from submissives to men who wanted you in every position in the *Karma Sutra*, men that spent their time just talking, fully dressed, while I stripped and played with myself until erupting in an orgasm deserving of an Oscar.

Before long, I had an appreciation for the one person naked and the other person dressed scenario. That added some kinky flair which reminded me of my repeat visits to Michael in his office and him letting me remove his clothing and give him a deep blow job. Those favourite erotic moments when I took control and he would have to stay fully dressed so that my nakedness felt extra naked as he would hold my legs wide apart, as wide as they would go. Just the anticipation of sex, the feeling of him stroking and fingering me as he wet his fingers with his mouth made me wish he was going down on me, giving me oral sex.

I wondered if this was what being tied up was all about: An erotic feeling of being wide open, so vulnerable and urgently craving penetration, and at that same moment going deep inside me hitting my G-spot with all the thrust I was dying for. I would get insanely wet and pretend that my hands were tied behind my back like an erotic bondage scenario and then feeling a great whoosh like my whole body had surrendered. I recalled for some years my days with Michael and having those similar experiences when being paid for it.

Certainly, the one person naked and the other person dressed scenario had many rewards but mostly it carried me away in the direction I wanted to go, taking on imaginative sex away from the boring.

As a prostitute you are there for a pure sexual experience. It is a deliberate erotic act and a way to explore your sexual limits. Things that I might have found awkward with a lover I could do in the sexual role as a hooker. It gave me a feeling of power and accomplishment and I could explore my own sexual limits, where I was not only allowed, but encouraged, to get as dirty as I wanted to be.

Sat at the bar one evening feeling no different from any other, a man approached me and introduced himself as Billy – he was to become my first husband.

I was immediately taken with him, small in stature but big in personality, with a cheeky grin and plenty of chat. A true Cockney, born within the sound of Bow Bells, he told me. A Londoner and proud of it. His claim to fame was playing professional football for West Ham United, and he had his testimonial at the Blue Angel Club. It seems cartilage problems had caused his early retirement. He was immaculately suited and booted. I had learnt to judge a man's worth by the shoes he wore.

I also learnt that eroticism is about making someone feel sexy without necessarily laying a finger on them, or if you do lay a finger on them, it is about transmitting the most powerful sensual sensations right through to the bone and making them positively light up. The power behind the touch depends on what you were thinking, and I was thinking, *You are quite a striking man and it's almost impossible to keep my hands off you.* Those thoughts would have transmitted through my touch, an 'accidental' touch, unnoticed by anyone, but him.

I was effective in creating an erotic tension when I joined him at the table he had reserved for dinner. His words were, 'You're lovely, come and have dinner with me,' and then giving me an impromptu kiss that sent a powerful message which was impossible to misunderstand.

He was dynamic, direct and hardly subtle, but I responded directly back and suddenly there were fireworks. Lazily stroking my arm while having conversation with another hostess, I assumed he had obviously paid for pleasure before. We sat in a cosy alcove away from the entertainment of the room. He went through all the courses but I declined a meal, not wanting the smell of food on my breath.

He was generous to the house with his money and ordered bottles of champagne that cost most working people their week's wages. We played footsie under the table while we chatted about anything and everything and by the time he paid the bill and looked after those that had looked after him with generous tips, we left the club. It was an automatic transition and there was no build up to it; he asked, 'Are you ready to leave?' and I said yes. I hadn't discussed the cost of my time or indeed what his sexual preferences were. I felt immediately that this was more than business.

We went to a casino where I joined him at the blackjack table, sitting next to him while he expertly won over the dealer. I felt aware that my dress was virtually transparent. The long black lace outfit was great for business in a hostess club but hardly suitable for a casino. Eventually, after some time, we left and as we did he threw a few chips across the table. He tipped everyone and I respected that.

It was after four in the morning when we pulled up outside my apartment. I remember it was raining, and being a gallant gent, he jumped out of the car, opened the door and covered me with his jacket till we reached the porch, then covering my face with gentle kisses until he rested on my lips. French kissing with tongues deep into my mouth, searching every part of it. I couldn't quite grasp that he intended to leave me there, on the steps to my home, but he did, going into his trouser pocket and coming up with a wad of notes. He didn't count how much he lay in my hand, he just palmed me with plenty and left after jotting down my number with a promise to phone me later that day.

It wasn't that day but the one after that I received a call from him. I had spent the time in between totally absorbed with thoughts of him, so much so, I didn't work that evening. When his call came I didn't ask any questions, instead eagerly took up his invitation for lunch. 'What plans do you have for the day?' he asked.

'Nothing that special,' was my reply. The truth was it would have taken an earthquake to stop me meeting him.

It seemed that everywhere we went there was female attention towards him, which I commented on while having lunch. 'I am not a handsome man,' he would say to me all the time and I would disagree. He was older than me by 13 years, his hair mostly dark with shots of steel grey. His nose had been broken but it added character to his face. Large hazel eyes added to his appeal, with perfectly shaped strong smooth hands that held a tight grip. I loved the laugh that rumbled out of him. He had the most infectious laugh.

Walking around after lunch in Soho, he stopped and pointed to an item in a shop window. They were there looking scary all on their own and a build-up of excitement and anxiety hit my stomach. 'I think we'll take those.' He was watching me with those deep hazel eyes and checking my reaction. I did a pretend shiver and there was that laugh rumbling out of him, as he put his arms around me and pulled me closer. 'We'll have some fun with these,' he said, and pressed his teeth to my ear so I could feel the hardness of them. The potential for a painful nip or a soft kiss, but not knowing is what scared and excited the most.

The salesgirl had a large collection on display and she slipped her hand inside the glass case and removed our item on show, next to all the ball-gags and whips, spurs, crops and paddles, of which I was used to seeing and using, but not these – the scariest of all. 'Put your hand out,' and he pressed his mouth to my hair and his hand to my back, trapping me and soothing me at the same time.

I don't like sharp things that can cut the skin, so when the weight of the leather gloves with steel tips hit my palm, I gave a shudder and made a whimpering sound that made Billy smile. 'How do they feel?' he asked, his hips pressed hard against mine and I felt his hardness.

He could have bent me over the counter and had me there and then, but I replied, 'They feel good.'

To the salesgirl he said, 'We'll take them.' I was full of anticipation and already I was wet. 'I think we'll take them to your bedroom and play,' he said as he guided me with a firm hand at the back of my waist.

The ride home in his Jaguar was short but he made sure he took his time, slowly and silently. I knew he was playing with me. I had thoughts of the steel tips which had me dreaming up all kinds of erotic thoughts.

He asked me not to move, and that is all he said. I stopped moving instantly and two things happened. I started to wet my panties and I was so aroused I could smell the scent but he smiled at me to show that he smelt it too. Full of anticipation and trying to catch my breath he stops the car, jumps out after kissing me on the neck, while telling me I will be fine. 'I don't even have to touch you to know you are wet,' he whispered and winked and then he was gone until the car door flew open and I was grateful for his hand as my legs had turned to jelly. Escorting me into my apartment, finding the bedroom and laying me out on the silk sheets, I must have looked like a starfish, my head between lots of pillows, hands up and out and legs spread apart while he slowly undressed me, standing over me unclasping his belt and exposing his erect penis. He had a beautiful penis.

The steel tips were used all over my body without slicing my skin. Digging in enough for me to feel the pleasure, without hurting me. It was much harder not being bound and keeping myself still. The only thing that bound me were his words and my control.

He was a man that knew his stuff and a man also clever enough to know that penetration from his beautiful penis was going to bring from me an enormous orgasm that soaked the bed.

It was the way he carried himself, the way he experimented sexually with me, the chances in life that he took, that helped to continue our amazing relationship.

Chapter 12

Rules of the Game

'If you must play, decide on three things at the start: The rules of the game, the stakes, and the quitting time.'

I had learned early on that life with Billy was going to be a rollercoaster of experiences, from the height of hedonism to the depths of despair and back again. One of the things I loved about him was his brain, when it wasn't drowned in alcohol. He was a constant heavy smoker but it didn't detract from his ability to play all forms of sport to a professional level. Everyone took to this cheeky chappie who had an enormous spirit for life. He had the ability to get where gas couldn't and before you knew it you would find yourself in the best celebrity company, from sport and film to minor royals.

It became obvious from the very beginning of our relationship that there were no objections to my continuing to work as a hostess, in fact, quite the opposite. I felt safe in his company having lived alone since Lexi's departure. It was comforting having someone to talk to on my level. We understood each other, we thrilled at living on the edge and, as time went on, we became soulmates as well as lovers. Soon he took charge of the money I was earning, but he would make sure I got whatever I needed, and always the best that money could buy. Jewellery would appear encrusted with precious stones, and when on occasion he would travel to Switzerland he would return with a fur coat, or the most expensive handbag and luggage. A new Porsche, wrapped up in an enormous ribbon, arrived at my door for my 23rd birthday. He had taken control and I was happy for him to do so.

A rule was laid down. No clients could be entertained at the apartment unless Billy was included in the deal. If not, it had to be visits to hotels only and when that happened he had to be informed in advance, so that he knew where I was and what time my business would be over. If he wasn't waiting outside for me, a friendly taxi driver would be – a perfect arrangement. When occasionally bringing an eager gentlemen home, fun was mixed with business, and a very eager Billy would be waiting there and a no-holds-barred sex session would sometimes last for hours as Billy increased his already huge sex drive by sniffing amyl nitrate, encouraging me and our guest to do the same. One sniff of amyl gets rid of any inhibitions and heightens the arousal and the orgasm. Clients soon relaxed and took part in erotic threesomes, all at great cost to them, of course.

I was heading towards my 23rd birthday when it was decided Billy would move in with me, arriving with bags and baggage it became clear there would not be enough wardrobes or space to fit his tailor-made suits, hand-made shirts, dozens of pairs of shoes and accessories, as well as his electrical gadgets, his skis and boots. By the time the delivery van was empty, the apartment had taken on a different look, but the arrangement suited me fine. He had brought a spirit into my home that had never been felt before. Every day was exciting and each one filled with surprises.

It had been a long time since Michael had ended his payments for the rent and as Billy intended to take care of that, I was in a comfortable position, a very happy bunny. I had guessed Billy was looking forward to living at a settled address, after living in hotels and serviced apartments. Relationships and marriage are tough enough to keep on track but when you are married to a Billy type of guy that relationship can be hard to handle and you have to be ahead of the game to keep it together. His marriage had collapsed but he still maintained a friendship with his former wife who had earned her living as a high class hooker before turning her talents to studying the art of rococo restoration while at the same time opening a number of blue cinema clubs in London's West End. You have to admire a girl that multi-tasks and when we were introduced we got on famously. I had been multi-tasking too, running a chaotic home, feeding a hungry lover with delicious delightful food, while continuing to work most evenings.

Only a few months after their divorce, Billy had got down on one knee and proposed to me, over-exaggerating the occasion. We laughed but, of course, I didn't hesitate in accepting. It was performed in a unique and sweet way on Valentine's, the day after my birthday. Like many other loving couples on this special day we were dining out and a cake flickering with candles took centre stage on the table. At first glance I thought it was a loving birthday gesture but when I looked closer there was a little gift box hidden among the decorative icing, and then I spotted it and took a gasp. I knew inside there would be a ring. I was besotted with this guy who had taken over my life and looked forward to spending the rest of my life with him.

Six weeks after I registered the marriage, Billy and I were married at Jacksons Row Register Office in Manchester on June 9, 1973. I had wanted to return to the place I still called home and hoped the news of deciding to settle down in marriage would somehow be agreeable to my parents and heal our estranged relationship. I was dreaming. Their wedding invitations were ignored and so I entered my marriage without their blessing, only witnessed by a few close friends. I wished so much that my mother could have seen me in that dress of pink lace but she was nowhere to be seen. Sometime later, I learned that my father had been across the road, watching the arrival of my wedding car but he couldn't bring himself to take the few steps to join me. How sad for him and how sad for me.

Monte Carlo is where we spent our honeymoon, arriving at the Hotel De Paris on the west side of Place Du Casino. Billy's knowledge of the history and culture of wherever we travelled was impressive. He explained that we had arrived at the crème de la crème of the gambling world and the Place Du Casino was the height of glamour. Take a map of Monte Carlo and you've hit the palmy Place Du Casino... location, location, location! Grouped together majestically, the vision of the Hotel De Paris, the Monte Carlo Casino, the Garnier Opera House and the Cafe De Paris.

I was then his princess wrapped up in cotton wool, dressed in diamonds and furs. Every evening he returned to our bedroom suite, money and chips thrown on the table, recklessly, allowing me to take whatever amount I wished. With an amazingly dazzling guest list we dined, danced and gambled with the elite. The casino, with its theatre for opera and ballet, opened my eyes to all I had been taught as a child. How I wished to have achieved those goals then, among the magnificent buildings that house it all.

A walk up the steps from the Place Du Casino and through the canopied entrance took you to the high-ceilinged lobby and the statue of Louis X1V, where gamblers seeking good luck rubbed the horse's right knee to a shine. Grand and glorious with marble floors and colonnades, wide archways and a magnificent domed glass skylight. To the left the Bar Americain, with seating swathed in leather, and where live jazz played nightly. My favourite restaurant was always Le Grill on the top floor, surrounded by walls of windows that looked out on to the Mediterranean, the ceiling opening to a starry sky.

Looking back, how we managed to last six months of this opulence is amazing in itself, but my new husband's expertise playing craps and poker won the day. I later realised he would bet on two flies climbing the wall and put everything on which reached the top first. Sex addiction is so much more rewarding than a gambling addiction.

Roulette, blackjack, craps, baccarat, stud poker, Billy was a master poker player. Among the gambling tables in the evening beautiful ladies would flaunt their cleavages and diamonds, attracting the attention of the visiting gambling elite gentlemen. This practice became a much needed hobby of mine towards the end of our stay. Of course, I was encouraged; Billy with a run of bad luck was not a pretty sight, and so I succumbed to my old ways and gentlemen were invited for champagne and canapés in our suite, the canapé delight being me.

Men on their own or accompanied by their lady friends, all were encouraged to taste sexual delights away from the gambling table. Tips to the hotel concierge to guide me towards possible candidates were a regular occurrence. I spent my days visiting the shops of Monte Carlo, buying dresses to impress and slipping away to St. Michel where I had befriended an American lady who took to the tables of the Monte Carlo Casino in the evening. Hugely wealthy, she looked like she had stepped out of a Hollywood movie, all boobs and bottom, with lips always painted scarlet red.

I became a friend with favours. Having gone through three husbands, retaining huge amounts of their wealth in divorce, she was looking for different pleasures and had formed an attraction towards me that Billy encouraged, and we naturally fell into a steamy episode that had me tracing my steps back to her home, where she would encourage me to relax naked in her pool. Cocktails would be served at poolside by her man servant after she had enjoyed towelling me down, oiling and fingering my body and laying kisses on my skin. I will never forget Edie. My urges towards a woman's pussy became alive for real there, on the Riviera.

I took pleasure in undressing and caressing some of the

most beautiful aristocratic women, who let their guard down with the touch of my hand or mouth, their gentlemen sharing the joy of the act with Billy, whose need of all forms of sexual perversions became obvious to me. Being bisexual himself, he was always eager to join in the fun – twosomes, threesomes, and a whole heap of money was passed our way for the pleasure but alas ended up as always on the gambling table, spewed away till eventually it was time to depart. A decision was made to return England. The mass of money had dwindled and all that was left was a collection of diamond and emerald jewellery, most of which had been won in our bedroom suite. We were returning home without even our car, which had quite literally been gambled away. As well as the jewellery, the only sign of exuberance and wealth was a large Louis Vuitton trunk crammed with clothes by Chanel, Dior, Givenchy and Yves Saint Laurent. Style and elegance at a price.

Chapter 13

Preston's Pleasure Dome

'Today will never come again.
Be a blessing.
Be a friend.
Encourage someone.
Take time to care.
Let your words heal, and not wound.'

I was 25 years old when we finally returned to England after our extended honeymoon. We were not in a good position financially so Billy had to make some moves very quickly, networking around the East End of London, where he based himself to renew his business contacts.

Meanwhile, I took the opportunity to contact uncle Harry and aunt Zara in Enfield, who welcomed me with open arms to stay with them. Billy had been in touch with his ex-wife and she generously introduced him to her people to help set himself up in the north of England with his first blue cinema club. It was to be the first of its kind outside the capital and the venture had excellent prospects. Did I trust his judgement when spending nights in her company? No, but we needed her contacts, so what if they fancied sex together? I knew he loved me and you soon discover when in the adult industry that there is a huge difference between making love and having sex.

It was on my first night in Enfield that I took a phone

call that stopped me in my tracks. Harry was expecting the call. It was my mother, who had finally decided to break the ice between us. Sadly, it wasn't for a pleasant chat – she had bad news for me. In between sobs of despair she managed to explain that her favourite sister Stella had only months to live after being diagnosed with lung cancer.

I packed my bags and took the first train back to Manchester, where cousins, aunts and uncles rejoiced in seeing me back with my parents at last, and for me the years of separation very quickly became a distant memory. My mother needed me and I was there to support her. It's amazing how a crisis can bring people together, closer than ever before. You realise nothing is more important in life than family.

Billy joined me immediately after he heard the news as life became focused on Stella. My sweet aunt had lost her beauty, her gorgeous face puffed up with drugs. I was thankful she was never told how poorly she really was, although perhaps she knew. However, the day we all had been dreading came and she died quietly, without a fuss, leaving us devastated. This was the first death in the family to have any real impact on me but my mother suffered the worst. Her darling sister was no more.

Billy had spent the months setting up his first cinema club in the city centre, frequented by men in macs who masturbated beneath them while watching porn. Eventually we moved into an apartment above what was to become our first brothel – Eros Massage Parlour on Moss Lane East, Moss Side. This was soon followed with parlours in Blackpool, Preston and Wigan and before long Billy had established himself as a main player in the industry. Did he sample the goods? Probably, but I never asked and never found out. Everyone was clever enough to know better than to kiss and tell.

Billy had the pick of the best of working girls, using his magnetic personality to perfection to entice them in.

During this early period I spent as much time as possible with my family and we became close to my cousin and her husband who lived in Whitefield, two steps up the ladder from the Jewish ghetto of Salford where we lived as kids. Billy the charmer had easily slipped into the Jewish way of life where the main topic of the day was football and racing for the boys and beauty salons and doting on our husbands for the girls, with a few hiccups in between: The occasional collapse of a marriage due to a husband's dalliance with another man's wife, or vice versa. Me? I had the man I wanted, I didn't need anyone else.

Before opening the business venture in Preston, Billy had lunch on a few occasions with the chief of police. It was important to know we were not going to be investing a heap of money in a massage parlour for it to be immediately closed down by the police. Turning a blind eye is easy if you were receiving generous back handers and once being given the go-ahead he wasted no time in choosing the right girls to work alongside me in the small venue in Preston, so we could open 12 hours a day, seven days a week. All the girls were desirable but two stood out.

Wendy was very dynamic and highly aware of her sexuality – a luscious 22-year-old Liverpudlian with platinum blonde hair worn cropped around her face. Her eyes were a vivid shade of green that ate you up when they focused on you. She wasn't petite but broad and fit, a lover of horses and a keen three-day eventer who would on occasion find herself riding alongside Prince Charles in the Cheshire Hunt. She had the upkeep of several horses and became a hooker in order to keep them.

She loved every aspect of her job and played a major part in the brothel's success. Wendy loved the power her style of sex gave her, devouring men, teasing them with her tongue, working her body all over them and allowing them to bring her to orgasm in any position they desired, simply because she desired it too. Her orgasms were never fake and they knew it, which heightened their lust for her. She was a brilliant dominatrix, playing the role to perfection when she felt in the mood to crack her whip across a man's bare arse. Arriving to work immaculately made up, with a suitcase full of outfits to vary her style to suit her clients' needs, she was the ultimate professional and her adoring clientele returned for more, time and time again.

In contrast, Patsy was submissive, tall and slender with fine features and perfect creamy smooth skin. Her auburn hair would be worn in a high bouffant style and no matter how rough a client could get in the throes of reaching their height of passion, her make-up always remained in perfect place. Her claim to fame were her breast implants, which were still a novelty in the 70s. She was also a brilliant actress, using a vibrating dildo that she carried in her purse, to whet their appetites, slowly inserting it deep inside her while squirming with desire.

These were the two girls I chose to work alongside, as I returned to the business of selling my body – and what a spectacular body it was. Toned and slender, with a tiny waist, great legs and a perfectly curved butt. I was tempted by Patsy's silicone-enhanced boobs, considering expanding my own breast size. But for now I retained the small pert breasts that perfectly balanced my body.

The decision to return to the sex industry was not easy. I was very happy surrounded by my family, involving myself as much as I could with their lives. I became very close to my cousin and her husband and children and my mother was at last content with her daughter. But these were tough times and I yearned for the luxury lifestyle that prostitution provided. I was surprised how easy it was to get back into the routine as I stepped into the parlour in Preston and in no time I had collected my own clientele who paid the extra money I demanded. It was financially a big step down, compared to what I had been receiving in London, but on Billy's advice I worked within the bounds of what his girls were charging. 'Trust your judgement,' he used to say, but I knew what he meant: 'Perform for those who tip you well.' Half an hour of my time would cost the equivalent of £100 today, and as my bookings improved, so did my enthusiasm for the job.

Favourite girls were often booked for a two-girl special, which delighted them both, not only for the generous tips they received but also because they loved to play with each other, their orgasms rocking the building as they fingered and fucked with their prize toy, the double-ended dildo, lying head-to-toe working this treasured toy inside them. Men were mesmerised as they watched and masturbated, totally engrossed with the vision before them.

If I was asked to choose a girl who did it for me, it was Patsy with her gentle touch. As I lay on the bed while she soaked me with baby oil. Judging by her reaction when a booking was made for us both to perform together, I guess the feeling was mutual. If I was present, her face lit up with childish delight. If I wasn't there I could expect to hear her sweet voice on the telephone, unable to contain herself, filled with excitement about the two-girl booking made for us.

Chapter 14

There's No Business Like Show Business

'People begin to be successful the minute they decide to be.'

Billy revelled in his new role as Mr Respectable and became a big part of the Whitefield society, playing football for the Maccarbi Jewish team and helping them win. His enthusiasm for all sport impressed many people and the wives of the husbands he had befriended loved his sense of humour. He was, indeed, an interesting, fun-loving character in whose company to be.

Meanwhile, his days were spent slowly building up his sex empire. He was bold and took chances that always seemed to pay off. Like the time he invited the entire Wigan football team to sample the delights of his brothel. When news got out, every man in Wigan was champing at the bit to get their rocks off with these beauties who expertly managed to give a man the ultimate sexual pleasure.

Brothels have a more desirable name and go under the disguise of a massage parlour. In those days saunas were installed with a room for gym equipment, so that if 'straight' customers called for a sauna and massage, that's all they received. All the girls were advised to learn to provide a therapeutic massage and many underwent training so that they could flaunt their certificates as proof they were legally a professional masseuse.

Advertising in newspapers followed the same pattern, sauna and massage being mentioned, and all these years later the same applies today. The reason was not so much to hide the fact from the police but to prevent members of the public from objecting and bringing the business to the attention of the boys in blue. It was vital for everyone not to let their guard down.

Within the same space of time a snooker hall and poker club in the city centre became another of my husband's ventures. His partner in this enterprise, Don Tony, was a man who many thought of as handsome. His taste in women usually leant towards the tall, beautiful black girls he met regularly at the Russell Club dance hall he owned in Moss Side, an area notorious for gun fights and drug busts. Don was a stocky, tough-talking white man who found it difficult to crack his face with a smile. But he was regarded as a white god in the Moss Side circles in which he moved, his soul club attracting black artists from throughout the UK and America.

The snooker hall became an instant success and attracted top players like a young Jimmy White, who was on the brink of success, and Alex Higgins, the number one snooker player at the time. Their exhibition games soon spiralled into incredible matches, with huge amounts of money being wagered. The poker room at the back of the club was reserved for professional players, who would arrive from all over the continent to sit at the table. It was serious stuff indeed, with poker sessions lasting through the night and until the crack of dawn. The atmosphere in the little room was electric, players gambling thousands on the turn of a card, often losing all their money, jewellery and more. It certainly wasn't a game for the faint-hearted.

Professional poker players would travel to take part in a game in if they knew Billy was in residence. Their need to strip him of his money and win the day was president. Little did they know that he had a trick up his sleeve and while wearing what seemed to be ordinary reading glasses he was actually straining his eyes beneath ultra-violet lenses that gave him the power to see the cards his contenders were holding.

The City Centre Snooker Hall and Poker Club was eventually turned into the City Centre Sauna.

It was an extravagant venture but one that paid off as a much more lucrative proposition. Open 24 hours, seven days a week, it was the first with all-night accommodation for the many men who had spent an evening in the city and not been able to find the right girl to share a bed with. It became Billy's flagship parlour, housing an array of beautiful girls. It seemed that between the Russell Club and its soul music artists and the City Centre Sauna, they had mastered the art of enticing every visiting artist, sportsman and celebrity when they were visiting Manchester.

The Wilton Hotel on Hyde Road, Gorton, was a favourite place to unwind. Two miles from the city centre and very conveniently situated for Old Trafford, it had less than two-star quality and the furnishings were very basic. Situated on a busy main road where the old cotton mills still stood, the lack of 'star' status didn't detract from the warm and friendly feeling that the 'in-house' proprietor Maureen gave its atmosphere. Maureen was a wonderful character and the same age as me. We enjoyed some great chats in the morning over the breakfast table as she provided food for all the revellers who had taken to the bedrooms after a heavy night of boozing. There wasn't the slightest bit of glamour to the place, other than the glamour that walked in at night after leaving club-land in the city centre.

Maureen was very fond of Billy and enjoyed his company. Anything she could do to make him comfortable, she did gladly. They both had something in common, a love of living life on the edge of gangster land. Her experiences had me riveted to the seat either at the bar in the evening or over the breakfast table the following morning.

One perfect example of experiencing a little drama involved the idolised Manchester United player George Best, known by many for his erratic behaviour when indulging in one of his favourite sports – alcohol. George, it seemed, had taken a particular liking to one of the City Centre Sauna's young ladies. I have to admit she was extremely pretty, blonde of course, just the way he liked them, and in her late teens, which was even more appealing. She was ripe and ready for the job she had chosen to do but with a sweet innocence that appealed to every guy that passed her way.

George had spotted her in our company one evening while pursuing the pleasures of nightlife in the city. His constant demands for her attention, however, fell on deaf ears. Carol was quite simply not interested. George's attitude towards women left much to be desired and being ignored was definitely not on the menu. Unable to control his temper, he traced her steps to the Wilton Hotel. It was past 2am one Saturday morning and Carol had tucked herself into bed in one of the rooms Maureen had allocated for her. Meanwhile, George had arrived at the hotel, fired up and impatient to see her. Maureen, who was an expert at dealing with close encounters, quickly calmed the situation down, simply stating she was sleeping like a baby in her bedroom.

The events that followed should have been recorded in *The Guinness Book of Records*! Stones that sounded like boulders where hurled at the bedroom windows by a distraught and very drunk George, demanding the attention of the young woman he wanted. Maureen immediately went into action, making an urgent call to her close friend Sandy Busby (Matt Busby's son) and within a short space of time he arrived to rescue the situation. Grabbing hold of George, he paced him up and down Hyde Road, taking it in turn with others, while Maureen laid on plenty of black coffee to straighten his head. There was an urgency – it was Saturday and the main event of the sporting day was the Manchester United play-off at Old Trafford. George, being their 'star' player, was naturally expected to produce a winning result. Would you have bet on him being able to achieve it? But George being George made the pitch his own only a few hours later, scoring a hatful of goals!

Chapter 15

A Sexy Soirée

'A man is like a novel: Until the very last page you don't know how it will end. Otherwise, it wouldn't be worth reading.'

Billy's business was booming and now was the time to take advantage of our improved financial status and invest in property.

It was a beautiful spring day in 1976 when we were handed the keys to Broseley Road, Firswood, making a quick cash payment after being introduced to a man who urgently needed to release his funds from his investment. It was within easy walking distance of Chorlton village, with its array of shops, restaurants and leisure outlets. Firswood was also convenient for Manchester United football ground, very near the lawn tennis club and 20 minutes' drive from the city centre of Manchester.

It was a lively, boisterous village which still retained its old world charm. Broseley Road consisted of semi-detached houses on a tree-lined road, which added to its appeal. Each home had three bedrooms with separate dining and sitting rooms, with plenty of room for entertaining guests. Shortly after we moved in, building work started and by the end of it we had transformed our home, which now stood out like a beacon from the rest and drew attention from our neighbours.

Naturally, I paid attention to the most important room in the house – my bedroom. An exotic bedroom is always essential to me and this one was no exception. It was both chic and a man magnet, decorated and designed by me, with a desire for it to be a long-term love nest. The bed held centre stage, comfortable and sexy, with a brocade upholstered headboard, a canopy and matching chaise longue, adding a luxurious touch and giving it a boudoir feel in a glamorous setting. Elaborately draped, pale blue heavy silk curtains sealed the opulence.

I love to dress a bed and crisp white Egyptian cotton sheets are a must to create a cool feel under my body, with just a single white sheet to cover me, if needed. The quilted blue silk embroidered eiderdown was always folded back, to reveal the whiteness of the sheets, sets of matching white pillows, with large blue silk cushions randomly laid on top, completed the comfort needed.

The walls were white, with the occasional framed antique painting here and there. A large freestanding mirror allowed us to watch ourselves when we were ready, stimulating our sex to greater heights. Two white French country-style bedside tables stood either side of the bed with large porcelain lamps standing grandly on top. My dressing table was Edwardian mahogany, with a matching chair, its top laid out with a selection of silver antique brushes and combs and an array of beautiful crystal perfume bottles, all adding to the elegance.

The room was softly illuminated with low, indirect light. Peacefulness and quiet is of paramount importance, giving a feeling of privacy, intimacy and cosiness. To dampen the sounds from the road outside, I laid Egyptian rugs over the wall-to-wall cream carpet. Finally lots of candles were a must. My bedroom was my haven, I just wanted to be in that bed!

I doubt Broseley Road, Firswood, had ever seen anything like what went on when the Waldens arrived. Our crazy sex parties, our outrageous arguments, one of which saw me running naked into a waiting cab after locking my husband in the bedroom, followed by him swinging like

Tarzan from the bedroom window on to the top of the porch below, wearing nothing more than his jock-strap.

Billy's ever-present need for sexual satisfaction, either privately or during drunken amyl-fuelled parties, led us into a whole new world of orgies with couples who were strangers. His advertising in select adult magazines returned good results and pretty soon we were taking part in encounters across the north of England.

Our first party experience was in Leeds, where Adele, a mature and worldly woman was the hostess with the mostess, being very attractive, good humoured, spontaneous and warm, and with a liking for sex with strangers. Her husband used to watch her with admiring eyes as she performed deep throat oral sex with the expertise of a prostitute. Her need for penis penetration extended to taking on every man at the party. She was a crazy nymphomaniac, who drank nothing but bubbly and played with her pussy when it wasn't in action elsewhere.

I loved Adele's parties and we attracted each other mentally and physically. Most couples arrived expecting 'wife swapping' sessions but the pure pleasure of grabbing a wife and teaching her to experience a woman's touch, to bring her to orgasm, gave Adele and I mutual excitement. Once we got a taste of this sexually stimulating lifestyle we moved on to hold parties at our home when weekends were free. Adele, with her husband in tow, never missed one and I loved her being there, as much for the fact that she was the star attraction, which left me to be the perfect hostess, serving drinks and tasty snacks, occasionally participating if my body desired it. Meanwhile, Billy was free to sniff amyl and fuck to his heart's content.

The anticipation before our first sexy soirée was excruciating. Our aim was to provide an environment where our guests could have mature conversations about their sexual fantasies, and be prepared to share their deepest secrets, and if desired, explore and enjoy sensual experiences.

Our guest list would only include hedonistic people, sybaritic gentlewomen, and sexually libertine men.

I had asked Adele to arrive a little early and was relieved to see her parking her car in the drive. As other guests arrived, she helped everyone relax with a drink or two until they were ready and aroused. When the conversation began to loosen up, I was listening to chatter about who had been to this party, who had enjoyed that experience. I overheard a woman called Laura, saying that she had 'come to watch the boys play'. Then my attention was drawn to another conversation about a strap-on, from a petite woman we thought would be arriving with her husband, instead choosing to bring along a young stud to play with. I confessed to being turned on by any group activity and a guy called Rob pressed me to be specific. Looking in the direction of his luscious wife, I described our tongues entwined around his stiff penis. My verbalising did the trick and I hoped we could be living this fantasy very soon. A flush was evident on his pretty wife's face and he gave a sign of delight, while checking out his already hard cock. We were in for a good party, I was certain of that.

A few people drifted off to the allocated party rooms, where Billy, who was already nude, was eyeing the perfect pussy to penetrate. I suggested to Jan, Rob's wife, that we should change into something more comfortable and as we passed the kitchen, we saw a woman laying on her back on the floor where her male companion, who was already on his knees and between her legs, was eating off her cream-smeared pussy. What fun!

I received nice compliments on the revealing chiffon gown I had chosen to wear. A lot of heavy breathing and moaning was coming from an occupied bedroom and I heard at least one female orgasm while drifting off into an available bedroom, holding Jan's hand and allowing it to press against my pubic bone. She knew I was wet and ready to have sex with her.

Laura had already occupied the bedroom sofa and invited Rob and a young man to join her. The three were tongue kissing while the guys were caressing her breasts. Jan and I lay on the bed, enjoying watching the entertainment, until she felt the need to take things further as she knelt on the bed nibbling her way up my thigh to heaven.

Laura had directed her attention to French kissing the young guy next to her, while Rob leaned across his new buddy's erection, tickling the head with his tongue. My head was about to explode, overwhelmed by the visual stimulation. I leaned forward and lowered Jan on to the bed. 'Are you having fun?' she asked, with a broad smile. I noticed her pearly white teeth and wished to be nibbled more by them, but instead her husband came over, planting his head near my knees. As she moved away, I raised my knees so he had access to me. I had laid a basket of condoms on the bedside table along with lube, a trick of my own, taking the tip of the condom between my tongue and the roof of my mouth, holding the rolled-up end against my lips, I bent over him and placed it on to the head of his penis with my mouth, using my lips to slowly roll it along his entire hard length.

Gripping my hips tightly, he placed me where he needed me, gliding his erection towards me. Determined to stay on target, I met Jan's gaze as she bent down to look closer at the action. 'At this rate you won't last long,' she said, and she was right. I was bursting to orgasm and as I slid myself, extremely wet, down his long shaft, the power of his thrusts forced me to scream with delight and my orgasm sparked the trigger for his explosion.

Everyone had been enjoying the show and, as we relaxed laughing together, I felt the party might be winding down. Eventually, after gathering myself together and allowing my entertaining guests to do the same, I left my bedroom, noticing that the other bedrooms were now empty.

I found Billy chatting away downstairs, a large Jack Daniels in one hand and our cairn terrier in the other. The dear little dog had been left to roam freely among everyone, and was being praised and treated to nibbles in the kitchen. Grinning from ear to ear, Billy put down his drink and the dog and came over, slipping his arm around me. 'You OK baby?' he asked.

'Absolutely wonderful,' I replied. And as everyone left, we knew it was more than likely that we would see them all again very soon.

Chapter 16

Gone in the Blink of an Eye

'We cannot stop the waves but we can learn how to surf.'

How can you forget the time when your life was nearly at its end? You can't and those moments are registered deep in my memory.

I had reduced my hours considerably at the Preston parlour, only taking bookings that I regarded as 'easy'. On this day there had been three bookings taken for me that I thought were easy enough and I figured that my last client would finish, quite literally, well in time for me to return to Manchester on the train, reaching home early in the evening.

The morning was chaotic. Billy and I had eaten and drunk too much the night before, taking ourselves into the city centre and meeting up with some gambling friends and their partners. We didn't get to bed until around 3am. My first appointment was booked for 1pm and from leaving the house to arriving at the parlour took around two hours. Billy had been banned from driving, so he had employed a friend to act as his chauffeur. He had a full day ahead: There was a poker game in a Blackpool casino in which he intended to take part.

When Paul rang the doorbell we were ready to roll and take on the day. I was a little hung-over but otherwise I felt good. Being driven to Victoria Station, I left Billy with a kiss and a wish for a good day and off I went, unaware that the next time I would see him I would be curled up in bed in agony.

It was a hot summer's day and the air in the parlour was heavy. I put the heat and my hangover down to the hot flushes I was experiencing. I was also working that day alone as Wendy had to leave early, cutting her shift short it was expected, as she needed to attend to something urgently and would be returning to join Patsy, who was due to arrive at 5pm. It meant that there would be two hours working alone but I had no problem with it and never felt in any danger.

Time with my two clients flowed easily enough. I knew their style and the type they were. The first was a successful and powerful businessman who was used to manipulating the men beneath him like a puppeteer. However, this daytime domineering for some reason made him feel insecure and as a balance to reality, he arrived being submissive. I employed my best acting skills to help him live out his fantasy. He needed first to be talked into a different world and while he lay blindfolded bound and helpless, I suggested he pay extra for Wendy to assist in binding his body, making sure he was totally under our control. Then both of us climbed on top with Wendy straddled over his by then, erect penis, teasing him by stroking her pussy over its bulging head and then pulling away, leaving him frantic for more.

I, in turn, sat over his face, virtually suffocating him and he lay in that state spluttering and gasping for air while sucking at the lips of my vagina. He adored the pleasure of sniffing my scent and the torment of Wendy only allowing the tip of his penis inside her and then quickly taking that feeling away from him, on-off-on-off until he couldn't contain himself any further and we would allow him to remove his condom and explode on her belly. Simple stuff really and whenever he made a booking you knew what style he desired.

Wendy left and my second client followed shortly after and he was a dream to entertain. His needs were always simple. He used to arrive so quietly you would hardly know he was there. Talking in whispers and looking adoringly after me, he would wait without a word until I showed him into my room and while I waited for him to shower he would constantly be staring at my body with lust in his eyes. I always looked forward to his visits as he was so easy to please. Everything was routine. I would lay on the bed face down, while he took his time massaging me with baby oil. If I was to be massaged I more often than not had them use baby oil rather than talc as it kept my skin soft and supple. Other girls preferred talc in case the oil touched their hair. I just piled it up on the top of my head and lay with my eyes closed enjoying the experience. He would meekly ask me to turn on my back while he massaged my toes, lightly working his hands up my legs and inner thighs, until he reached my breasts.

His massage technique was quite professional and certainly stimulating and although he was a squat, unattractive man I had no problem achieving an orgasm when I let him stroke my pussy, and after I squirted my juice the excitement was always too much for him. After the condom went on it only took a couple of strokes before he exploded inside it. I then would join him in the shower where he soaped me and washed me down. He was in a way my little slave and when all was done he would creep away as quietly as he had arrived, tipping me on his exit.

Wendy had left and I was working on my own, I felt a little lifeless, tired and hot, but I didn't have any concerns while waiting for my last booking to arrive. After I would relax and wait for Wendy to return and Patsy's arrival, meanwhile taking bookings for them then have a girly chat before leaving for home. That was the plan.

He was a little late and as his time was short he rushed into the massage room without delay. He tried to avoid having a shower but I insisted. It was necessary, no-one wants a stale smelly body to work on. He had booked me several times before, a young strapping guy that loved to talk the talk about how girls were all over him for sex. I never questioned why he needed my services. I knew why – he loved the energy of my body and the way I bounced on top of him, circling and pounding him deep inside me. It was always purely by luck than judgement that the condom didn't burst but the truth was I looked forward to sex with him and the way he explored all the positions he could get my body into. Being paid well for all this pleasure was an extra bonus.

So here I found myself jumping up and down on his penis until a pain struck my stomach so hard everything went blurry and I lost consciousness. Sadly, he fled, leaving me there naked, in a mess and alone. I felt ready to faint again and I am sure I did. It was a miracle that I managed to crawl to the door, raise myself enough to flip the door handle and continue to claw my way down a small flight of stairs to the gym below, where I managed some weak knocks on the base of the door. Steven immediately closed his gym and tended to me, carrying me back into the parlour and dressing me, while insisting I drank as much water as I could manage. The pain I felt in my stomach was like nothing else I had experienced and I was gushing clots of blood. It was as though I was miscarrying a baby and I thought that was indeed what was happening.

Steven wanted to take me to Preston Infirmary immediately and I wanted Billy to come for me but as much as we tried we couldn't raise him. Listening to my pleas to be taken home, Steven did as I wished and, leaving the parlour as it was, he locked up and carried me to his car. He drove so carefully avoiding any jerks or bumps and eventually I reached home and he lay me on my bed and tended to me until Billy and Paul arrived. It was only then that Steven left my side and out of my life forever. Never did our paths cross again. I remember Billy's despair at the sight he was looking at, as by this time I was hanging on to the bedpost in agony. An ambulance was immediately called and as I was stretchered into it and off to Park Hospital with sirens blazing, and Billy full speed behind.

I was whisked into the operating theatre as an emergency and I remember thinking, *I am not going to survive this*, but thankfully I did. I had a benign growth in my fallopian tube, which had grown so big it had burst, allowing septicaemia to take over my body.

When eventually I was well enough to listen to the prognosis, I was told that when admitted I had around 30 minutes to live and it was a miracle they had operated in time. I was also told I would be unable to have children as everything had congealed inside me and had to be removed. It left me with no ovaries, no fallopian tubes, no womb and no appendix. I was 26 years old with all my insides out.

Chapter 17

Ring the Bell to Paradise

'Now is not the time to think about what you had but what you can do with what you have.'

Arriving at my hospital bedside with a very anxious mother at his side and two hours late for their visit, it seemed that Billy, in his haste to get to me, had crashed the car and both had arrived in a state of disrepair.

With tears in their eyes, they viewed in front of them the vision of someone on death's door. In fact I had just avoided walking through it. Eventually, when the day came and I was allowed to leave hospital, my weight had plummeted to less than eight stone, a mere shadow of my former self. It took six months of my mother's care, making sure I rested and ate the right foods, and I wallowed in her arms while she babied me, often sitting me on her knee, like a little girl. I weighed very little more than that. Eventually regaining my strength, I overcame the loss I felt of never being able to bear a child, and gradually as my health returned my enthusiasm for life was also restored.

When I was a child I had no control over what happened around me. If things were painful or difficult, I was at the mercy of those adults in my life, and when I grew to be an adult myself, I responded by finding ways of controlling myself and others. But being in a loving relationship meant that I couldn't control things in the way that I could when I was on my own.

It didn't take long before Billy was enthused with our next venture. There was a difference with this business plan though. He had driven past a Victorian end of terrace house for sale in Radcliffe. Liking what he saw, he took me to view it. The position was indeed perfect for our profession, being on the end of a terrace with an adjacent car park and discreet side entrance. He had already obtained the keys from the estate agent and so we took a look inside. We knew immediately that the layout was perfect.

His plan was to buy the property and put it in my name. This would be independent of the rest of his business empire and all mine to own and work in. Billy wasn't stupid and he knew that after my extended break he would have to dangle a carrot and his plan worked, as after extensive refurbishments were made, transforming the living room into the reception area, completely mirroring the two massage rooms and installing impulse showers, a sauna and gym, decorating and adding fixtures and fittings, I was ready to step back into my work mode. Our exciting new venture was in the next village to where my family lived – so near and yet so far. At no point did my parents enquire into the nature of my business, something I still find amazing to this day.

I christened my parlour Aquarius, my zodiac sign. I was 27 years old and it was in this little parlour that I walked through the doors 'controlled' and walked out some years later 'in control'. Aquarius helped me to regain my independence and confidence to make my own decisions and override those with which I didn't agree.

Out of business hours my personal world became a mixture of Jewish family life, the occasional trauma within Billy's empire and his ever-present need for sexual stimulation that he chose to have privately or in booze and amyl-fuelled parties. Each of these three things were kept strictly separate, and I found myself bringing from within me three different personalities to suit the three lives I was living.

I intended from the start to stamp my style on Aquarius, so that the day I opened its doors visitors who called and were potential clients were immediately amazed with the vision on front of them. I took the nude woman out of the privacy of the massage room and displayed myself almost naked immediately as they set eyes on me – the stripper was re-born. Into the dustbin went the white overalls which were standard dress and a rule for every massage parlour. It was supposed to give a look of legitimate respectability but it did nothing to whet the appetite. I had discovered the art of knowing how to sell the value of my services to make the most money in another style and place way back in London and some elaborate burlesque outfits came out of mothballs. I changed my outfits to suit the client I was with or simply because I loved to display different erotic looks to please myself.

My private room, with its tinted mirrored walls, had a vintage dressing table and wardrobe which added to a French boudoir style. The outfits in my wardrobe consisted of basques, various uniforms, lingerie and a selection of stilettos and boots, some PVC and rubber wear. The drawers of the dressing table were filled with stockings, suspenders and bras of all sizes, for myself and my clients. I encouraged the fem in the man, if it was there, to come out and express itself. Before long I had acquired an interesting collection of whips, canes and paddles which I used to good effect on my masochistic clients who paid considerably more for the privilege. With vibrators for the men and separate ones for me, I had every angle covered.

When you walked up to the main entrance, there was a sign that read 'RING THE BELL TO PARADISE'. Once buzzed, the door would open and a short walkway led to a dark red-tinted glass door where you entered to be either greeted by myself or left to read my message framed in gilt on the wall, explaining to sit and relax for a while. Most waited, being entranced with the seductive background music and the colour of red which drew them in. Very few could break away to leave. The walls were decorated with abstract paintings of naked women in all forms of pose. Essence sticks were continually burning – sensual smells to stimulate the body and brain. The atmosphere kept them there and once they had become familiar with the layout, they knew to take a drink from the bar or go to the changing rooms, undress and steam away in the sauna till it was their turn for more stimulating pleasure.

Red, being my favourite colour, was present everywhere, with red velvet couches and upholstered bar stools, elaborate red velvet drapes hung from ceiling to floor. The colour red depicts sex, danger, heat and fire and wearing the colour lights up a woman's energy and spirit. This energy and spirit expanded in many ways to help promote my little business. I encouraged cab drivers to bring new clients to my door by tipping them five per cent of the entrance fee. All hotel concierges were on alert to spot a potential client eager for some female company and send them my way. The entrance fee would be charged on arrival but the most important decoration was displayed in a gilt frame on the wall in my private room displaying tempting delights to whet the appetite. It would take a strong willed man to resist a menu that read:

Yvonne style: (my choice)

69 party: (mutual oral sex)

Tantric sex: (massage, synchronized breathing, eye gazing, sex)

Love at the Y: (Cunnilingus)

Sauna Steamer: (Sex in the sauna – last appointment only)

Fetish & Fantasy: (Light spanking and bondage, whippings, wearing fetish outfits)

Whipped cream party: 1 hour only (A tasteful experience)

All prices to be negotiated on arrival.

I had learnt at an early age, you miss 100 per cent of the shots you don't take and I was prepared and ready not to miss one.

Chapter 18

Never Trust A Woman Like Patricia

'The secret in life is to appreciate the pleasure of being terribly, terribly deceived.' - Oscar Wilde

Patricia, a blonde, attractive, vivacious wheeler-dealer, came into our lives in the summer of 1977 and it quickly became clear that her aim was to steal my husband away from me in any way she could.

A self-assured 36-year-old who considered herself a beautiful man-magnet. Slender, she carried herself with perfect poise and every move she made had a purpose, both physically and mentally. As a spoilt child of a widowed father who was a leading jeweller dealing in London's Hatton Garden, she was pampered, protected and wealthy.

For a time it seemed that wherever we were she was, too, and pretty soon she was never out of our bed. When you are sharing your husband's body with another woman the friendship becomes extremely close. There was no doubt in my mind that he fancied her but I didn't regard her as a threat to my marriage.

Patricia introduced Billy to contacts, expanding his network of business opportunities. One example was the T-shirt printing machine franchise in which he invested. It was a novel idea at the time and used in a clever way. The machines would be installed at venues where professional sports events would be taking place, the main draw being a football match or charity event where famous footballers would pose with their adoring fans to have a picture taken. It would then quickly become a colourful reminder on a T-shirt, to the delight of the paying youngsters. Former Liverpool footballers John Toshack and Ray Clemence, who were idols at the time, started the ball rolling at the launch venue, the Walton Festive Show in Liverpool, and from that point Billy knew he had landed on a little gold mine, all thanks to Patricia, of course.

Despite our busy lives, professional and personal, we managed holiday escapes for a well-earned rest and relaxation. Spain, Portugal, Morocco, Geneva, ski trips to the Italian mountains, Patricia came too and when we were at home, she lingered around the City Centre Sauna, attached to Billy's coat tails.

On one occasion, after spending some quality time shopping till I was dropping in the city, and laden with my prize purchases, I decided to pay them a visit. There she was, stuck to him like glue, chatting merrily to the girls and, what I immediately thought, making her mark on her target. I allowed Billy to encourage me to take her in a massage room and with the waiting client's permission ask if he minded if I gave him a massage in place of the girl he had chosen. Of course, he was delighted and more so when he had the presence of a blonde beauty at his side. Patricia refused politely to participate in finishing the job with me, preferring to watch as I lay my hands expertly, bringing him to a full blown climax, rather than laying her hands on the goods herself. It was at that point I began to detest her.

There was only one man she wanted to lay her hands on and it was only ever Billy. She was after my man and would leave no stone unturned until she got him and he was willingly going like a lamb to the slaughter – or so I thought.

A short time into this 'friendship' Billy and I were dining alone in a city centre restaurant where he revealed his plan for the next chapter in our lives. Patricia had been given the gift of a villa in Spain, generously provided by a previous lover. His intentions were to travel there with her, then make sure she transferred the deeds into his name. Here was his plan: 'I will have Patricia convinced that I will be hers once she transfers the deeds,' he said. 'Give me four months and the villa will be ours. When it is I will phone you and I want you to come straight over to me.' I asked no questions. I didn't need to. His words proved where his loyalty was. He loved me and all Patricia had planned was about to fail miserably. So I sat there quietly gloating and looking forward to her downfall.

Give or take a month or so, he was as good as his word. 'I have the deeds to the villa – it's ours,' he said, in a hasty phone call from Spain. 'Take the address and name of where to go and who to introduce yourself to when you arrive.' My destination was La Cepa Bar in the square of Fuengirola – the owners, Diane and Mark, would be expecting me.

My bags were packed in no time and the following evening I walked into La Cepa, introducing myself to the man and woman behind the bar. Diane, blonde and beautiful with a smile that lit up her face, welcomed me with a warm Welsh accent, while her husband Mark immediately asked what I would like to drink. They were fully aware of the circumstances surrounding my arrival. Both it seemed were involved in other relationships, but although their marriage had collapsed, they still remained a loving couple. Diane's current squeeze was a tall, good-looking guy called John, a London cockney who, judging by his muscular body, had the power to sort out any problems.

I was told that Patricia was expected to show her face at some point and Billy had received a phone call that I had arrived, so I settled at the bar drinking all that was offered to me, while regular customers warmly introduced themselves. I immediately felt at home. I didn't need to wait too long before my love rival sauntered into the bar, her hair tied back away from her face, dressed casually in trousers and a little top. She spotted me out of the corner of her eye while ordering a drink from Mark and hastily knocked it back in her grand manner. It was obvious from her flushed, shocked expression that she hadn't expected to see me. Approaching, her remark was direct and simply put. 'What are YOU doing here? Didn't you know I have been fucking your husband and he is about to ask you for a divorce?'

My reply was simply put, too. 'A fuck's a fuck, but he loves me. I'm going nowhere.'

I was prepared for a drink to be thrown over me, knowing her temper. I expected a tussle, but a tussle with a knife – never! Her reaction was quick, the knife appeared from nowhere, holding it to my stomach, telling me to step outside.

In a flash, John, who had been watching her every move, jumped from the side of the bar and grabbed her around the neck from behind with a force that made her drop the knife. She was then frog-marched outside, still held tightly around the neck. Everyone in the bar rallied around me while Mark and Diane assured me Patricia wouldn't trouble me again. The truth is, she hadn't troubled me at all. I was quite prepared to handle her – it was the knife that was the problem. John returned with Billy after what seemed hours. There would be no more trouble. Patricia had been taken to the villa, where she was made to pack her suitcase and from where she left without too much fuss.

I was told that when she realised she had been duped her main reaction was shock. Her pride took a battering too but the London gangland members who included John were not to be messed with. Add that to the total disinterest of the Guardia Civil and it was clearly impossible for her to argue the toss. After all, she had not really been robbed. She had walked into the situation eagerly and willingly with her eyes wide open, hoping that transferring the deeds into Billy's name would get her man – it didn't. I believe she stayed on the coast for a few days before returning to England. She never crossed my path again and Billy and I moved on with our life as though she had never existed.

We were now the proud owners of a beautiful villa. It might seem strange to you that Patricia handed over the keys to the villa without a fuss but let me explain more about the Spain we were venturing into.

Although it was 1978, a visit to southern Spain, certainly Malaga, was like returning to the 1950s. It was rumoured that the mayor was wanted for collaborating with the Nazis, and thought we were still in the Second World War. He spent his time riding the hills around Mijas on a donkey with panniers strapped to its sides. The ventas (cafes) in the hills didn't have proper toilets. Instead you had to go to an outside corrugated shed and squat over a hole in the ground to relieve yourself. A lager was seven pesetas (threepence in pre-decimal money). The local police force, the Guardia Civil, were very friendly with Billy, quite often joining him for a drink in La Cepa Bar. They welcomed the influx of Brits making Spain their home, bringing them wealth like the country had never seen.

These were the early days of UK gangsters buying Spanish properties for holidays or permanent use, and the country was happy to accommodate them. The British and American contacts Patricia had made in Spain became Billy's friends. He also renewed acquaintance with members of the London gangland world who were living in the area and had made La Cepa Bar their bolt hole. A little taste of England within the Fuengirola square. This was where our new life in the sun was just beginning.

Chapter 19

Villa Christina

'Work like you don't need the money, live like you have never been hurt and dance like no-one is watching.'

The turn off to the Villa Christina was just off the most dangerous road in Europe, notorious for the number of deaths of motorists speeding along the carretara highway, heading for Marbella.

Turning right at the castle coming out of Fuengirola, you took your life in your hands. The villa was dramatically built at the top of a hill, with views over the beautiful coastline. Visitors approached up a long winding road and as the huge gates opened and they drove the long gravel driveway they caught the first sight of this magnificent building, its whitewashed walls covered with pink bougainvillea. It took your breath away.

Once inside, you found typical traditional Spanish decor, the large sitting room filled with antique English furniture that had been included in the deal. We loved to entertain in the barbecue pit next to the swimming pool and many happy hours were spent there, in great company. Everyone brought food and wine and we took turns to cook al fresco, laughing and joking through the day. As you sat in the pear-shaped swimming pool looking towards the sea, it seemed as if it was an extension of the blue ocean waters stretching out in front of you.

Fun, frolics and frothy frivolity, with a mix of gothic and a taste of the bizarre describes party time at Villa Christina.

Our parties were unique, in the style of the *Rocky Horror Show*, where men dressed in corsets and garter belts, with make-up plastered on their faces, looking as if they had stepped out of a drag horror movie. Perhaps at this point I should introduce you to the players around this period.

Diane and Mark were always a required ingredient to help host and choose a theme for any party, usually outrageous, and their inspiration helped inspire me in later years when holding parties in my brothels. There were two differences though. In those days in Spain you had to use your imagination as you had to make everything by hand. Another important point was that although these parties were sexually themed, they were enjoyed without indulging in sex. No-one wanted it, no-one needed it. A party was simply that and after consuming lots of amazing home-cooked food and alcohol, no-one was fit enough for anything more strenuous. But the characters who attended were crazy fun-loving people who knew how to keep everyone entertained.

The brilliant owners of the La Cepa Bar made the perfect double act, bouncing off each other with jokes that had everyone in stitches. Diane was the perfect hostess, either behind the bar or helping to host a party. She was a blonde beauty who knew how to show off her good points to the best effect. When she was tipsy she was a nightmare, with a nasty side to her personality, but when she was sober she was humorous, intelligent and witty.

Mark was possibly one of the funniest men I have ever known. His humour was unscripted, as he reeled out one joke after another, entertaining everyone as he held court behind the bar. He was an alcoholic with no intention of seeking a cure. Bacardi and Coke was his diet, morning, afternoon and evening. How he managed to entertain as well was often impossible. Everyone expected to find him in all sorts of disarray. It added to the class act as he partnered Diane behind the bar. He would have been handsome before addiction took hold of his body but by the time we arrived in Fuengirola his looks had long disappeared. When sober, he was a charming gentleman and it was clear he loved Diane until his long suffering liver eventually gave up on him.

Sally was Mark's girlfriend, a bubbly, plump, pretty blonde Australian, who had stopped off on her travels around Europe. She was in her early twenties, many years younger than Mark, but they attached themselves to each other and enjoyed steamy sessions of sex with carefree abandonment. She pandered to his every need, for which Diane was thankful and although she had originally planned to make only a short stopover in Spain, she ended up staying there until they split up a year or two before he died.

Elaina and Peter were our closest neighbours, living in a villa nearby. She had obviously been a very good-looking woman but over the years in Spain had let herself deteriorate. Occasionally when I popped over I would be confronted with her dishevelled appearance as she emerged from the bedroom after long sessions of sex. I would then be regaled with detailed descriptions of all they had achieved between the sheets, nothing spared.

Her expertise at describing her sexual activities was equalled by her expertise at cooking. Her food was delicious and her imagination amazing when it came to painstakingly making party outfits for herself and Peter. They always outshone everyone. Elaina came from San Diego, California, with a troupe of children who always seemed to take second place to her love-making. Raucous and loud, she managed to live a grand lifestyle on the back of a past marriage. I much later discovered that there was a very explosive story behind her need to leave America and live far away in a distant land.

She had been married to a top policeman who had an early death. But there had been suspicions around the way he died.

In 1963 he had been a police escort on that fateful day in Dallas when John F. Kennedy was shot dead. The suspicion was that Lee Harvey Oswald did not fire the shot that killed him. Her husband, along with six others, had evidence that backed up that claim. He was called in front of the head of the Warren Commission and told in no uncertain terms to back off as it wasn't in his health interests to relay the information he had. He died suspiciously some weeks later, shot by an unknown assailant. Rumour had it that it was an inside job and that Kennedy was murdered by the American mafia. Another theory was that Cuban president Fidel Castro and other interested parties like Jimmy Hoffa, who was the head of the Teamsters' Union with a millionaire lifestyle, worked for the mafia and collaborated to end Kennedy's life. Hoffa eventually disappeared, amid even more rumours that he ended up in a lump of concrete.

Elaina's future life was decided by the American government to make sure she didn't collaborate with people who had evidence that would never come to light. Hence her grand lifestyle in America.

Peter, her partner, always stayed in the background, allowing Elaina to take centre stage. It was obvious he was allowed to stay in her home as long as the sex he gave her was often and inventive. Something he seemed to gladly provide. He was tall and skinny and reminded me of a client who delighted in grovelling to the needs of his mistress. He claimed to have come from an upper crust Canadian background but I always had a feeling he lied to impress. You could never really get to the bottom of his tales. It was obvious where their style of living came from. It was never provided from his income, only from hers. He was a sponger of the first degree.

Jill and Richard were another interesting couple. She was loud-mouthed but extremely kind and hailed from a middle-class family in Tetbury, Gloucestershire. Her skinny legs showed off her extremely large, natural breasts which she loved to display, regularly bouncing them around topless at any given barbecue gathering. Jill's delicious food added greatly to the table and she often entertained at her villa, putting out delicious delights that everyone looked forward to taste. Her husband, Richard, was an Osage Indian chief, straight off the reservation. He got paid large amounts of money every month by the American government, in compensation for the authorities stealing his land. It seemed to me that the American government had a lot to answer for.

At over six feet tall with Indian good looks he was proud of his heritage and could often be found in Fuengirola square performing a 'rain dance' which always brought on a storm that was desperately needed in the height of summertime, when the scorching heat dust would drift over from Morocco. Everyone who watched this humorous display of ritual dance stood back in amazement.

Wonderful days were spent on a ranch across the hill from our villa, where we stabled our horse, Angelo, christened by a friend after Billy suggested his name be changed from Perla. He was bought from some travelling gypsies, after Billy spotted him tied up to a tree on the beach, looking very sad. He came home and spent the first night at the bottom of our garden, where he was much happier. The following day we found the ranch and soon discovered that Angelo was excellent at dressage and we took every opportunity to show off his skills. From then on many hours were spent at the ranch, drinking from the vats of wine and dining al fresco on food washed down with Rioja. How I loved those hazy crazy days, grooming and riding.

Our carefree days in Spain quite often included a trip to the bullring, cheering on our favourite matador. Billy's fascination with this bloodsport was encouraged by an US ex-army flight lieutenant called Harry, who owned a bar named after him, hidden away in a little side street off the Fuengirola square.

Harry's Bar was a regular bolt-hole for many American visitors and ex-pats. He entertained us all with stories of close encounters he had experienced while running with the bulls in Pabloma. This was a venture Billy wanted to experience and Harry would take him along whenever the occasion arose. I hardly understood the thrills that they got from a near-death experience of a bull's horns piercing their body but the achievement of escaping this danger was their reward, then returning to the safety of Fuengirola to thankfully face another day.

This period of life in Spain was certainly filled with magic moments, but for me they were short-lived, as to pay for this idyllic lifestyle I had to return to England and get back to making some serious money.

Chapter 20

The Biz

'With every action there is a reaction.'

Returning to England wasn't all work. I found plenty of time to play and one of my favourite places was the Showbiz, known to all who frequented it as 'The Biz', a late-night drinking bar in Alness Road, Whalley Range. Officially called The Clifton Grange Hotel, with its tree-lined avenue, expanse of parkland and rich variety of architecture, it had an atmosphere of rural tranquillity, even though it was just minutes away from the city centre.

The Biz was run by Phyllis, mother of Phil Lynott, the lead singer with Thin Lizzy, who lived there with her partner Dennis. They welcomed anyone who came knocking after first checking their identity through a small sliding panel in the door. All very cloak-and-dagger but in those unenlightened times it was illegal to sell alcohol after a certain time. If you did, you could expect a raid from the boys in blue. How stupid that all seems today, when you can pop into a supermarket 24 hours a day to buy your liquor.

Phil and his band members regularly turned up at The Biz, as did many showbiz people. It was normal to see actors, artists, conjurers and strippers, even a transsexual ventriloquist at the bar. The Sex Pistols regularly drank there in their early days as a punk band, along with various American musicians who were appearing on stage in Manchester. George Best was often seen propping up the bar. With both Phyllis and George being from Ireland, I guess they had a lot in common.

Although it was a working bed and breakfast hotel, this and the showbiz side of entertainment were kept totally separate when The Biz came alive from 1am to 7am. Phyllis was a stunning looking woman and certainly gave the place a magical touch.

After being buzzed into the huge Victorian property, you found yourself in a reception hall, its high ornate ceiling decorated with original gilded plaster cornices. A plush carpet and oriental rugs covered the floors, rococo gilded mirrors hung everywhere, antique furniture was scattered around and china cabinets filled with beautiful porcelain. Taking centre stage was a large mahogany table and there stood a huge crystal vase filled with sweetly scented fresh flowers. Phyllis spoke with pride of the huge bouquets sent weekly to her via Interflora by the American actor Gregory Peck, rumoured to have been a previous lover.

The first thing you noticed when entering the lounge was the impressive array of crystal drinking glasses sparkling on display at the back of the bar, where the hosts served the best cognac and whiskey from crystal decanters. It was total decadence with a feel that you were in a very special place.

Most of the time the glamour that The Biz exuded was lost in a haze of alcohol consumption, as by the time you had left a city centre club and managed to walk through the door at 1am everything was blurred. There was no better place to continue through the night with a mixture of personalities that easily gelled together. Not many in the know could resist it and I am sure that high on spirits many deals were done and many friendships sealed. The Showbiz was certainly the biz, full of atmosphere, you never knew who would arrive to add to the entertainment and it was certainly one of my favourite places to hang out when wanting to continue downing my favourite vodka martinis in a very spirited mood.

I was in that mood some weeks after Billy had come home from Spain and returned to my bed early one morning after a night at the poker table in the city, playing a professional game of stud poker against men with deep pockets. He was on a winning streak, returning with a beautiful bit of bling he'd taken off the finger of a fellow player. He produced the item with its perfect white diamond, the size of which I had never before set sight on, six carats sparkling in a gent's setting. That diamond was about to become mine.

I had arrived home only a few short hours ahead of him after not being able to resist a visit to The Biz and not quite fully compos mentis after a trip home on the back of a milk float that had been delivering the morning pints at Alness Road. Hardly a ladylike way to make an exit or to arrive home, to the amazement of those that were up early enough to watch. It took some minutes for me to realise he had stripped his opponent of his money and also his ring. Billy suggested that the diamond should come out of its flashy gent's setting and be re-modelled for me. Some weeks later this very expensive ornament was slipped on my finger and wherever I was, it was there decorating my hand. I couldn't wait to show it off, and what better place than The Showbiz. It was a short time later after Billy had returned to Spain that I ventured there again. The lounge bar was full of the usual regular faces, sport and entertainment mingling with everyone else. George Best was once again chatting to Phyllis at the end of the bar. Bunny Lewis, the drag queen, was holding court at the other and, as I took my seat, I made sure my ring was noticed. As it turned out that bit of flashy exhibitionism proved very costly.

Two days later with Billy still in Spain, I was alone in the house, about 5pm, having just returned from a shopping trip with my girlfriends. It had been a glorious summer's day, the sun was still shining and my spirits were high.

It wasn't long after I had put my shopping down that the doorbell rang and there on the doorstep were two men in balaclavas. Before I had time to think, they had pushed me into the hall, spun me round marched me up the stairs towards my bedroom. 'Where's the money?' they demanded and I could feel the pressure of a hard object pressed against my back. I was told it was a gun. Okay, it could have been a bluff but was I going to call it?

I knew Billy had deposited all of the cash in our safe deposit before he left for Spain but I also knew I had to keep my head and somehow manage to apply my best acting skills and calmly steer them away from my front bedroom where, stashed away in the wardrobe, was a fortune worth of jewellery which had been transferred from Customs at Heathrow Airport – by arrangement, of course. Some of the jewellery was intended for the American soul singer George Benson, who was due to appear at the Russell Club.

It's amazing where you find the strength when you need it and using my head I alerted them to the fact that we had very nosey neighbours and they should keep to the back of the house, if they didn't want to alarm them. Luckily, they took the bait, pushing me into the rear bedroom, ordering me to lie face down on the bed while they tied my hands to the headboard. Stretched out defenceless with my eyes firmly shut, trying to escape from watching what was taking place, their constant demands for money grew to fever pitch. At that point I never thought I would open my eyes again. Then it happened. They spotted it, sparkling on my finger, a stunning six carat diamond ring, worth much more than they ever imagined to realise in cash.

It took no more than a second for it to be ripped off my finger. But only a second later there were stones that sounded like boulders being hurled at the windows by a very anxious neighbour, panicking them that they had been spotted, with the police on their way. 'Leave her alone. The police have been called,' came this loud woman's voice from nowhere.

Thank God for nosey neighbours! One happened to be looking through her window at the time they arrived on my doorstep. Her voice was music to my ears as they registered her screams and hastily took off down the stairs and out through the rear kitchen door, escaping over the fields beyond, with my ring still firmly in their grasp. This wonderful neighbour, who ran into the bedroom and freed me from the restraints around my wrists, is still a dear friend today. It is, of course, a very special friendship that now has sustained the ups and downs of many years, with hopefully many more 'ups' to come.

It was true that the police had been called. David, a beat bobby, lived next door to her and had been alerted, following in pursuit, but to no avail. It wasn't easy explaining to Billy long distance on the telephone all that had happened. In fact, I was more concerned about explaining the loss of the ring, than how it had gone. Billy's reaction to the news was calm, his main concern being for me, thankfully the loss of the ring secondary. He must have made a dash to Malaga airport, because he was back in Broseley Road early the next morning, ready for action.

First came the reward, put out loud and clear for anyone with information as to the whereabouts of my ring. Secondly, who had planned the robbery and, most importantly, who had attacked me? Nothing came from it. There were rumours, of course, but nothing concrete, and after a while we put it to the back of our minds and life went on as normal – normal for us anyway.

Chapter 21

The Taste of a Fine Cigar

'Anyone who lives within their means suffers from a lack of imagination.'

With Billy back home to look after me following the robbery and to ensure the safety of his jewellery hoard, we decided maybe our days at Broseley Road had come to an end and it was time to find another home.

Nipper Lane was a tree-lined suburb to the north of Manchester, with cute terraced houses. We found a perfect place there and I had great pleasure in using my designer skills once again to transform it into a home that could easily have featured in an upmarket property magazine. When I could, I took time to visit auction houses, where I enjoyed joining the professionals to bid on antique furniture. Upholstered fabrics and wallpaper from the most expensive designers were chosen to match. The bedroom was transformed, with a tented ceiling and walls covered with exotic fabric. Gilded mirrors, a four-poster bed and a dressing table from the art deco period completed the romantic picture. It was the perfect room to relax in, to express my passion, or simply to escape into dreamland.

Meanwhile, Billy had invested his time and our money in a cigar enterprise. This little number had been active for about two years, gaining many influential contacts around the city. Everyone wanted a piece of the action. Being married to a wheeler-dealer whose adrenalin is pumping 24 hours a day, you learn to expect the unexpected. Billy knew to keep his business connections close and there was an unwritten rule never to ask any questions when activities were highly illegal. I guess depriving the English cigar wholesalers of business, by becoming a main dealer for King Edward imports, all done behind the backs of the Customs and Excise men, fell into that category.

Billy's partner in crime looked after the London end. His role at Heathrow Airport gave him carte blanche to do as he wished, without being observed. He was extremely careful to protect his identity and apart from Billy, myself, and one other close confidante, no-one knew how the cigars came into the country or who was involved. I was told briefly they were coming off a plane in huge cartons, labelled as prayer books, which I thought quite hilarious. I guess it was his contact, a well-spoken, educated young guy with a hippy outlook and laid-back manner, who had the idea. Billy didn't leave the collection of such important cartons to anyone else, only occasionally employing a trusted friend who would travel with him in the dead of night in a hired van to meet the link man at Heathrow, load up the merchandise and return home.

Both our houses in Broseley Road and Nipper Lane were just large enough to store the number of cartons which arrived on a regular basis. I learned to put up with the disruption for a short time – the boxes were generally gone within a day of being delivered. For a time, though, we had King Edward cigars everywhere and those selected to sell them on were well rewarded, Billy's policy being 'everyone has to earn', and because of that attitude he sold out more or less immediately, meaning the goods were never hanging around our home for long enough to draw attention. He was heading towards becoming the sole distributor of King Edward's in the north, and everywhere you went, there were his cigars. Clubs, pubs and restaurants, hanging out of virtually every guy's mouth.

Cigars became the only thing to smoke.

Three dogs featured in my life with Billy, but no-one became as special as the last one. Muppet, a beautiful Bichon Frisé who lived the life of luxury, added to the contentment we felt at home, and he certainly stole the show. He was loved by friends and family, adored by his master, and the feeling was mutual. This period was further enhanced by happy weekends with all my family, particularly with my cousin, her husband and their two sons, to whom I became close. We enjoyed sitting around their kitchen dining table, the hub of the house, making small talk with other visitors, talking business and football, eating tasty kosher delights served throughout the day. Sunday evenings were regularly spent dining in a restaurant frequented by all the Whitefield Jewish society. Later in the evening, Billy and I would leave that little world and drive to Moss Side, where the Russell Club, owned by Billy's partner, Don Tony, would be jam-packed with people enjoying the soul singers performing on stage.

Occasionally my cousin and her family would holiday with us in our villa in Spain. My parents took their first overseas holiday there, along with aunts and uncles, all enjoying the delights of the Costa del Sol. It still amazes me that even though I was spending my weekdays indulging in the skills of prostitution, it was accepted by everyone. Not a word was said and no nasty gossip reached our ears. The industry we were in was, to all intents and purposes, normal.

While taking time out in Spain escaping from the winter blues we took in a daily dose of gossip at the La Cepa Bar and there we got chatting to a charming couple who were new to the scene of Fuengirola bar life. They had ventured down from a villa they had built and just moved into up in the hills of Mijas. From that first meeting Mike and Sue became our very dear friends, we hit it off so well. Opposites attract, so they say, and we were so very different, from backgrounds to business to social circles that we mixed in, but somehow nothing mattered as much as being together whenever possible and enjoying each other's company. It was a very welcome change, as our friendship was formed on everything except sex.

We learned along the way that they intended to put their apartment on the coast in Fuengirola up for sale and Billy took the opportunity of asking to view it, which we did just before returning to England. We immediately liked what we saw and as our intentions were to at some point sell our villa, as we were spending less and less time there, perhaps this was the opportunity to make the move into something less committing. Asking for some time to think about it, we arranged to visit them at their estate in Surrey as soon as we could make some time. It wasn't long before we received an invitation to visit them in Cobham for the weekend. It didn't surprise me to find their home to be palatial. It was magnificent and suited their style, which was always impeccable. Mike, being a self-made merchant banker, was as tough as the business world he lived in, but in his private time he was a humorous, fun-loving man who was proud of his girlfriend Sue. They had lived together for years, never marrying, which suited them just fine.

While we were enjoying their company they asked us to join them in the royal enclosure for the five-day Royal Ascot meeting held annually in June. The royal enclosure was an invitation-only area and you had to be proposed by a member to gain admittance. I then did my homework, finding out more about this race meeting that is classed as the best in the world. I was amazed to learn that until 1955, divorcees were not allowed and still to this day, anyone with a criminal record or those who have been declared bankrupt are barred.

Before the race begins the royal party arrives through the gates of Windsor Great Park in open carriages, drawn by Windsor Greys, where they are conveyed through cheering crowds. Gathering all this information and knowing the importance of the invitation, I spent every opportunity from there on in, travelling to the shopping streets of Knightsbridge to find the outfits and especially the hats that would set my style for the occasion.

Sue had been very clear on certain points. Formal wear is a must. For men that means morning dress – a tip, never call it 'morning suit' or you will be shown up as a bluffer and your elite status will probably be withdrawn quicker than you can say 'coach park 11'. Billy chose a grey jacket and trousers with a matching waistcoat, white shirt and black tie and the essential grey top hat, which by some miracle he managed to keep on his head all day. For women, I was told in no uncertain terms, dresses and skirts should be a modest length, just above the knee, or longer. Strapless or off the shoulder dresses were an absolute no-no, midriffs must be covered and hats worn at all times. So many rules and regulations, it was hard to keep track, and so it happened that for Ladies' Day, and my chance encounter with the Queen, I had wished I had worn the chiffon ensemble I had chosen earlier in the week. It was feminine, discreet, full-flowing, with a high neckline, the skirt resting well below the knees. Fabulous, luscious and light, in beautiful tones of pink and lilac with a matching turban adorned with a large flower display, stiletto shoes and a little clasp-bag completed the chic and feminine style – just perfect. But I got it the wrong way round and ended up dressed in a cowboy-style suede dress and jacket with long edging on the hem that opened the skirt up to my thighs. A suede stetson and matching stiletto cowboy boots finished my risky look.

While wishing to check the horses in the paddock, this sexy, stylish cowgirl found herself walking yards in front of the Queen, wondering why all the men were doffing their hats at me. A total misdemeanour on my part, hardly etiquette, hardly clever, hardly appropriate. Did I care? Not at all. I was full of the day and loving it.

Mike loved his buck's fizz breakfasts, followed by the most delightful food and wine. We took our lunch baskets prepared for us by Fortnum & Mason and spent every day at the number 1 car park, in the company of Henry Cecil & Co. I soon discovered things not to do when in the royal enclosure. Never say 'pleased to meet you' when being introduced. If you have no idea who they are, then you are not pleased to meet them. Don't say 'pardon' when you mishear, just say 'sorry' – I was told that saying 'pardon' was worse than saying 'fuck' in that company. After absorbing all these rules of etiquette, I threw caution to the wind and did what Viv does best – being myself.

Chapter 22

Age of Aquarius

'Success is the experience of rising to the level of your true greatness.'

It was a beautiful sunny day, one of those days when you are thankful to be alive to breathe in the warm, fragrant air. Every country has a different smell and driving off the ferry that took us from Dover to Calais you could smell the different fragrance of the country.

We had stayed overnight in Dover and woke up refreshed and ready to take on the long journey ahead on stretches of toll motorway to the Spanish border, and occasionally picking a town to venture through en route. From Reims, to Toyes, Dijon, Valence and after spending a fun-filled day of discovery, we took to the highway well before dusk to continue our journey to arrive on route at Montpellier. This carefree journey was taken on with relish and with France being a beautiful country we had no wish to step up a beat and rush to our destination. This was intended to be a little holiday escape before arriving in Spain to again check out the apartment our friend Mike had for sale.

Out of the corner of my eye I saw the curve in the road ahead. It was there in front of us before we knew it. We had no time to look at each other and no time to say a word but we knew just before we took the bend that danger was ahead. It seemed ages before the car stopped spinning on a road that was slippery from the day's heat. Billy, in his efforts to realign the car, put his foot down hard on the brake. The impact forced my head through the windscreen. The next thing I remember is the blood dripping down my face, covering my dress, and Billy's shocked expression when looking at me.

He had escaped unharmed but I knew I hadn't. I didn't need the mirror to know it, I felt it. Within a flash, people came to our rescue and I faintly remember being driven with my husband calmly supporting me to the nearest hospital.

The medics, after an extensive examination of the damage to my face, suggested surgery, which I immediately refused, instead allowing them to painstakingly pluck the splintered glass out of my skin and clean me up, which reluctantly they agreed to do. I had no interest in checking myself in the mirror, I wanted out of there, rapido!

Sat outside on our suitcases, looking like two dishevelled orphans, unable to continue our journey by car, Billy asked whether I wanted to go back home, or continue to Spain. 'Onwards to Spain, of course,' was my hasty reply and so he hailed a cab, unconcerned about the cost, to take us over the border. The journey would have cost the same as a flight home, so no difference which route we took, but as he looked at the mess I was in, on that long journey to Spain, he had decided there and then, we were buying the apartment.

On our arrival in Spain my mother was phoned and informed about the accident and immediately she took the first flight to be with me. Billy's beloved Jag looked like I felt, with a concertinaed bonnet and battered body up in the hills of Mijas. It sat in the garage of our villa, awaiting the arrival of Colin, Billy's mechanic, who was whipped over to take it back home, where a reconstruction eventually had it looking better than ever. My face healed well too, apart from a little minor scarring, and nothing a tan couldn't disguise. During that brief respite in Spain we settled, Billy, my mother and I, into enjoying our future apartment nestled beachside amidst Fuengirola village life. It convinced us the purchase was the right decision and we wasted no more time before buying it.

In late December 1980 and while the Christmas and New Year festivities had brought on a rush for sales of cigars, I left my husband at home and travelled to London in a blizzard, staying overnight with Mike and Sue. I was flying out the next day, with a friend joining me for the trip, to finalise the deeds to the apartment, which were to be in my name. This was a move that Billy had decided would be for the best, considering the delicacy of the business moves he was involved in. Then our New Year's Eve celebrations in Fuengirola began, partying in the square till late into New Year's Day.

Sadly, it wasn't long before we would be leaving the sun and fun of Spain, hung over and exhausted, arriving at Heathrow to be greeted by more blizzards and fog. The weather conditions had halted most flights, including ours to Manchester, and so we took the offer of what the airport had laid on hand, a slow coach trip home. The journey seemed to take forever, with stops for much-needed refreshments, trudging in snow nearly knee-high, wrapped up against the freezing fog. But, as always, my friend and I made light of a bad situation, settling back into the coach eventually to see the blurred distant lights that lit up Manchester Airport. The tired driver, unable to see clearly, unfortunately took an approach route that was much too low for the coach, causing the glass roof to smash down on our heads, which was by this time an experience that was nothing new to me.

One evening, as we were relaxing at home with a couple of bottles of wine, the peace was broken by a loud ringing of the front door bell. There stood four plain-clothes policemen, who searched our home and found what they were looking for - a number of cigar containers.

We later learned that Billy's name had been found in

the address book of his Heathrow Airport contact and so the game was up. After being read his rights, he was led away into a waiting police van, the officers having great difficulty getting him through the door, with an angry Muppet dog snapping at their ankles.

We were left to spend a restless night, Muppet and I, cuddled close together, while I tried in vain to contact our solicitor. When I managed to track him down early the next morning, he quickly jumped into action, drove to the police station were Billy was being held and arranged his bail. There was no question he would be honouring his bail conditions for long, especially as our solicitor explained that he could be facing years in prison, with the likelihood of a fine for hundreds of thousands of pounds.

Shortly afterwards, he hatched a plan to escape, using an Irish passport that he had gained in a false name and concocting his disguise. Then after kissing me goodbye, he disappeared into the night, only contacting me when he was safely in Spain. We had told family and friends of his decision to flee and everyone reacted with concern for him. Few were worried about the crime he had committed. It was smuggling cigars, hardly a murder, which was precisely my parents' thoughts, too.

Almost as soon as he had arrived, word was sent that he wanted two things sent over from England. The first was Muppet and so I made arrangements for him to be flown over, after he had spent six months penned up in quarantine. He was as tough as his master and emerged unscathed to enjoy his new home. Billy's second request was for his treasured E-Type Jag. Our friendly mechanic Colin jumped at the chance of two weeks all expenses paid in the sun. He knew that everything would be laid on to make sure he enjoyed every minute of his stay.

It didn't take Billy long to settle in and within weeks he called me to say he was thinking of buying into a car hire company. It was of course *our* money he was investing. As a result, he became an equal partner with a guy from the south of England who had moved to Spain with his family some years earlier. The offices of Wheels Car Hire Company in Torremolinos hired scooters as well as new Fiat Punto convertible cars and Robert, a quiet, somewhat unsociable guy, made a wise move taking Billy as his partner. He needed his get up and go to advertise the business and make it a success. Soon Billy had taken Wheels to great heights. Everyone used his company, including several major holiday travel companies,

I was addicted to this man who controlled my life and I encouraged his vision of making a grand lifestyle even grander, simply by staying put in my parlour and bringing in the money. I knew no different and as he continued to show me the proof of his success, I continued to work to enhance it. But while all this was progressing, so was his consumption of his favourite tipple, Jack Daniels.

His drinking eventually led to the decline of his relationship with Robert, the sober astute businessman, whose only concern was that the books balanced.

Billy, meanwhile, was interested mainly in socialising to get more business. You might think that this was the perfect partnership, but unfortunately it led to arguments, with one partner worse for wear from booze. 'Nothing sinks quicker than a partnership', so the saying goes. It was destined to fail. The two men eventually parted, with an amicable divvying up of the profits, and a payout that Billy requested in lieu of his share.

Back home in England, I was gaining control of my life and the confidence to realise that I held the key to success. Suddenly I knew he needed me more than I needed him. The feeling of power increased as my popularity in business grew. As well as Billy, I was also addicted to my job. I never wanted to leave, no matter what the day brought and every new dawn I rose to the challenge of bringing my dreams to life. I was not discouraged by setbacks, but nourished by them. At last I knew the truth of another well-known saying: *'Success is the experience of rising to the level of your true greatness'*.

Chapter 23

The Cast of a Dead Man's Teeth –
Porn, Prostitution, Police

'We flatter those we scarcely know, we please the fleeting guest, and deal full many a thoughtless blow, to those who love us best.' – Ella Wheeler Wilcox

Part of my reign at Aquarius from 1979 to 1984 coincided with a time when the Yorkshire Ripper, Peter Sutcliffe, was on the loose in Manchester. He only attacked working girls in the streets but anyone in the sex industry in the city was well aware of the potential dangers. However, it was no more of a threat to me. I refused to let it distract me from the job I had chosen and loved.

The Ripper murdered 13 prostitutes in a five-year period from 1975 and in 1980, at the height of the serial killer scare a Harley Street dentist, Dr Mace Joffe, was brought in by police to take a cast of Jimmy Savile's teeth, to check against bite marks on the Ripper's victims. He was told by the police that Savile was known to prostitutes and that he was a potential suspect. In fact, two of Sutcliffe's victims were found near the DJ's flat. More surprising was that Savile visited Sutcliffe in prison after his conviction and they were seen as friends during his later visits to Broadmoor Hospital, where the Ripper is still incarcerated.

The following year, when Sutcliffe was arrested and subsequently locked up for life, he said in a statement he had moved to Manchester when it became too hot for him in Leeds and Bradford. One of his victims, a street prostitute called Jean Hordan, was murdered after he picked her up in Moss Side and took her to a secluded spot on Princess Street, Chorlton. Her mutilated body was found a week later by two allotment holders, one of whom was Bruce Jones, who went on to play Les Battersby in the TV soap *Coronation Street*.

In spite of this frightening backdrop to my world, I felt empowered as I stepped through my parlour door. OK, somewhere out there was a monster who lurked the streets and massage parlours around Manchester but I couldn't allow myself to be troubled by him. If I had, my business would have suffered, my clients would have been unhappy with my service and taken their bodies elsewhere. I am sure I was not the only working girl with these thoughts.

I loved working at my Aquarius. The hours were not long, so I was always on top form for my clients. It was at this time I realised that giving the pleasure of sex, however it was needed, gave me enormous pleasure too. I don't mean physically, having orgasm after orgasm, but the pleasure of knowing that the men who came in like mice left feeling like kings. In a way I was a sex therapist, as there was much more to the job than satisfying the body. It was much more rewarding satisfying the mind.

A man who rushed in wanting to expose himself in front of me, did not then expose himself in the street, saving girls and women the distress of the unwanted encounter. Other clients I catered for included the young virgin, who wanted a sexual experience before he stepped out and looked for love. An invalid being wheeled in by a friend, sometimes their wife, needed to be treated like a fully fit man. Guys who loved to dress as a woman but couldn't show this side of their personality at home. Husbands who were not short of sex at home but lusted after something fresh.

Paying for sex with a hooker, rather than going out clubbing or pubbing to find a 'straight girl' to release his sperm in or on, can end up more expensive anyway and threatens to wreck a marriage. Once you leave a prostitute's room you never need to return – unless you want too. Love and sex are two different things. I took everyone who respected me and my services and I claim, in all modesty, that I performed a very good service. It wasn't a typical wham-bam-thank-you-ma'am. I really enjoyed my work and I loved the sex. I very rarely had to fake my pleasure and never rushed my client into achieving his orgasm. All my attention to detail paid off and it was incredibly rewarding to know that men were queuing down the road for a share of the action – I kid you not!

As a prostitute you are there for a pure sexual experience, a deliberate erotic act. Things I might have found awkward with a lover, I could do in the role of a working girl, hooker, whore, whatever name fitted the bill. It gave me a feeling of power and accomplishment and I could explore my own sexual limits, where I was not only allowed, but actively encouraged, to act as dirty as I wanted.

When you choose to sell your body, you have to learn to be tough and handle all situations.

Eventually, you build a strength that no-one can destroy, no matter what level you work at. Believe me, the sweetest, most innocent looking hooker has inside her a toughness like no other. It goes with the territory.

It's very rare to find a client who is completely loyal. You have to be totally dedicated to their needs, if you are doing the job right. This is no marriage; once he leaves, he has no reason to return, unless the service he receives is thrilling enough for him to come back for more. So Peter Sutcliffe be dammed! I never allowed him to trouble my mind. The power of the money I was earning took precedence over everything else and, like the rest of working girls, I took comfort in knowing that the enormous efforts the police, who were for once on our side, were putting into his capture, would result in his arrest, sooner rather than later.

However, the official police attitude was in stark contrast to the beliefs of the Chief Constable of Greater Manchester, James Anderton. His time in the job from 1975 to 1991 covered all my years in the brothel/massage parlour industry, both with Billy and later without him. One of his first acts as chief constable was a drive against pornography and prostitution. A special vice squad raided 284 bookshops, confiscated a total 160,000 magazines, including *The Sun Page Three Annual*.

The crackdown received support from feminists and anti-porn campaigners but was criticised as a moral crusade. Anderton replied to his critics that he was responding to public complaints, a total fabrication. It was his campaign alone. It had been argued that organised crime gangs in Manchester controlled the sale and distribution of pornographic material, as well as running brothels and street prostitution. He obviously hadn't studied our business, which had no connection with gangland. Still, whenever he cracked his whip and dropped a pin on the advertisements for massage parlours in the *Manchester Evening News*, the premises would receive an immediate raid from the vice squad.

At the same time there was a drive against late-night drinking in the city centre, with the focus on illegal drinking clubs and after-hour bars and clubs. As a result, 24 nightclubs had their licences revoked by magistrates. Regular patrols were also conducted in the 'red light' district of the city, with a special check on the homosexual community. Consequently, Manchester city centre was deserted after 10pm.

Anderton was also very vocal about his faith and became known as 'God's Copper', supporting among other things castration of rapists and child abusers, one of the few beliefs he had right. He was an authoritarian, who endorsed hard policies. In 1986 his remark that homosexuals, drug addicts and prostitutes were 'swirling around in a cesspit of their own making', led to widespread criticism. His extreme language and religious overtones made him his own worst enemy. The Happy Mondays' song *God's Cop* targeted Anderton, who was still in office at the time.

He was also the inspiration for various fictional characters, including the satirical novel *Lord Horror*. In 1989 a remark by him about the Aids virus was quoted, replacing the word 'homosexuals' with 'Jews'. As a result the book was banned and the author imprisoned for four months, proving nothing good can come from bad. Describing Anderton helps to explain the harsh regime Billy and I were working under, expecting a visit from the vice squad at any time and never being surprised when it happened. We were fortunate to have constantly on standby a solicitor who was respected by the police and knew how to deal in their language. He found it easy to get us released from police cells with a low bail after a quickie court appearance the day after the raid, so we took it all in our stride and life went on, hardly missing a beat.

Working alone, I had always kept my wits about me. Actually, I was rarely completely alone as Aquarius had become a lively parlour, where clients came to relax and mingle, enjoying their time away from the routine of the day, talking to others as they waited their turn in my boudoir of pleasure. It became impossible for me to have a moment to relax. A constant flow of clients streamed in throughout the day and as one left fulfilled another would immediately step into the privacy of my room, ready for action. The reception area took on the appearance of a doctor's surgery, with all seats taken. I had never adopted an appointment system, preferring to use the first-in-first-served approach.

It was the week before Christmas and the parlour was seasonally decorated and sparkly. In he came as I was booking in the last client before closing time. He was slightly drunk but nothing more than I thought I could cope with. Alcohol is to blame for the bad behaviour of most men in a parlour but I was in a good mood, thinking happily about my Christmas break abroad only a few days away, so I joined him in a festive drink. It turned out to be my biggest mistake. He had visited me before and was normally easy to handle. But this time was different, only I didn't see the warning signs. Suddenly, there he was, stripped and ready to go, expecting to be taken not just round the world but to the far side of the moon and back.

'I want my money's worth,' he demanded. My fees depended on what the client wanted, although sometimes I made exceptions, depending on how I felt about them. Some were so nice I wished I could give them the world on a silver platter but that wasn't the case with him. I knew I had to handle him with kid gloves but clearly my radar wasn't working properly that day or I would have realised sooner that he was big trouble.

There was something sinister about his eyes. I can usually tell a lot by a man's eyes but that day I got my signals wrong. After working in vain on his limp prick, trying to raise an erection underneath the sheath, he shouted angrily, 'Take it off and do it bare.' This request was taboo and I told him in no uncertain terms, suggesting he gave up and left it for another time. I had already been in the room much longer than the time he had paid for. Without a word, he leaped off the bed and lunged at me. Too late, I saw the sadistic look in his eyes and before I could jump out of his way, he grabbed me by the throat and forced me back against the mirrored wall, smashing my head, grabbing my hair and violently punching my breasts and groin. He had gone berserk. I managed to whack my knee into his balls so hard that for a moment his breath was taken away. Immediately I took my chance to escape into the street, virtually naked.

Luckily, the driver of a passing car was alerted by my distress, pulled up with his passenger seat door already open for me to jump in. The police were called but when we returned to the parlour, it was no surprise to find he had left the building. By some miracle, he was caught later that day and was held in police cells for being drunk and disorderly. The following day the same officers were stood at my parlour door. 'Do you want to press charges or let him go?' they asked.

I decided to release some Christmas spirit. 'Let him go, it's Christmas after all,' was my instant and generous reply.

During my time in Aquarius it was rare that I crossed the line to allow a punter to become a friend with whom I looked forward to having sex. Eddie the media mogul was one. His chauffeur popped his head around the reception door just as I was closing shop one day and asked, 'Can you stay open for my boss?' Seeing the uniform I guessed his boss was important.

His boss, who owned a now-defunct newspaper, had revolutionised the industry by taking on the print unions. Half Iranian, big in body, with a handsome face. He became a regular visitor to the parlour, bringing brandy and champagne to drink while we sweated it out in the sauna before heading to my boudoir for amazing sex. I'd have had him for free.

He was a master of control, very charming, with lots of charisma. You only had to look at him to know he was powerful and that power was taken through into the privacy of my room. His ever-present need for a cigar, even in the heat of the sauna, amused me and the power and control of the job he held added to the attraction.

A man has control of your pussy when he possesses the art of knowing how to lick and suck it. He knew how to do those two things perfectly. He had control over his body, too, and sex with him was always energetic. He had a perfect penis, quite wonderful in shape and large enough to give great satisfaction when he entered me with slow, deep, penetrative movements. His need of taking me in every position was more to show his prowess as a stud and hearing me reach orgasm was never as important as feeling his own. He was indeed a rough rider but I loved being in a sexual battle that he would always win.

His finale was always to flip me over and take me on all fours from behind, pounding away until he had me at screaming pitch and he reached his orgasm with a lion's roar. When he regained his demeanour, he kissed, re-lit his familiar cigar and said goodbye. I always knew his handsome face would be clamped between my legs again, sometime soon.

So many good-looking guys came my way but my next client had the broadest smile and huge dark eyes which focused on mine as I walked into reception. He was sitting quietly on his own, while the other two men chatted happily. As I dealt with the two clients before him, I felt excited at the thought of what was to come. His first visit consisted of lots of French kissing, his tongue insisting on searching my mouth. He was a passionate young man of 23, 11 years younger than me, and he played professional football. It wasn't Premier League stuff but he became a first-class lover and was soon frequenting Aquarius twice a week after practice on the pitch. My massage room with him became my bedroom as we set about our sex sessions, starting with long hand orgasms as I lay next to him, touching his cock. Sometimes when he was bringing me to orgasm, he would keep my hands from his penis, despite me longing to get down there. I slowly learned to accept this concept of uninterrupted concentration, although it was quite different from my normal play. I liked sensations all over my body and I'd gladly have had his penis in my hand or mouth while he was working on me. However, it became clear he was a 'one trip at a time pony', so I kept my hands from his precious jewels until I received the signal. This way, providing I didn't distract him, I got to go on his wild orgasm-giving rides. So no complaints from me, I went with the flow.

When I played with his penis it got deliciously rock hard very quickly and his super hardness always managed to take me by surprise. Suddenly, he would mount me and start screwing for all his worth, and my tongue would be drawn to tracing his neck and face. With him my mouth always wanted what my pussy had. It was indeed a strange attraction I had towards him. I had no interest in his background, although he found it easy to tell me about it, including the fact that he was in the process of getting married. None of that was important. He was a punter visiting a prostitute. There was no threat to anyone.

Occasionally before Billy's escape out of England, we would sometimes spend an evening in a favourite country club and among the mass of clubbers all dressed to impress, I would spot him taking notice of me and we would acknowledge each other. He would refer to my closeness with my husband as unusual. He didn't quite understand how two people could be so obviously attached to each other after years of marriage. He eventually disappeared out of my life after having the pleasure of his body in my bed at home. I couldn't resist that attraction he held.

I didn't want my life in Aquarius to end. I loved my parlour and was very settled with my life at home, enjoying leisure-time trips to the countryside with Muppet. But my dog by then had been taken abroad to join his master and his master had become very eager for me to retire, sell our home and business and join him permanently in Spain. So leave I did and Billy got his wish.

Chapter 24

The Two B's – Days of Wine and Wanting

'Life isn't defined by how many breaths you take.
But how many moments take your breath away.'

Two things happened to encourage me to retire, sell up and move abroad. The first was receiving a phone call from Billy. 'I've found a palace for you to live in,' he said. Those words took my breath away. He dangled that carrot again and it worked. I quickly arranged to take two weeks respite and, as it was approaching Christmas, I left England with its gloomy weather and arrived loaded up with decorations and presents, stepping off the plane and feeling the warmth of the sun. Even the smell of the country was more inviting and seeing Billy waiting for me at the little terminal thrilled me to bits. His energy for life was ever-present and, as he whisked me away to our Diamante apartment, he made it very clear that my working days had to be over and that ahead lay a new life with new friends and a wonderful villa in which to enjoy the years ahead.

Muppet made such a fuss of me when I walked through the door of the apartment, his tail wagging, yelping for a cuddle and saturating me with his kisses. I discovered there wasn't a dog more loved and spoilt in Spain. He and his master were inseparable, he was at Billy's side constantly and became a little celebrity among the

Costa del Sol crowd. Cooked chickens were bought for him to eat – no ordinary dog food for this pampered pooch. He'd dine out with us, sitting well-behaved beside his master and even went clubbing. Muppet had his own cute character, not unlike Billy.

The second thing that happened to encourage me to retire was falling in love with the villa as soon as I saw it. The land it was on took my breath away. Driving up the main Mijas road where that little village rested, the local donkeys decorated in colourful ribbons, drawing behind them carriages to transport holidaymakers around its quaint village and stunning countryside. The tavernas had not had a lick of paint for many years, retaining their originality. I was in heaven.

The villa had been ticked to purchase before I arrived but when Billy saw the pleasure in my face he had signed and paid for it before the end of my holiday. Work needed to be done and much money needed to be spent to get it the way I wanted. My designer skills were evident by the end of the interior construction. Our bedroom looked like it belonged in the Hollywood 1940s era, with its whitewashed walls, black cast iron chandeliers and wall lights. Naturally, an enormous bed was a must, and a giant black lacquered headboard with gold painted leaves and colourful birds gave it an oriental style. Its matching dressing table had a huge carved mirror, the sugar pink drapes and bedspread with co-ordinating birds of paradise in the pattern and the sugar pink carpet thick enough to bury your feet completed the exotic style. The en-suite bathroom had an adjacent wet room with a jacuzzi the size of a small swimming pool, the walls of pale pink mirror giving it a romantic feel.

We had the huge kitchen ripped out and designer units made and brought over from Germany at vast expense. The only areas that we left untouched – apart from decorating – were the dining and lounge areas. On the wall in the dining room were original tiles dating back to the art deco period that the previous owners had erected, and in the centre of this was a wall fountain where a wonderful water display erupted with the flick of a switch. From there you walked down steps into the lounge below, with its open fire lit from wood collected from trees chopped down in the forest just metres away. The floors were dug up and reconstructed with white marble, and the glass floor-to-ceiling doors opened on to the patio, pool and barbecue area, with views of the countryside beyond. The whole reconstruction took months to achieve and when completed – and after several weekend visits by me to help oversee the work – I took the necessary steps to leave my Aquarius and retire, selling my business and property for a good profit and putting all the money made from the sale towards the cost of the villa.

When I departed England I left nothing behind after selling my home there too. The only thing I knew I would miss were my friends and family but Spain was a just two-hour flight away, as easy in time as Manchester to London by train and so it was comforting to know they could all visit and I could return whenever I wished.

Our time in the second villa was divided three ways and life became a mixture, with friends down the hill in Fuengirola, Lew Hoad's Tennis Ranch crowd, and friends Billy had amassed in and around Puerto Banus in Marbella. Friends from the ranch hardly ever mixed but there was a camaraderie between friends in Marbella and Fuengirola.

Costa del Sol had been christened Costa del Crime in the British press, with many villains escaping the hands of the law in England. For those on the run, the south of Spain had become a respectable place to reside and many leading gangsters and those who were on the fringes lived there happily. Tough gangsters have as much attraction as movie stars and they were celebrities in their own right. Billy had happily placed himself on the periphery and friendships had been struck up before my arrival, so gradually I was introduced as we moved around, socialising in Fuengirola and Puerto Banus.

Vinnie was a car dealer with connections. His past life as part of the 'Quality Street Gang' in Manchester gave him enormous standing. His time living with us while his yacht, docked in Puerto Banus, was refurbished was a very pleasant one. He was easy going and I admired his strength of character. He could spot a faker immediately and although always polite, he had no time for anything other than genuine.

As well as his strength of mind he had a strength of body too. I always felt that if he was forced to venture into battle he would win hands down. With all this power he had a lovely way and was a true gent with an unassuming manner. He hated to stand out in a crowd and was always happier standing back. Those who knew him, respected him, not only for his manner, but also because of who he was. One day Billy and I visited Vinnie on his yacht and while he was down in the bowels of the boat doing repair work a row was erupting in the cabin above. As I sat unaware, taking in the sun, temperatures were rising. It didn't surprise me that my husband was on the end of a good ticking off. He had been opening his mouth too much about notorious gangster Ronnie Knight who was personally putting him in his place. You certainly didn't mess with Ronnie but Billy under the influence of booze was loose-lipped and dangerous when in that condition. Fortunately for him he came away unscathed and while the commotion was reaching its heights, Vinnie had joined me on the deck to ease my worries, keeping away from the commotion himself.

Occasionally, Sue, Ronnie's girlfriend, would arrange to join me at Lew Hoad's for a session of aerobic lessons. I liked her company, with her easy-going style and bubbly personality, she was an attractive blonde from the East

End of London who never once let her man down. When we eventually held our house-warming party in the gardens of the villa, Ronnie and Sue were invited, plus others of equal or more standing. The fact that the Guardia Civil were placed to protect our gated entrance relays the importance of those who were inside.

Lew Hoad's Campo de Tennis, located amid several acres of botanical gardens, was built in the style of an Andalusian farmhouse in the foothills of Mijas, between Malaga and Marbella. There were numerous tennis courts, including a clubhouse court seated arena where tournaments and other main tennis events took place. The Mediterranean Restaurant and Terrace Bar, whose patio overlooked the clubhouse court, was a regular meeting place day and night for ex-pats and locals and the occasional celebrity tennis player or movie star. Sean Connery could be seen there on many an occasion. My move across the water was an easy transition once Aquarius had worked out of my skin. The pure thought of living that villa lifestyle and waking each morning to the magnificent mountain views that were the backdrop to Mijas – who would hesitate leaving the dullness of north Manchester? The nearest you got to nature was Heaton Park and the ducks in the muddy pond.

Billy's social skills were ever-active and after becoming a member of the tennis ranch he developed as a very popular character whose laughter you could hear well before you could see him. He also proved to everyone that he was not just good company but also someone against whom to test your tennis skills as he excelled at all ball games and was an excellent tennis player, winning many amateur tournaments.

As for me, I fell into the role again of being a supportive unobtrusive wife, leaving everything to him. Organising social meetings and events were his forte, so I played the part of a subservient wife very well. I was losing myself again but it was easy to do as the thrills and excitement in life came from his ability to attract interesting people to him like a magnet. So I sat back and let him lead the way.

My tennis started off poorly and lessons were booked with Denis, a quiet, white-haired, skinny, unassuming ex-pat and one of the professional coaches at the club. I bought up nearly every designer tennis outfit from the boutique and woke early most mornings for my lesson. If I were to explain how wonderful the feeling was taking that early morning walk as the mist cleared to reveal a bright blue sky, the smell of the blossom and birds singing in my ears, well, it would be impossible to explain how good that feeling was. Life became a constant social whirl and many a morning we woke with sore heads after a night of too much alcohol consumption. Sometimes in our own bed and sometimes not.

Barry and Marlana were introduced to me before I actually saw them. It happened during a phone call I received late one night from Billy before my move to Spain. He was out taking in some evening entertainment and, after consuming many Jack Daniels, was just about sober enough to introduce me to this couple he had already been having threesomes with. 'Bring over as many bottles of Courvoisier brandy as you can, it's their favourite tipple,' he asked.

I knew then what he might have had planned once I had arrived and settled, and I was right, I knew my man. Both Barry and Billy, the two B's as I called them, were juicing up with the thought of Marlana and me eating and fingering each other's pussy. I had little desire to enter this three-way stretch. I was tired of using my body to please my man but a sexual extravaganza had been arranged well before my arrival and there they were the two B's discussing tactics.

Thankfully, Marlana and I got on like a house on fire.

She was pleasing her man to reach her goal of getting that wedding band placed on her finger and I had learnt the art of being a lady in the living room and a whore in the bedroom. When Billy and I arrived at their villa she was stepping out of the swimming pool naked, a vision to be seen, with her slender svelte figure tanned and toned. I was drawn to the water dripping off the ends of her breasts and memories of an old friend called nipples came flooding back. Never would I have thought a woman could possess anything larger, but Marlana's nipples were like huge brown corkscrews. A good lady of the night is a good actress but with her I knew I would be natural. She had a touch of class and I liked her style, from the swing of her hips to her dulcet tones.

Barry and Billy had disappeared into insignificance as I asked her to give me a guided tour of the villa, which she did after pouring large brandies for us all from a crystal decanter. Everything about her was tasteful and I guess she found me tasteful too. 'Do you want to go through the motions of making love to me or would you prefer not?' she teased. Those were the first words out of her mouth as we moved towards the bedroom. Putting it that way I guess she was used to acting her way through planned moments of lust. I was pleasantly surprised at the question but, realising the need to entertain our men was of the foremost importance, I agreed to play the part of a whore in the bedroom. But it took little persuasion. She was naturally seductive and I still had my actress head on, so no problems my end.

In came the men, strutting like peacocks, displaying their naked bodies and it was then that I realised Barry was one of my kin. Looking down, I noticed his circumcised penis of not bad proportions. A tasty bit of meat for a Shabbos dinner. When I said it we both burst into laughter and the ice was broken.

How is it that most men think they touch a woman in

the right places instantly and yet seem to take forever fumbling and fingering around in foreplay never hitting the G-spot? Oh, for a man that knows where your spot is! Like the young stud I had left behind in England. I discovered that Marlana was a bigger actress than I was as we lay next to each other on their bed while our men had swapped partners and were making the most of pumping our bodies. Here I was back in work mode. Had I retired at all!? I immediately got into the sensation of laughing and talking and fucking without feeling and anyway, I needed my daily orgasm.

Fun at Lew Hoad's tennis courts was kept separate from our private times together but sometimes other couples were invited to a 'wife' swapping evening. I always regarded this as a truly chauvinistic saying. Why not call it a husband swapping evening instead?

When the two B's set their bait nobody needed much persuasion and very soon we would all be stripped naked, swimming in the pool, drinking and dining round the barbecue in carefree abandonment. Times like this, I always let the wine take over my head and I would easily end up on the grass, floor, or tied up in bed sheets, sucking, fucking, laughing and climaxing, hot and perspiring, and so I would shower, swap and do it all again. I got caught in the abandonment of the whole experience and when joints were brought out to puff on, I willingly let myself relax next to Marlana's body, purring like a kitten while she kissed and finger-fucked me all the way to heaven.

I liked to please or be pleased by a woman but I have to admit that coming towards an orgasm while being pleased this way, it is the dreamy vision of a man's penis that brings me off the most. For me the pleasure with a woman was more towards giving pleasure without feeling it myself. Mentally, yes, but physically no, for that I had to have a man. Sex between two women can be the most beautiful thing without the use of artificial devices. They have more in common than men and women have more understanding of each other's bodies, less selfish and more gentle.

Marlana, Barry, Billy and I became very close friends in and out of the bedroom, enjoying lazy hazy days in the sun, playing tennis, meeting up with Lew and others for our daily dose of gossip on the ranch, going to many tennis club events. Sex was taken over by a great friendship that lasted till after Billy's death.

Eddie Avoth was another gentle giant but he had an attraction for women like no other. His personality was equally as big as his body. Although he had been a world class champion boxer he had a gentle manner. Both Vinnie and Eddie were proof that strong powerful men didn't need to throw their weight around.

Eddie was very protective of Billy when needed, which it seemed was quite often while I was in England. Never being a man to hold his booze, he was fortunate to have Eddie around to ward off any foreseeable problems. They became very close friends for a time and he had the most charming of girlfriends who was also from his home town of Cardiff. They made a very handsome couple and often would travel to either our villa or the La Cepa Bar in Fuengirola village centre where all the great characters collected. They mingled easily with everyone and I was thankful that Billy had not crossed the line to suggest a rumbling in the bed sheets together. I think if he had, Eddie would have laid him out flat with one punch.

The future Linda Pleasance was one of the many attracted to him but his eyes were firmly on her gorgeous daughter, as many men's eyes were. Being much too young and with Linda watching her, they understood the rules – look but don't touch. Linda was a Manchester girl through and through and a former stripper herself. In Fuengirola she had gained status by becoming the live-in lover of the British actor Donald Pleasance. She was a crazy cuckoo redhead that Donald fondly called his Eliza Dolittle. He loved her to bits and I could see all he saw in her, streetwise and crafty, but also surprisingly she was very well read, with a library of books on all subjects in their home.

Their relationship was obviously serious as they eventually married. But before that, with or without him, she was most days present in La Cepa Bar, where Donald would sit quietly and she would be on her best behaviour. But whenever he was away filming the mouse came out to play. Linda would revert into a vamp and a tempestuous side of her character would appear after downing a few San Miguel's, a habit I shared after a bottle of Rioja wine when the stripper emerged from inside us and everyone got a show for free. Who cared? I can look back on those days of complete abandonment as adding colourful pages to my life.

Mingling with the colourful characters in Fuengirola were the Brink's-Mat boys. No-one asked details or even if they were using their real names. No-one cared. The case of the Brink's-Mat was without doubt colourful. An ex-cop ended up with an axe in his head, and a Great Train Robber was shot dead in Marbella. Heathrow Airport was certainly active again in November 1983, when inside one of their nondescript warehouses was one of Britain's biggest secure vaults used to store currency, precious metals and other high-value consignments. The Brink's-Mat bullion remains the biggest and most notorious heist ever to take place on UK soil.

Spending some time back in England, I received a call from Billy asking me to meet Charlie Wilson at Manchester's Piccadilly train station. He had flown in from Spain to visit a friend in the city's Strangeways Prison. A colleague of ours wanted the privilege of driving the car in which I collected him. The visit over, we went for lunch at a club and he left the same day. I found him unassuming and the fact that he was one of the Great Train Robbers back in the 1960s didn't really impress me. I just made sure his visit was sweet and away he went. I read many years later in the 1990s that Charlie Wilson the Great Train Robber, who lost three million of Brink's-Mat money on a drugs shipment, was shot dead leaving his villa in Marbella. The Brink's-Mat gold has claimed more than 20 lives so far, with some shot dead as a warning to the rest of the underworld, and as the 30th anniversary has passed, there is no sign that the killings are going to stop.

Chapter 25

For the Love of Billy

'It's not the load that breaks you down, it's the way you carry it.'

Life in Spain was just one long party. But even that can get boring after a while. Then one day I received a phone call from a friend I hadn't seen for some years. My first introduction to Lauren happened when she was sweet 16 and I was some 12 years older. She was employed part-time selling and stacking shoes in my cousin's shop in Cheetham Hill. The family took to her sweet nature and she would often be sat around the kitchen table mingling with the rest, the family home being a hive of activity.

I hadn't viewed her in any other light until one morning at breakfast, after returning from an early morning aerobics class, I took a long distance phone call from Australia. In her urgency to contact me she had obtained the villa phone number from my mother. I listened while she explained the reason for the call. She had been working in a Sydney escort agency and just happened to wonder if I could help set her up in her own massage parlour when she returned to England. Listening to her story, I realised she needed help financially. It had been two years since I had retired and sold my business and I'd had no contact with the industry since that time.

Firstly, I needed her to post me over an edition of the *Manchester Evening News* where a full page of massage parlour advertising would be on view. I could then check out the competition and get the feel of the business again.

This she agreed to do and I asked her to phone me a week later and I would give her my decision. When I put the phone down I mentioned to Billy the conversation and we both agreed that if the paper arrived we would know she was serious with her intentions. Were we not at all surprised she had taken a road into prostitution, no. She was always ambitious and the fact that she had been using her good looks and figure to enhance her lifestyle, good for her!

She must have put on her roller-skates to grab a newspaper and post it, as within a week it popped through the letterbox and just days later I was on a plane out of Spain and looking forward to seeing my family, meeting up with friends and intrigued with what might come from meeting Lauren. We quickly got down to business and as I had studied the competition through the small ads of the paper I thought it a good idea to open a parlour in Whitefield, that's how confident I was that my family's knowledge of the business would present no problems to them.

'Fantasia' opened its doors on Bury Old Road within two months. Never being one to miss a trick, I jumped on the opportunity of earning my own money again, only this time someone else was working her body. A contract was formed on the basis that I would lay out the money to set her up and for that I expected a payment of £500 per week for six months to offset the £2,000 start-up costs. Working as an escort was totally different to working a massage parlour and I gave her my expert advice on prices to charge and how to run her business, explaining the way for her to earn maximum money.

My knowledge was worth what I was charging, so I felt I had done well by her and in turn I left her a very happy bunny. She was a gutsy girl as she too intended to work alone. It's amazing how the power of money can affect the risks you are prepared to take in life. Her only other ally was her mother, who took on the role of cleaning the parlour, which I am sure gave her some security after I returned to Spain. Before leaving, I felt in no hurry to collect my money and had left it some months before I was back in England. You can imagine my shock when I discovered she wouldn't immediately be able to pay me. Why? Lauren had invested not only her own money, but mine as well, in a stocks and shares account in her name that could not be accessed immediately. Everyone learns by their mistakes and her lesson was hard for her to take as I insisted in no uncertain terms, 'Pay up or go to your mother for it.' I was not leaving empty handed. Within a week I had my money and we moved on to calmer waters.

Lauren completed the six-month contract and worked another six months before she retired from the business and sold out to another girl eager to take her place. We then moved on together into a completely new venture, the fashion industry. Our new partnership was fun as we established a boutique where all of Whitefield and Prestwich and areas beyond called to buy and where Lauren's buying skills were excellent. Like any business venture I threw myself into helping with its success. Fashion shows were organised, where retired catwalk models, who had married well and had become 'ladies that lunch' were delighted to step back on the catwalk again, for charity of course.

I was fully enjoying my days involving myself in my boutique and indulging myself listening to the gossip when the ladies popped in for a chat and coffee, hopefully to leave with a purchase or two. Gossip not being my style, you know to keep your mouth shut in the world of prostitution, unless you need to open it for other reasons. So I listened to conversations on love, marriage, designer shopping, holidays and, of course, gossip on who might be fucking whose partner. Gossip is dangerous, especially on questions of loyalty. I also found humour in hearing about the men in question and wondered if they had added to their list a visit to a massage parlour, as if they had it was more than likely they had ventured my way.

I had added another business title along with Madam and Prostitute. I was now also a director of a boutique and had established myself in the clothing industry. What fun! Two new business ventures followed shortly after, one south side in Denton and the other locally in Prestwich, as Lauren and I opened massage parlours one after the other. We had developed a skill of spotting an ideal place, knowing the most important ingredient required – position, position, position. Her need of taking no risks meant we had to be extra cautious, only having one girl working a shift. According to the rule book, it is legal for one girl working with a maid. Two or more working girls is classed as a brothel and thus illegal. Who said the law is an ass?

Both these businesses had a short lease of life, as Lauren's love life became serious. She, unlike me, kept this part of her business life away from the man in her life. However, a good thing came from the venture, for me anyway: Jilly, who worked shifts in the Denton parlour, had proved her worth as a friend as well as a work colleague and was there when I needed her in the not too distant future. As for Lauren, our future was not too rosy, when a friendship eventually became damaged and lost, as well as our partnership.

Billy had actually become very ill in his 48th year. I was away so much in England mixing business with pleasure within my family circle that I had decided to invest in a home in Whitefield, a cute black and white rendered cottage that I once again took pleasure refurbishing, money being no object. Lauren and I were doing well and when I returned to Spain I was shocked with Billy's weight loss. He was no longer playing tennis and although tanned, it couldn't hide his deteriorated appearance. Maybe there was something wrong but it didn't seem to concern him. Either that or he was hiding it well. Instead, he told me he had had enough of Spain and I organised a meeting with our solicitor in Amsterdam where they discussed putting a deal on the table that would be accepted by the police and allow Billy to come home.

Amsterdam, well-known for its red light area, would surely have been a treat for Billy's solicitor and the perfect place to mix business with pleasure. On his return to Spain, within a few days Billy received the news. A deal had been struck and it took him no time to pack and get to the airport as fast as he could to return to the land he had missed so much. It didn't take long for Billy to renew friendships and he quickly gained access to the executive suite at Manchester United's football ground for a home match. He was back in the fold where he wanted to be, among family and friends and gambling buddies at Don Tony's new gaming club, and all was happy for a while.

Employing the renowned George Carmen QC, he walked into the crown court some weeks later to face his sentence, leaving me with a kiss and, 'See you soon baby.' That was his style, prepared to take the inevitable on the chin. He received a very generous six-month prison sentence and served his time locally at Strangeways in Manchester. Within days I received a visiting order and with it a letter asking for, among other things, sports socks, as he intended to play in the prison football team.

Lauren on one occasion joined me on a visit. We still had parlour interests together and she was concerned that when Billy was released he would want me to sever those ties. During that visit I noticed his sadness when I explained to him that my business arrangements would continue with Lauren independent to whatever he did. I had at last become independent myself, at least for the moment. That moment didn't last and on his release I immediately forgot my independence and like any loving wife, my loyalty had to be with my husband.

Another property, 467A Chorley Road, entered our lives.

Billy found and rented it and within weeks it was up and running. Tiny in comparison to any other massage parlour, before long it was big in popularity. When you have a busy place with many customers it's like any business, you attract the best of staff. It was obvious even in those early days that 467A Chorley Road would become famous.

Being on a main road opposite a pub and a skip and a jump from the local police station, it was hardly hidden. The front door on to the street was left permanently open, visitors having to immediately climb a steep flight of stairs. To the right was a small reception room with two sofas and a coffee table, TV and video for showing porn, and a compact bar that also acted as a reception desk, all crammed together. Through a curtained entrance were two small rooms with showers and built-in single beds on which the girls entertained. To the left of the stairs you walked immediately into a tiny kitchen with just a kettle perched on top of a small kitchen unit, and immediately from there through a door into the toilet area. It was basic, without a sign of a sex toy to stimulate the imagination. Exon was Billy's final parlour and the one he loved the most.

His health became of huge concern and his coughing seemed to go on forever. One night while spending an evening out with Don Tony and his current squeeze, a bout of coughing started that he struggled to stop.

Don and I glanced at each other and we knew then he was not well. A hospital appointment confirmed a malignant tumour and he was whisked in for an operation. Only hours before going down to theatre he asked to speak to the surgeon, who came out of the operating theatre still in his robes where he explained that there was a very good possibility that the cancer was contained in one lung. 'People can live with one lung,' I told him.

'OK but what if not and the air gets in and the cancer spreads Viv, what then?' he asked. My reply persuaded him to trust in the judgement of the surgeons and continue to theatre. On his return we knew the answer. The surgeon had opened him up and closed him up again. His prognosis: six months to live.

At first when hearing the news I was in total denial and my first port of call was the boutique where Lauren was waiting to hear the news. I explained the situation. I would not be able to concentrate on anything but the care of my husband for however long it was needed. How could I put a time on it?

Her reply took me by surprise. It was sharp and direct to the point and her words were uttered without any emotion. The partnership could not survive without my input and therefore a price would have to be arranged for her to buy my share of the business. I didn't react. Billy was sitting in the car outside and I needed to keep things calm. I wanted to scream – a price! If the boot had been on the other foot she would have been told to go away with my blessing, everything would run fine without her. Thinking about it sometime later, I guess the hard line she took with me was in a way her payback for me being hard on her with my early investment during her parlour working days. Broaching the subject some weeks later, her reply confirmed my thoughts and was simply said: 'Yes, but I had a good teacher.'

The following few weeks were a daily blur of just mechanically getting on with things. It wasn't easy as Billy took to drowning his sorrows in alcohol, making arrangements with girls in the parlour to party with him, even driving along Cheetham Hill Road where all the street hookers hung out, looking to take a decent-looking girl off the street, which resulted in a knock at the door of our home one evening. When I answered I was surprised to see two policemen ready to arrest him for kerb-crawling. After explaining he was a dying man and would be dead before he got to court, they apologised and left without making a charge. How generous of them!

The girls at the parlour were very supportive, Jilly in particular. She loved Billy and had joined the team after I had kept in touch with her when the Denton parlour closed. Every day he would visit, struggling on his walking sticks for a chat with his girls, every day he made it to Don Tony's club for a game of poker. Sympathetic players would understand his spaced out appearance due to the amount of drugs he was taking.

Nick Thatcher was his consultant at Wythenshawe Hospital, which has a reputation for being one of the best National Health hospitals for treating cancer and heart disease. Billy actually had a choice to go privately but Nick was adamant that his skills were there for everyone, rich or poor. Billy liked his manner and had a great respect for him and so there was no decision to make. Nick was his man and Nick in turn was always available to give advice, especially to me who was at a loss and still in denial. He told me not to be concerned about his excess drinking as it wouldn't last long as his body wouldn't be able to take it, which proved to be true.

Shortly after he found out his destiny he took me to Capri, the island of love. Sat having breakfast on the hotel terrace one morning an American lady asked if she could join us at our table. In conversation she told us an amazing story of how she was in the process of working on a thesis about a Brazilian man who had the power to heal sick people with the laying of his hands. Without any hesitation she quite simply asked if Billy was terminally ill. This question was quite amazing, as not knowing him before you would never have been aware of his weight loss, plus we had super tans that gave him a glow that hid any sign of illness. The conclusion to this conversation was her leaving her telephone number where she was staying in Chelsea for us to contact her if we wished to travel back with her to Brazil.

Billy took a lot of persuasion. His thoughts were, why

waste money when his mind was concentrated on collecting all he could for me before he died? My constant nagging worked. I'd have grasped at any straw to keep him alive. Contacts in Brazil were made through Mike in Cobham who knew a couple of guys who lived there. We confirmed that we would make the trip, phoning the American lady and before much time passed we were on a flight from Heathrow, arriving in Brazil and heading for the Rio Palace hotel opposite Copacabana Beach.

Rio was an amazing place, with a huge strip on the beach for volleyball games and a line on the promenade for daily joggers. Everything was directed around keeping fit. The bodies of the girls on the beach had to be the best in the world, wearing tiny bikini tops just covering their nipples and G-strings exposing their perfectly pert bottoms. I was one of the few European girls among them that could match up to their sexiness, my body able to compete with the best.

We had fun. Billy had no problem with communication, the common language of Portuguese being similar to Spanish. We had fun too, as best we could. Who could resist that Brazilian style of partying?

One day we visited a sex motel, driving into a block of town houses and paying an entrance fee at the guarded gateway, then driving into the basement where we entered the townhouse from the private garage. Each of the three floors focused on sexual pleasure. On the ground floor a huge spa with every sweet smelling potion and lotion to hand. Easy listening music played constantly, huge plants and flowers edged the spa and a hot sauna to use if you wished. The next floor, the dining room, with a menu left in the centre of the table and food cooked by your own chef, ordering your choice of meal was done by telephone and the food delivered up to you on a pulley that arrived when you heard a bell ring, open the cupboard door and hey presto, there it was.

Finally the bedroom with its huge screen playing constant porn, an enormous bed with black silk sheets and every type of sex toy and lubricated condoms stashed in the bedside cabinets, all neatly packaged. We took pleasure in using every room, while Billy filmed me stripping to the music, then he did his best to make love to me before tiredness took over his body. 'The film is for posterity,' he said, and I still have it to this day. We arrived without being seen and left the same way.

Days turned into weeks and still there was no word for Billy to be seen by this man from the mountains who seemed to have the powers of Moses or Jesus himself. We decided that I should return home and Billy would continue being looked after by his friends, who by this time had become very protective of him.

Returning home to the comfort of Livesey Street I was thankful for the constant support of family and neighbours who supported me through my days of anguish, waiting and hoping for some miracle to happen. Eventually a phone call came, Billy had been taken in a coma on a stretcher up the mountain to Protropolus to meet this man of miracles. The following day he phoned from a hotel and, trying to hold back his tears, he told me his tumours couldn't be atomised out of his body as they were surrounded with fluid, so by the laying of hands he had moved them to a place where there would be no pain. And so he returned home carrying with him phials of liquid to sip to slow down the cancer. He came with stories of amazing things. Twins that had brain tumours, after the laying of hands the tumours had disappeared. People who were unable to walk, miraculously walking again. This man had powers that were a mystery to everyone, including scientists at NASA's Kennedy Space Centre who were there monitoring him.

Billy found the strength to return to Spain and sign away the deeds to the villa, happy on his return that he had completed all he needed to do. I remember him walking towards me at Manchester Airport, refusing wheelchair help. He was so brave. Within a few weeks I drove him on his last journey to the hospital. He, unlike me, knew it was his time. Nick Thatcher, who now is head of Christies Hospital, had told me that as much as Billy wished to die at home, it would be better if he was in hospital care. And so he died there in the F6 ward at Wythenshawe, inside a room with torn curtains and old bedding. This was what dying people could expect for their final hours.

Those that have had a loved one go through the stages of cancer are well aware of the emotional rollercoaster and how you cope with it is just as important as how they deal with it. We were no different. It's normal to feel resentment when cancer has intruded your relationship but the resentment is targeted towards the cancer, not your loved one. We found it important to give the cancer an identity, a name we could point a finger at.

Thankfully I found the strength I had gained before in times of despair and I seemed to float through from beginning to end, being carried all the way. A little advice: focus on the qualities you love so much about the person who is ill, their strength of character, a contagious laugh, a lovely smile, their compassion for others. You will find these qualities are still there. The actress Pat Phoenix who played Elsie Tanner in the soap opera *Coronation Street*, had recently died of lung cancer in a private hospital but while she was ill she put her name to the Buy A Brick Appeal to improve the conditions of the F6 Ward and provide another building for terminally ill patients and their families at Wythenshawe hospital. We had joined that cause.

Billy's funeral was amazing. His precious dog Muppet never left his master's side, sitting under the coffin when he was brought home. The tiny cobbled street where we lived in Whitefield couldn't cope with the traffic from the number of mourners wanting to pay their respects, people from all walks of life. It was a wonderful send off. At the end of his life, Billy had redeemed himself and Muppet, who so missed his master, pined himself away and died in my father's arms six months later.

Chapter 26

The Merry Widow

'You can be much more alone with other people than you can on your own – even with people that you love.'

I was 37 and widowed. I felt I had lost my safety net. I had reached a point where it was time to assess the 'friends' I had around me, while assessing myself too. I drew comfort in knowing that I had often been told I had a good disposition, proved I suppose, in my forgiveness of Lauren's hard-nosed attitude over the boutique I had invested in. It took a good disposition to walk away without taking a penny for my share of a successful business but at the time she knew I had no fight in me and therefore took advantage of the opportunity to own 100 per cent, knowing I couldn't put the hours in while Billy was dying.

The loss and respect of a friend is one of the tragedies of life. The fact that I allowed her to continue as a 'friend' is part down to a good disposition and part knowing that it was more than likely her payback time in response to how hard I had been with her regarding payment in her massage parlour those years before. Either way, deep down, respect for her was never regained. Within six months I had taken stock on my life and all that had gone before it.

Letters of condolence poured through my door, all relaying their personal feelings of loss, touching words that lifted my spirits just enough. It may seem quite surprising but the recovery from the loss of Billy wasn't as hard as I expected. I didn't really know how I should feel but I shed no tears. They say you can never be prepared for the loss of a loved one but it really wasn't that hard. In the weeks running up to his inevitable death, we had prepared ourselves and talked all we had to talk to each other. He left me, loving me, and that alone gave me strength to take on the days ahead without him. Either that or God was carrying me.

I had been left a wealthy woman and I did as Billy suggested, sold his business interests but kept hold of the Swinton parlour, although I had little interest in climbing those stairs that he had trod. Instead I rented it out. Jilly had been one of Billy's rock solid girls. Reliable and honest with a great sense of humour. A busty bubbly blonde, she was respected and in return had respect for other girls who worked with her. How thankful I was that she had come into my life to work in the Denton parlour those months before and her offer of taking the weight off my shoulders with my Swinton parlour I gladly accepted and a suitable rent was arranged. But the importance of the rent I received was never as important as knowing that Swinton's door was open and it was alive and kicking.

I had detached myself completely from pleasures of the body. Instead I focused on strengthening friendships and a close friendship had been formed with my neighbours Barbara and Hugh, and it was Barbara with whom I chose to venture into business, opening a children's boutique doors away from the ladies boutique I had shared with Lauren. Abstaining from sex came easy to me. I wasn't ready to be penetrated where Billy had been – part of the grieving process maybe. It wasn't something I did deliberately but it just seemed easy to fall into that state of mind.

I was active enough, indulging in the pleasures of nightly booze-fuelled partying, either at home or clubbing in the city. My parties at home were always theme-inspired, inventing all sorts of reasons. Bonfire Night wood was collected and a fire the size of a house lit on the fields adjacent to my garden. No neighbours complained, they were all invited. Birthday, Christmas, New Year, summer fun parties, anything to keep myself busy and not alone.

A close set had been formed, which included the Prestwich and Whitefield few that loved to party. Days were never as important as the nights, which were the only time of the day to which I looked forward. I woke most mornings needing the 'hair of the dog' to get me functioning, employing a cleaner in my little home, and venturing every day to choose a new outfit to wear instead of laundering what I had worn the day before. I was on a decline and if anyone noticed it, no-one did anything about it and neither could they have tried. In the wake of the children's boutique, a gents' boutique followed, buying the property and completing a trio. It was an impulsive move for sure but everything I was doing was impulsive and without much thought. Adrian had come into my life while I was dancing like a woman possessed in front of his DJ stand. He was a young good-looking mixed race guy, who spun his discs with perfection and his choice of music had everyone on the floor moving to his music. He noticed me while I was noticing him and beckoned me towards him to slip a telephone number into my hand. From that brief encounter a friendship followed and I discovered his sole desire was to enter the fashion world opening a designer men's clothes shop. As I had a vacant property that suited the purpose, I helped him towards that goal, not having any real interest in the running of it, other than an arrangement of weekly payments for the money I had invested, with a little interest, of course. This arrangement he honoured and swiftly paid off his debt to me without a problem.

Around the same time I reformed a friendship with a girl who used to work for Billy in the Preston massage parlour. Wendy had spirit that I liked, a top-class hooker herself, with a private life that she kept separate from her business life. Her love of sex was only equalled by her love of the equestrian sport of three-day eventing and riding with the Cheshire Hunt. She proudly showed off her buttons, enabling her to ride up in front with the best, including on occasion Prince Charles. She had returned to the fold briefly in Billy's final days, visiting him when she was in town and we had formed a close friendship.

Wendy had an uncomplicated personal sex life and never had the time to be tempted with a loving relationship, preferring to choose young athletic studs to attend to her constant sexual needs. The young stud who was servicing her was constantly under her command as she held the purse strings and if he happened not to be in attendance an array of dildos of all shapes and sizes were to hand under her bed to attain her much-needed daily dose of orgasms.

Coming from a conservative middle-class background with no siblings and a frail mother she had a difficult relationship with, her family time, rare as it was, was spent making sure that her two nieces, who her mother was devoted to, would not end up with her estate. She had a successful sauna/massage parlour in Chester, as successful as mine in Swinton, and together we combined the two. We both had good reason. The tax man was on her back and she needed an escape for a while, and I needed to escape from Swinton for obvious reasons.

Our plan was set and put into place and she immediately took the opportunity of taking over Swinton, working herself most days and leaving the days she chose not to work to Gilly. Changing the name from Exon to Danielle's French, she immediately stamped her style in my Swinton parlour.

Now was the time for my resurrection and with that my old spirit came alive again. Pinkies was a parlour in

Chester and Wendy had put plenty of flair into her business but I found the interior unimpressive. Everything was immaculately presented and contained within the premises. The laundering of towels was done on the spot, unlike Swinton where the ladies from the launderette next door used to pop in to collect and deliver. Her idea of having vanity sinks installed in the massage rooms as well as showers made it easier and much quicker if a simple wrist action with hand relief was all that was required. No need for undressing completely so no need to shower. In my view, Pinkies style was clinical without a sign of a sex toy until it appeared out of the handbag of the girl providing the service. But like Swinton a sex menu was on hand so that a client could choose which service he fancied.

Wendy always preferred to work alone, with her svelte-like figure and being that much older than her competition, she took no chances of being overlooked. She needn't have worried, her service was always second to none. When she took over at Swinton her dominant presence had men under her control with the click of her finger or the crack of her whip.

It wasn't long before we discussed widening our horizons by opening the first escort agency in Manchester. What better place to have a business discussion than on a trip to New York on the QE2? Climbing aboard at Southampton dock was thrilling, watching the balloons fly into the sky as we sailed out to sea. We had booked a cabin below deck but using our social skills it didn't take long before we were installed in a suite on the Queen's Deck, thanks to the captain of the ship and we gladly accepted his invitation to join him at his table for dinner, which was regarded as a real honour.

Unfortunately, within two days of the four-day journey we hit Hurricane Gilbert and life on deck for the remainder of the journey was a nightmare. The enormous ship was tossed at sea like a little fishing boat, with huge waves crashing over the decks. After a day spent with my head in the toilet and Wendy braving the storms wobbling on stilettos from bar to bar, I took an injection in my bottom to relieve my sickness and joined her. By the time we had thankfully set foot on dry land I was weather-beaten and £5,000 lighter after spending my time in the on-board Louis Vuitton department store. Luggage and bags of all shapes and sizes were bought, a totally enjoyable extravagance.

The aim of our trip was to see Michael Crawford perform in *Phantom of the Opera*. Missing his stage performances in London's West End, we chose to follow him to New York. What better way to do it than taking the QE2 out and flying back by Concorde. By the time we arrived at the Manhattan theatre and joined the line waiting to enter, news reached our ears. Michael Crawford had laryngitis and would not be performing, a substitute replacing him. Feeling thoroughly robbed and dejected, we cashed in our return flight. Concorde could hardly have lifted our spirits and we returned to England dejected on a regular flight.

Exon Escort Agency on Deansgate provided company for men and women worldwide, with male and female escorts. We had found a prime position in the city centre and the location attracted the best of escorts, with attractive receptionists manning the phones. Gay, straight, everything was provided to suit what was needed.

John, an effeminate blonde, arranged the male side of the business. It amazed me how many 'straight' men wanted the pleasure of a pretty gay young guy. The girls were hand-picked and beautiful and bookings came in from near and far. A credit card machine came into play and extra machines were carried with the escort to their destination. Clients were pleased to pay this way, booking their pleasure time as 'lunch' or 'dinner' meant they could put the cost down as expenses without a question being raised. Before long trips abroad were being arranged, with their cost running into thousands of pounds. This was the late 1980s when a regular overnight booking was a mere £850.

Blondie was given the name by Wendy. She was an excellent receptionist but with gentle persuasion by Wendy, eager to get her body into action, she ended up working in the parlour in Chester. What encouraged this move was my gradual annoyance at having a partner who spent her time either skiing in the Alps or on a beach somewhere in a distant land. The straw eventually broke the camel's back after she took off on her travels after only a week's return in England. My actions were direct and simple. I took control of the escort agency and my Swinton parlour and withdrew my interest in Chester. There would be no argument unless she wanted a battle on her hands. So she left, taking Blondie with her.

Within a year Blondie was dead, alone and unprotected. It seems Wendy had refused to pay for a receptionist and not wishing to pay the cost herself she took the chance of working alone. That decision cost her life. One stab that was so fierce it passed through her body and instantly killed her while she was bent over the vanity sink, knickerless in her massage room. With her face looking over her shoulder up to her assailant, she took her last breath. Did she know who attacked her? We would never find out. After two extensive reports of the incident on the TV programme *Crimewatch*, to this day the monster who murdered her is still at large. Did Wendy attend the funeral? No. Did she send a message of condolence? No, not a word.

Chapter 27

A Guy Like Robbie

'The easiest thing to be in the world is you. The most difficult thing to be is what other people want you to be.'

Making an unannounced visit to my escort agency early one evening, no-one was more surprised at my arrival than the young man sitting among the girls on the sofa. There was no mistaking his amazing good looks and the girls seemed thrilled to have his company, laughing and joking and generally enjoying themselves. It occurred to me that their attention was more on him than on whether they would be chosen for a job that evening.

After a brief discussion with my receptionist, I asked who he was and where he had come from, hoping he was there to apply for a job. On learning that he was spending some free time away from the model agency down the hallway, where he was one of the star attractions, I gave him his marching orders, telling him to come back when he wanted to feature on the books of our escort agency. He rose from the sofa with perfect grace, did a low bow like you do for royalty, and swiftly left, to the dismay of everyone except me. I thought him cheeky but it was a moment's thought and I quickly turned my attention to business.

During a meeting sometime the following week, while sat having rare gossip time with John behind the reception desk, I learned that the model who had sat among them the week before would indeed be interested in escort work. As I was there it might be an opportunity to interview him, not only because he was a striking young man, but also because he had obviously formed a friendship among the escort staff and I needed to keep my eye on the situation. I was right with my assumption, he was in the building, at the Jet Set Model Agency where he was being given the run down on his next modelling assignment for a catalogue shoot. John got a message through to him and within a short space of time he walked briskly into our office, pulled up a chair next to me at the desk and spoke while not taking his focus off my eyes. My immediate impression was that this was a young man capable of handling any situation, something needed when working as an escort.

He was certainly incredibly good-looking but could never be mistaken as pretty. He had a face that sculptors would want to make a cast of. He was mesmerizingly handsome. Six feet tall and slender, mixed race of Irish and Jamaican blood, which turned out for him to be a perfect mix. I was drawn to him immediately as an immense asset for my business, while settling into an evening of discovering Robbie over a bottle of wine to relax the atmosphere. It was an open interview as the office had started to fill up with girls coming to take their place, hoping to be picked for work and all phones manned, with receptionists answering many calls. But it was as if no-one else was in the room as he answered all of my questions with complete honesty.

I discovered that Robbie was asexual and, not understanding the term, he explained that he didn't look at people of either gender and think 'mmm, I'd like sex with you'. That just didn't happen for him. He told me that in his personal life having his looks mostly worked against him as girls especially would try their best to compromise him with, 'If you don't try it how do you know?' He always made himself clear: he may have experienced sex with opposite or same gender people, but he didn't enjoy it and wasn't interested in it, regardless of having tried it or not.

I became engrossed in finding out more as he explained asexuality is an orientation, which is a choice totally different to celibacy, and also there is a difference between aromantic asexuals and romantic asexuals. Aromantic asexuals don't have any romantic attractions, so quite often do not want to be touched, or have physical intimacy. Romantic asexuals don't experience sexual attraction but they do experience romantic attractions, so they will look at someone and won't respond sexually to them, but they may want to get closer and find out more about them, to share things with them.

This was true of Robbie: he was a romantic asexual and, although having no interest in sex, was still attracted to people. Before the end of the interview, which lasted all evening, he had developed an attraction with me, and I welcomed this 'different' young man into my life and gained a different outlook as, like him, I didn't just fall in lust anymore, which wasn't such a bad thing, really.

We immediately attached ourselves to each other and I discovered that he had been through a very difficult childhood, where as a young boy he had been physically abused by a next door neighbour, taking the brunt of these sexual attacks to protect his siblings from suffering the same fate. The children were left to their own devices, as their mother left them on many occasions to fend for themselves. It was a hard upbringing which in turn made him a hard young man. It made me think that perhaps it was the rapes and body abuse I had suffered in my teens which had turned me into such a tough woman. Robbie's psychological problems most certainly arose because of his dislike of sex, and by pronouncing himself asexual it made sense to anyone thinking him homosexual or heterosexual.

It was through him that I had a name for my state of mind. I had become asexual too. My reasons were obvious to him. I had worked nearly all my life in or around the sex

171

industry and been prodded by many men and some women too, combined with the loss of Billy and all the trauma I had experienced with his demise. I was left without any feeling for intimacy, apart from a kiss and a cuddle.

Before long we were inseparable. He had become my little guardian angel. His streetwise attitude had no bounds when it came to protecting his Vivien and we went forward into a part of my life that certainly became exciting and very different. As he was protective of me I also offered the same protection when he occasionally worked as an escort. It was only occasionally as the client he was escorting had to pay top money to have his company and they also had to understand that a 'no sex policy' applied. Look and enjoy but don't touch. He was not living at my home but we felt a constant need to keep tabs on each other and as he became important in my life everyone around me had to accept him without question.

Still with Billy very much in the forefront of my mind, I discussed with my receptionists at the escort agency the idea of holding a charity event with all the proceeds coming from the ticket sales and auction going to the Buy a Brick Appeal for Wythenshawe Hospital. Everyone was enthusiastic, but Adrian at his boutique was quite perturbed when I flounced into the shop with Roger, while he chose a selection of outfits to wear for the fashion show.

We managed to secure appearances from members of the *Coronation Street* cast, with actress Helen Worth, who played Gail Tilsley, making a speech. The star turns appearing gave their time for free. Frank 'Foo Foo' Lamar, the legendary drag queen, who had captivated audiences at his palace on the east side of Manchester city centre for years, was more than willing. I had known Frank for some time. The frocks were just his working clothes and out of drag he was a very handsome guy. He used to say that if he could have gained love and recognition in his showbiz life, not as Foo Foo, but as Frank, he would have given up the

£4,000 frocks. But his fame was as Foo Foo and a lot of his wealth was donated to charity.

Without a shadow of doubt Robbie stole the show, his catwalk presence attracting offers of work for magazines and television. Many famous faces attended the evening, including the now disgraced television presenter Stuart Hall. The charity event was a huge success, raising thousands of pounds for the hospital. Billy's cancer specialist, Nick Thatcher, was there to accept the cheque. When I discovered him sitting at the bar with a whisky in one hand and a cigarette in the other I sat and joined him with a cigarette myself, not wishing to make a comment about our 'habit'. He was a top man with a very demanding life-saving job. I guess a cigarette was needed.

Robbie's career was moving in the right direction and I loved being a part of it. There were also other propositions put to him that night but he used his brain and took advantage of dinner and drinks, I am sure leaving the company with just a kiss on the cheek. Stuart Hall was his pursuer, the same man that was convicted and imprisoned for his unlawful conduct with underage girls. It seems his lust for forbidden fruit travelled in different directions. Whether Rob realised it or not, this attitude of distancing himself from anything physical actually paid off, as his company was requested more and more. When Oscar Wilde wrote 'I can resist anything but temptation', he could have intended those words for Robbie.

It is without doubt that I was fascinated with him and a caring nurturing side came out in me, where I became my mother. By that I mean I wanted his success, not just an ordinary success, but one that took him to the top of the ladder. For me he was a budding superstar and I thought that everyone who met him would be looking through the same rose-coloured spectacles as mine. I became like my mother so much I sent him for elocution and singing lessons to develop his already wonderful voice. I discovered to my amazement that Rob possessed many talents. His impressions of Diana Ross and Michael Jackson fascinated me. He moved and danced in their style and at home would dress up as Diana and when he had transformed himself by putting on his slap and squeezing into an evening gown with a luscious wig to finish the look, it was 'Diana' personified.

In 1989 the Happy Mondays were the talk of Manchester, while Robbie was recording in the Bury studios. My only concern was that he continued to attend elocution to improve his speaking voice and the recording studios to improve his vocals, with a hope that very soon they would have something to get him a recording deal. Looking back, what planet was I on? A fantasy planet for sure.

Life had become a whirl of social events that year coming up to 1990 and among the fun and entertainment were very special occasions with my shining star. I had become so wrapped up with his amazing ability to transform himself into a woman. This ability was incorporated into his escort work, at my suggestion. His company was expensive and a high price was set to accompany a client for a dinner date dressed as a woman. If they had ideas that this show would continue in their hotel suite they would be very mistaken but the bill for his time would already have been settled, so making his excuses to leave made no difference.

Was I encouraging him a stage too far? Maybe I was but he was willing and up for the venture. One night I drove him to a hotel, watching him walk up the street, wobbling on his stilettos, while swinging his hips, his long wig perfectly in place, dressed and made up as a beautiful woman. He just had the knack of transforming himself into something stunning. If there was a high to be achieved, I reached it on those occasions.

It was around this time that we took things a stage

further and got our kicks out of crossdressing together and venturing out into a town where we were unknown. Choosing always an elegantly stylish hotel to book into with the pure intention of taking over their restaurant dressed as a man and woman – only he was the woman and I was the man. He would pick a role model to emulate, spoke in a soft voice, and walked a woman's walk, swaying his hips and using his arms more. He enjoyed paying attention to detail. His exposed body hair was waxed and his eyebrows well sculptured. He gave himself a manicure and painted his nails cherry red. We both took great delight in searching through my accessories of belts, necklaces and earrings to complete 'her' look. He played around with his features, contouring with make-up, creating an illusion of making his nose narrower, his cheekbones higher, emphasising his already cute full lips with a cupid's bow. His mask of make-up became complete by applying false eyelashes, mascara, eye shadow and lipstick and finally his precious wig. When he had finished he had created the ultimate feminine look. Of course, he didn't have the curves of a woman, so he used my waist cinching corsets to achieve an hour-glass look. His rather large package had to disappear and so a pantie hose and tape were used. One of my bras would be stuffed with socks and somehow he managed to achieve a cleavage of sorts. Tucking his testicles in and taping his penis back, when everything was complete he looked at his reflection in the mirror and loved the creation he had made.

While he was creating his look I was creating mine by hanging a pair of his jeans low, wearing his shirt and jacket that fitted loose. I used a tight-fitting swimming costume to hold my breasts as flat as possible. I tied my hair in a ponytail at the base of my neck and I sat patiently while he made my eyebrows bushier with mascara. Flat brogue shoes completed my look.

All through this process we would invade the hotel

suite fridge, drinking its contents of wine and champagne until I was confident enough to walk into the restaurant with this stunning woman at my side. We would dine and drink the evening away with what felt like the eyes of the world upon us. Later, drunk with the thrill of what we had achieved, we slipped away to the privacy of our suite where we spent the rest of the night, giggling, cuddling and kissing and then falling asleep without any sex at all.

This thrill that I had with him was never repeated with anyone else. It was special, it was different, and after all there could only ever have been one Robbie, as there could only ever have been one Billy. It seems my love of the unusual was what thrilled me the most. It started as a jovial acceptance. How often Robbie loved to emulate a woman, then I discovered how much more fun life was for him after his gender bend. Sometimes I thought he never wanted to go back and that he felt better off in that other gender than he felt as his own true self.

Chapter 28

The Marriage Compact

'The road to hell is paved with good intentions.'

A lady proposing to a man is hardly the done thing. Proposing to a boy is even worse. But I did, there in my bed, cuddled up as usual after a night of extreme frivolity in the gay village in Manchester.

It's not only the company of gay people that I love but the atmosphere and music in those clubs, and when the mood takes you they are the best place to let your hair down. I love it with a passion.

Back in the bed we decided to be even more risky. I brought up the subject as a joke and he took the bait and, overflowing with excitement, jumped from beneath the duvet and out the door as fast as his feet would carry him. His family had to know the news.

Within days his mother had enrolled herself on my team, starting as my cleaner at the house and parlours and eventually moving on to reception work, to finally becoming a manageress of the establishments in Manchester. Small beginnings, but Julie knew how to make her moves with her eye on the target. I had amassed a great business in Swinton and on that ride I had started two more massage parlours, one cheekily opened in the building on Deansgate, a floor below the escort agency and the floor above a Mormon church. Little did the devout congregation who gathered there every week know what was happening above them when they were looking up saying their prayers.

The second massage parlour was in the back streets of Piccadilly in the city centre. Femme Fatale had a different style and feel to the Swinton parlour, which was always my favourite, remembering some of Billy's last advice. 'Swinton is your baby and it will always look after you,' he would tell me. I carried those words forever and kept its seedy style and winning formula and, like Julie, I had my eye on a target too. Robbie's success in the entertainment world would be my success. I had become my mother after all.

My wedding day had to be as flamboyant as the couple it was representing and to set the pace a wedding that reflected our style was a must. Here enters Anthony Price who made his name dressing rock 'n' roll royalty. The designer who bestowed an iconic look upon Roxy Music, styled the Rolling Stones, convinced David Bowie to wear a lounge suit, and designed the white lace mini dress worn by Jerry Hall when she tied the knot with Mick Jagger. That same creation I chose for my wedding day, too, instead choosing a deep crème lace rather than virginal white, and while glamorous rock 'n' roll marriages don't often last the test of time, unlike the continuing success of Anthony Price, I was about to head towards the same disaster.

I chose a Jamaican holiday for two reasons. I wanted a Caribbean tan to set off my wedding dress, I wanted to glow on the day. The second reason being Robbie had relatives in Jamaica who he was encouraged to visit and so we boarded the plane loaded down with our cast-off clothing for which his relatives from the ghetto would be thankful. Montego Bay was our destination and after a rocky flight we were transported to our hotel which was fronted by a white ribbon of sand, gently shelving into the turquoise waters of the Caribbean Sea. It was breathtakingly beautiful and I fell instantly in love with Jamaica.

As soon as we were escorted to our hotel suite I stepped out on to the balcony breathing in the sweet scented air. I was anxious to quickly strip, grab the first bikini from my luggage and venture out. Robbie was not feeling that way inclined. A little shook up from the flight that had been far from smooth, I thought, so I left him to recover and made my way out to survey the surroundings. I had chosen the most expensive hotel in Montego Bay, what else? And after being approached by an attendant that had the body of a gladiator I was happy enough to allow him to escort me around the hotel complex, while he offered me lessons on windsurfing, sailing and snorkelling, courtesy of the hotel, of course.

As I was anxious to soak up the sun, he led me towards a suitable position where the plumped-up cushions on a sunbed were shaded by parasols facing the sea. Offering to bring me refreshments, I quickly realised there would be more available to me than a liquid refreshment, if I so desired. Having confidence with my body in a bikini, I knew attention would be paid to my boobs and butt. However, to those who looked and wanted to know, nothing would be available, not with this girl anyway.

After drenching my body in sun oil and allowing the rays to penetrate my pale skin, I tired of that and took to the swimming pool, drifting on my back with my face up to the sun, then swimming up to the pool bar where I sat among others, drinking their golden rum and looking forward to whiling away the few days ahead stretched out on the sun bleached sand. But what lay ahead for me was a totally different picture, fraught with uneasiness. Robbie had little appetite for exploring the island with me, or doing anything with me at all. He had no real interest in involving himself in activities of any kind, his sparkle had disappeared and what was left of the fun-loving, exciting person I knew was nowhere to be seen.

I did what I was good at and buried my head in the sand, hoping this was a momentary blip. The following morning while I was resting, he was running around organising a boat ride for himself. Where was the boat heading? The beach nearest to the ghetto where his grandmother lived, and so I watched as he sailed off in a tiny rowing boat, till he appeared as a dot on the ocean, and wondered what dangers were ahead, not only for him on his sea journey but also for myself. Boy, did this girl like to take some punishment. I could have simply ended everything by packing my bags, leaving him to his devices and booking into another hotel. But I didn't. I stayed and as always as Viv does, tried to work it out.

When Robbie returned late into the evening, not by boat but by a reggae bus, he had company with him. Aunts, uncles, nieces and a little grandmother arrived with him from the ghetto into this five star hotel that was used to a much more sedate clientele. By the time they left with the clothes they had come for, and a promise that there would be more to come after my return to England, I was ready to down that golden rum till the cows came home.

The first time I found white powder it was hidden in tissue in the bathroom of our hotel suite. When had he started sniffing coke? Who knows? It could have been well before I had met him. He was made aware of my concerns and immediately flushed it down the toilet while giving me unconvincing excuses as to what it was doing there in the first place. I only had to look at his eyes and agitated manner to know there was more to it. There was a change in him – he was fidgety and edgy and would disappear without a word. His usual amazing social skills were evaporating, too, preferring to have room service rather than dining out. He was taking a dive for sure and all I could think about was the money that Lauren was rolling over with Viv's wish to spend, spend, spend. The truth was, I was more interested in the party following the wedding vows than the vows I was about to be taking.

Lauren received my phone call the following day. On hearing a very anxious Viv on the other end of the phone planning to cancel her wedding plans, her reply was simply, 'You can't, you are too far in.' She had done what I had requested and blown a whole heap of money to get the show on the road. 'It will be easy enough to get out of it if you really need to.' – How wrong she was! It doesn't take much guessing to know I listened to her advice rather than what my head was telling me: *Get out while you can, Viv.* I look back on that decision and know I needed help myself. Both Robbie and I were on a road to disaster.

The wedding was attended by new and old buddies. Even close friends of Billy's had turned up. Surely they must have known I had lost my mind completely.

Normally the bride is a little late for the wedding but not this wedding. While the bride was waiting in the registrar's office surrounded by friends and family, Robbie was running around Moss Side in his wedding limousine, together with a very concerned John from the escort agency, who was his best man. It seems that obtaining the drugs he needed was more important than his wedding day. The whole day was a sham but everyone enjoyed themselves, apart from the anxious glowing bride. The evening was also a nightmare after I spent it sat at the bar of the Ramada Hotel, where the honeymoon suite had been booked, being entertained by an Australian cricket player who was there with his team mates. Robbie had left my side at the wedding reception in a heap of sweat. He couldn't even make it through to the night-time. I left for home the following day, hung over but otherwise intact and as if the day before had never happened. It was only the signing of a bit of paper after all. Life would go on.

Heroin was the monkey on Robbie's back. I was devastated but it all made sense. Missing days, lack of money after all he had been earning, not turning up for job commitments, why had I not seen it before? Those who have been involved in a heroin addict's life know there is no short road to recovery, if there is a recovery at all. You just live in hope that one day they will be clean and then you give up when they don't. While Robbie went through rehab after rehab, one minute winning, the next minute losing, I was on a rollercoaster myself. At first I was convinced I would find the power to cure him, even taking steps one night to virtually tie him to the bed while he went cold turkey, then ending up driving him to Moss Side after he pleaded and begged for just a little of the drug his body was craving. Then ending up back in rehab again with a promise he would stay clean when he came out.

The most frightening time came when I received a phone call to tell me Robbie was perched on the balcony of the 14th floor bedroom suite in a Birmingham hotel, intent on throwing himself over after cutting his wrists. By some miracle the American soul singer Luther Vandross was in the adjacent suite and, seeing a young man balanced on the balcony, he sent his bodyguard to coax him down. Thank God for Luther!

How I managed to keep my business afloat through all this trauma was a miracle itself. Thankfully, I had girls who had been with me in the good times before these troubles and they had no intention of jumping ship. Why didn't I go overboard myself? There were a few good reasons for that. The first was that when I asked Robbie what had sent him down this road of no return, he looked at me and I never imagined I would the words that came out of his mouth. 'It was you Viv, just to get through the days facing elocution lessons, knowing I was dyslexic and unable to properly understand the words in front of me and not wanting to disappoint you with all the expectations you had for me. I needed the drugs just to get through the day.'

Nothing had prepared me for that. It was some years later that I found out he had lied. His addiction to all forms of drugs had happened years before we had met. I eventually gained my divorce but it didn't come easy, as Robbie did everything in his power to stop it. Threatening me with exposure as a madam running a brothel in the city centre if I went ahead with the divorce. 'I married you and made a commitment for life. You married me just for the fun of it.' What fun?

Chapter 29

Profumo's Secret Passion

'He's a politician. It's like being a hooker. You can't be one unless you can pretend to like people while you are fucking them.'

John Profumo was tipped to be Prime Minister in the early 1960s, until he was exposed in a sex scandal which shook society and nearly brought down the government. At the time, he was notorious, his name plastered over the front pages of every newspaper and on every TV broadcast in the UK.

Thirty years later, when he walked into one of my most popular massage parlours in Manchester, John Profumo had reinvented himself as a respectable member of society, being made a CBE in 1975 for his charity work with the poor people in the East End of London. Did the general public know he was still in need of a sexual fix, right up to his death in 2006? I doubt it.

Profumo fell dramatically from grace in 1963, after an affair with Christine Keeler, a glamorous call girl and the reputed mistress of an alleged Soviet spy. He was forced to resign and the resulting scandal shook Prime Minister Harold Macmillan's government. At Femme Fatale, the salon I ran on the back streets of Piccadilly in Manchester in 1994, he found a favourite in my star hooker Sugar and would make sure he booked at least an hour with her whenever he was in town in search of a good time.

Femme Fatale was open 24 hours a day, seven days a week, with four girls working each shift and three shifts a day. It was in the perfect spot, hidden among fashion warehouses and occupying the whole of a basement building. It was ultra-modern, with every convenience, including a small spa pool and intercom system in each room, in case of emergencies.

The intimate sleeping area was always occupied at weekends, reminding me of the days at the City Centre Sauna all those years earlier, when men of all ages had been out on the town, on the lookout for a pretty girl to bed. Femme Fatale had a different style and feel to the other parlours and it brought in the most money.

For several months, until he was confident enough in our relationship to reveal his true identity, our mystery client was known to us only as 'Jack'. Certainly, he didn't seem to think or care that he was taking any risks in visiting the salon. Like many men, the need of sexual fulfilment was his highest priority.

Sugar had an ease and grace the other girls did not have. She was beautiful and intelligent, with a sweet nature, and was considered a gold star experience, with many visitors lusting for her company. So popular was she that she was permanently on hourly bookings, hardly able to take a breath. Yet her popularity never fazed the others because, as often as possible, she encouraged her client to have a two-girl experience, making sure the money was spread around.

Sugar reeked sex, from top to toe, and her biggest thrill was giving men the most pleasurable sexual experience. When you looked at her, you focused first on her full and luscious mouth and her expertise at sucking cock led to regular requests for more. Her very long, honey blonde hair, usually worn loose around her shoulders, would be artistically tied back off her face to perform the sex act she was so good at, but it was her agility in positioning her body in any acrobatic style for sex which made her so popular with every customer with a rock hard penis.

Men in high-powered jobs, be it in government or industry, seem at some point to feel the need to seek the pleasure of a prostitute's company. The two lifestyles fit perfectly. It wasn't unusual for a famous face to hunt out the incredible delights of the beautiful girls in my parlour and 'Jack' Profumo was no exception.

I first met him when I called at the salon on my return from an afternoon's shopping in the city centre. His posh voice and suave manner immediately attracted my attention and it was obvious he was particularly confident in the company of young and beautiful girls. He displayed the flirtatious arrogance of knowing what brought him pleasure.

His appearance was severe but he had natural sexiness and charm, with a naughty sense of humour that my receptionist Julie encouraged. She welcomed everyone in the same way, prince or pauper, and it was clear he felt very much at home.

As we were introduced, I noticed he had already relaxed into the atmosphere, having taken off his coat and secured it in a locker with his briefcase. I asked what he did and, clearly cautious at our first meeting, he told me he was the director of an engineering company taking time out for sexual pleasure, after completing his business in Manchester.

I took no more interest in the newcomer than I did with the other men who were relaxing there that day. I had reached a point in my life where, for once, there was something more important than the business – sorting out the mess of my fateful marriage. So even when Julie revealed that 'Jack' was John Profumo and that he had promised to return in a couple of weeks, I still had no urge to get to know him better.

The fact that nobody in my brothel paid any extra attention to him pleased 'Jack' and made it easier for him to trust us to be discreet. Who cared, anyway? He was just a client like any other. John Profumo? So what?

Sugar had the ability to arouse his desires and feed his constant need of new thrills and she played the game so well for him. At the end of each session, 'Jack' would leave her with a kiss and instructions for the part he wanted her to act next time, including how she should dress. Perhaps it would be the cute and sexy maid, strutting her stuff in the tiniest of outfits. Whatever his fancy, she entered the spirit of the game and going panty-less was a must. For this hour of fantasy, she would receive good rewards, too. She admitted she was drawn in by his erotic imagination, which was immense and inexhaustible. He was always in total control.

This was no impassive lover but a man of 70 years and well past his prime, who was still very passionate and Sugar professed that the sex with him was always pleasurable and that he was also kind and very loving. After enjoying his time at the salon, he would pass Julie a tip as he left as quietly as he had arrived.

It might have been foolish for 'Jack' to confess his true identity but he had come to trust Julie in making sure he got what he wanted from his visit. He also knew that the 1960s were long gone and that only someone of her age would remember who he was, unlike the younger girls.

About a year after I had met him, it became clear that 'Jack' had been fully accepted back into the Establishment. In 1975, after decades of charity work among the poor people of the East End of London, he had been made a CBE and in 1995, there he was, sitting next to the Queen on the top table of a dinner in celebration of former Prime Minister Margaret Thatcher's 70th birthday.

The Bishop of Bath and Wells, a friend of Profumo's, once said of him: 'No-one judges Jack more harshly than he does himself.' He says he has never known a day since it happened when he has not felt real shame. By that did he mean the orgies and whipping parties or almost being responsible for the downfall of the Conservative Government, of which he was an important part? Who knows?

Despite this quiet VIP visitor who was entertained in my parlour, I continued to juggle work and my personal life and the balancing act began to take its toll on my health.

I had turned to alcohol and soon it was needed to calm my nerves morning, afternoon and night. Friends tried to rescue me but it was impossible for me to escape Robbie's drug-infused binges. Court orders taken out to remind him of the boundaries he couldn't cross fell on deaf ears. He had easy access to me, not only at home, but also at Femme Fatale, where his mother Julie was now my manageress. My efforts over the years to stop him in his tracks had been in vain and he had become my constant nightmare. Even a court order ordering him to stay away from me was ignored.

Under all this stress, early one evening after a few too many mind-numbing drinks, I jeopardised my freedom by exiting through the back door and jumping into my car to make my escape. Robbie was at the front door, fired up with anger and anxious to stop me. The rush hour traffic had ended, so I had no problem putting my foot down on the accelerator pedal to speed my getaway.

I have never been as relieved to see the blue flashing lights of a police car ordering me to pull over to the kerb. In fact, when the officer approached the car and asked me to step out for a breath test, I told him how thankful I was, giving him a brief outline of the circumstances which had caused me to take to the road.

I knew a short prison sentence beckoned because of the number of times I'd already been up before the magistrates on drink-driving charges. Employing the best solicitor in the country for the job, Nick Freeman, 'Mr Loophole' himself, I was left in no doubt that I would receive a custodial sentence. My friends had anxiously been watching my downfall and if a psychiatrist had got hold of me, they probably would have questioned my mental stability. But crazy though it sounds, the prospect of disappearing off the face of the earth for a while didn't bother me a bit.

It took a year for the case to come to court and I was thankful for the time to sort out my affairs. I sold my home in Prestwich and rented one in Timperley, Cheshire to be close to two dear friends whose companionship extended back to life around the Lew Hoad Tennis Ranch in Spain all those years before.

My divorce finally came through and with help I got through the waiting period. Karen, a close and trustworthy friend had moved into my home, which suited us both. So when I got sentenced to a four-month prison sentence and entered the cell underneath the courtroom with the words 'send her down' ringing in my ears, I knew I had everything in place.

Chapter 30

Send Her Down Please!

'You've got to take the good with the bad, smile with the sad.
Love what you've got, and remember what you had.
Always forgive, but never forget.
Learn from mistakes, but never regret.'

'Send her down.' Those words were ringing in my ears after the magistrates sentenced me to four months in prison.

I entered the cell underneath the courtroom knowing I had everything in place. When you are cooped up in a tiny cell, hardly able to move, while travelling a long road in a prison van you have enough time for regrets and on that journey I had many. Her Majesty's Prison Drake Hall in Staffordshire was certainly a long journey and by the time I was given my prison number and shown to my cell I had mentally prepared myself for the weeks ahead. My time in confinement would be six weeks with good behaviour. There was no way I intended to be bad.

I had been charged under the name Yvonne Carla Rossi, my business name, a cute move on my part. Rossi MG0410 was the name I answered to. It took my true identity away and I was happy to become that other person while in prison. Immediately before I was transferred to Drake Hall, which was an open prison, I was locked away in Styal Prison in Cheshire. If I ever needed a wake-up call, spending 24 hours at Styal was it. Being locked up with the hardest of women imprisoned on long-term sentences for more serious stuff, it only took a second to work out I had to watch my back.

Styal is also a holding prison where women are assessed and moved on. Thankfully, this process happened within that 24 hours and then I was whisked off with some other thankful women to the more relaxed regime of an open prison and virtual freedom.

I guess Drake Hall was no different to any other prison, rules made to be upheld. When the bell rang at 6am you had to be up, make your bed, shower and dress and be stood to attention in line to answer to your name and number just one hour later. This may seem easy enough but knowing that if you were just one minute late extra days would be added to your sentence made it seem so much harder. That threat hung over your head like a noose every time that bell rang for any number of reasons.

Everyone seemed to form their own little groups on their induction day and you stuck like glue to your new friendships, each one looking out for each other, keeping away from trouble, being supportive over problems left behind in the outside world. Things that had little importance in normal life became of the utmost importance in prison. The cell block you were allocated to spend your time was important. More like stark bedrooms than prison cells, you could pretty them up as you wished by asking your visitors to bring things with them to make life easier. Long-term prisoners were the ones who took advantage of this and when you noticed a cell decked with rugs and curtains you knew that woman was possibly there for murder and had been transferred there when reaching the end of her sentence, a stage towards getting used to life on the outside. These long-term prisoners tended to stick together and away from novices like myself.

Pauline, my closest friend and confidante, had been sent down for benefit fraud, of which she professed to be completely innocent. The Government had got it wrong. Nearly everyone had a tale of innocence and you listened and believed their version of the facts with great interest. What else did you have to do? I found Pauline to be a breath of normality amid so many others who had major psychological problems and she took on a 'mother' role within our group. We made sure we stuck together, although our cells were apart, and we jointly managed to get into art classes, which took us away from thoughts of prison for an hour a day.

My first job was mopping the passageways around the cells, eventually making it to the library. This was regarded as a top job and you received the maximum wage of £4 a week, which I spent on the ever-needed cigarettes, sweets and toiletries from the prison shop. You would sell your soul for a cigarette and many favours were given in exchange for that wonderful weed. Receiving a fortnightly visit from the people you had chosen on your visiting order was looked forward to with relish. Just hearing word about the outside world and being told that everything was OK was all that was needed to help the weeks pass and in between we would wait in anticipation for our names to be called out each day, hoping to receive a letter from family or friend. Little messages of support: '*I am thinking about you and look forward to seeing you soon, keep your head down and your chin up*', and another, '*please try and get through it anyway you can and get this nightmare behind you, remember nothing is bad forever*'.

Letters of love and support came in daily. We all prepared ourselves for visiting day, prettying ourselves with make-up and styling our hair. Women anxious to look their best for their man – I was so very thankful not to have that problem. My main concern was my father, who by this time was in the early stages of dementia. I had arranged for a trustworthy friend to check on him daily and make sure he was in good spirits. I had given him no warning of what was to come but as always he was supportive and as long as he heard my voice daily on the prison phone he could rest easy.

There is a fear of leaving prison, known as 'gate fever', and I was told everyone, no matter how short their prison spell, experiences it. The reason for this is simply that you are cushioned, the system takes control of any problems you may have on the outside and so returning to that outside world without support can be daunting.

When the time came for my release I felt that fever, too, waiting with a large brown bag that contained all my possessions. I seemed to have been sat waiting for an eternity until Karen arrived to drive me home. Bloomsbury Lane had never looked so good. When I arrived home and opened the front door, I felt as if I was walking into a palace. Everything that I had taken for granted before was suddenly so very special. I threw off my shoes and felt the luxury of the carpet beneath my feet, taking a shower and wrapping myself in my fluffy bathrobe, lying on my cosy comfy bed and realising how fortunate I was to be free to sleep and wake when I wished and free to make changes in my life. I had all the summer ahead and many good times to come.

It was 1995 when I stepped back into my Swinton parlour and took control. It was an easy transition and I was eager to get rid of any memories of Wendy and connections to Robbie. The name had to be changed immediately once I had severed all my ties. Money always talks and I paid off Julie to exit from my life sooner rather than later – in a polite way of course. The girls who remained had waited anxiously for my return, hoping and praying one day it would happen. I didn't let them down.

Bouncing through the door, full of the joys of spring, free in every way at last! It only took a day to realise my precious parlour had been badly neglected in my absence. The takings had dropped appallingly and my girls, as much as they tried to work along with a manageress who had deteriorated and took the club along with her, were sat more on the sofa than laying on the bed. No 'punter' wants to enter a brothel where the manageress is obviously worse for wear with booze, no matter how tempting the girls are. So unprofessional. How they worked in those conditions is testament to their loyalty to me and a smile appeared back in their faces as soon as they saw me jump into action.

Decorators were taken on immediately to refresh the building. I kept all the girls on board as a thank-you for their loyalty and when they put out that the boss was back in business, new girls would be eager to join us. We needed to take some time away till the decorating was complete, but on that first day our Swinton parlour was christened with a new name to bring it alive again.

Anita actually returns to the pages of my book towards the end, when we met in very different circumstances, but for now she was here, sat opposite me on the sofa while we tossed around new names. 'Call it *The Toucan*, get it? 'Two can',' she said in a flurry of excitement at her invention. *What a genius*, I thought, and immediately visualised the Guinness bird being the club's logo and this emblem eventually becoming famous for our club as well as a pint of the black stuff.

Here started my favourite of all parlours: 'The Toucan at Swinton', recalling once again some of Billy's last advice. 'Swinton is your baby and it will always look after you.'

Bringing you back to the present time for the moment, while writing my memoirs I found myself searching through old items of paperwork that stirred my memory back to those early days at my precious Swinton brothel, and I came across this: '*THE BIBLE*'. Set out in rough form, were the rules of the house each new girl had to follow. A grin appeared on my face recalling the time but then it was serious stuff.

1. *Please be in work no later than 11am to be ready for business at 12 noon.*

2. *Be ready for a client to come in up till 12 midnight.* **Do not** *get changed before that time.*

3. **Always** *let me know if you can't come in to work so I have time to get another girl to cover your shift.*

4. *Your receptionist is not expected to go to the shops for anything, so bring what you need with you.*

5. **No visitors** *to call in to see you during working hours.*

6. *Have anyone calling to take you home wait in the pub car park, not outside the entrance.*

7. *Regularly buy new outfits to wear so you have different lingerie changes.*

8. *Full make-up is a* **must** *at all times.*

9. **The Massage Rooms:** *To be tidied after each client; clothes rails tidied, beds freshened and left neat with a men's magazine placed among the pillows.*

10. *Always make sure there is oil, talc and tissues, plus air freshener, in rooms.*

11. *Stay in the room until client is leaving and see him to the door.* **Don't rush the massage.**

12. *Take all that you need in the room with you so that you don't have to leave the room, leaving the client on his own.*

13. *If the client has to wait in the room, offer him a drink.*

14. *Tell your receptionist if anything is needed for the massage rooms when stocks run low.*

15. ***All toys must be left clean.***

16. **No** *personal phone calls received, except for emergencies.*

17. **No** *personal phone calls made unless it is an emergency.*

18. *No-one to work anywhere else in Manchester while with* **Toucan**.

END OF BIBLE

Suffice to say there were a whole heap of instructions for the receptionists too. I won't bore you with the details except to mention the most important one: 'make sure the money is safe'.

In Toucan the girls walked around in the naughtiest of outfits, exposing their breasts and baring their bottoms, dressed in PVC, rubber, leather or baby doll lingerie. Other parlours were more cautious and had a rule that their girls wore white overalls, like a beautician or a genuine masseuse. Why, when it would be not what you wore, but the act that you did that got you arrested? And anyway it was much more fun our way. Customers loved the naughtiness. That's what a massage parlour is supposed to be – naughty. I had girls of all ages, above the legal limit, of course. Different to Femme Fatale where they were all babes from the age of 18 to 25 and not above.

Fay was with me before Swinton became the famous Toucan Club and she was still with me 17 years later. On interview I wasn't so sure whether to take her on. Did I need to go down the mature road? I was so thankful to a customer who had met her in a previous parlour telling me that I should, as she was the best in the business, which proved very true. Mature and stunning, nothing fazed her. She knew how to give a man or woman the ultimate orgasm and showing them how much they turned her on by returning the pleasure. So it became standard that a new recruit gained their education from Fay and ended up with her lust for the job.

Toucan became well known for having girls who got down to it. 'Dirty', I guess, is the word. Don't men love it! Of course they do. Sat in the little reception room, crowded out with impatient men, listening to the moans and groans of girls reaching their orgasm, was music to their ears, the walls being very thin. Toucan became that famous the police use to call every Christmas asking for a donation towards the Police Charity Fund. We felt totally protected. But even we experienced a few nerve-wracking moments. What follows is an example:

'The Dog' was christened by the girls, not only in my parlour but others he had visited. He was detested but providing what was needed helped whoever had to deal with him release their total distaste of him. One of the things he requested was to be put on all fours with a dog collar around his neck and a lead attached to drag him around while given orders to beg. He had a taste for used condoms and so rubbish bins were emptied in him and over him. The man was an animal, for sure. How the girls chosen stopped from vomiting is proof of their professionalism but I am sure they threw up after he had disappeared from sight.

Then he moved onto something different to come off on. Being chained up and severely whipped or caned. This act was not for the faint-hearted, so Fay was allocated to do the job. She knew how to whip a man without scarring or making him bleed.

I had popped in when least expected and out of the domination room came Dog with the youngest girl at the parlour. Being concerned about this I questioned her, expressing my concern that she was not expert enough to deal with him. She insisted she was, it wasn't the first time he had chosen her. I then asked to be informed the next time he visited but, more by luck than judgment, I visited there again without any warning and arrived to chaos.

It seems that after connecting his dog collar to chains

dangling from the ceiling he had raised himself on a chair. While being whipped, he kicked the chair from underneath him and dropped with the collar tight around his neck. He had for the moment stopped breathing. The girl screamed for help and Fay with a bewildered customer ran into the room. They untied his restraints and Fay placed her mouth over his to administer the kiss of life. He came around in a pool of his own excrement, he was that close to death.

Auto-erotic asphyxiation is not a new thing, Michael Hutchence, the Australian rock star and front man of INXS, had been found dead in a hotel room in Sydney, as had the American actor and martial artist David Carradine. The practice is of sexual masochism and involves reducing the oxygen to the brain while masturbating to achieve a heightened orgasm. It seems there is a fine line between lack of oxygen in the brain and death and it's in that state that whoever practises this deviance becomes highly aroused, and it's this that allows them to orgasm.

The poor girl had no idea that his plan was to involve her in the act. I lost my temper so much with him, I was quite prepared to finish off the job. Thanks to Fay, an ambulance wasn't needed and he scuffled out, head bowed, after being ordered to clean up his mess, only to phone the next day apologising and asking if he would be allowed to return as he had enjoyed the experience so much. The answer: 'Not in your lifetime.'

Pondering events, I was sure this animal must have had a very normal, decent wife and children at home. Which proves how important massage parlours and the like are for keeping this from them.

I have often been asked if being a madam is tough. Being a madam can be stressful at times but I never found it tough. OK, there were a few occasions when I had to handle myself after dismissing a girl from the premises. I was always regarded as a madam who was firm but fair and dismissals would never be made without good reason.

Making sure all the girls on the premises were drug-free sometimes was stressful, especially when you had suspicions that drugs were being taken and brought in by men with a mission to share it with his chosen girl in the privacy of her room. That sort of situation was stressful but never tough.

Having your entrance doors busted open by masked men demanding your money, that's tough. But it only happened once and the money was passed over, one's life being far more important than any amount of money. Finding your premises have been robbed, the safe broken open and the contents taken, that's tough. Keeping on top of competition could be stressful at times but never tough.

In all the years of being a madam, I found it mostly pleasurable and extremely rewarding.

Chapter 31

The Business of Sex

'Scandal is gossip made tedious by morality.'

Georgie Ellis. I had guessed from the first time I met her that she was mentally a wreck. Then I discovered that the better term would be 'eccentric'. Then from that, you would meet up with her again and she would be incredibly articulate with a sweet speaking voice. It's always well-spoken voices that do it for me.

I found it amazing that a woman who had lived through so many tragedies, born to an alcoholic wife-beating father and having to grow up and live her life with the stigma of her mother being the last woman hanged, could be in the shape she was. It was miraculous.

That night when I met her, she was out of her head on booze but sadly without anyone giving her a second glance. It seemed a regular occurrence for her to be in that inebriated state. I found her raucous, rowdy and a little rude and we got on like a house on fire. I quickly learned that her love of the 'gangster' type of life was really the only one she enjoyed.

She had been mistreated by men in her early life and vowed it never would happen again but, hearing the lifestyle she chose, it could never be guaranteed. We discovered we were similar in our thoughts. We saw sex as a means to an end, in other words we knew our bodies were a saleable commodity and, with that conclusion, had no regrets.

Georgie had no problem in entering into conversation regarding 'Ruth' and always called her by her first name, never Mum, Mummy or Mother. I discovered much later that in her mind she was the same as her mother, who felt the worst fate for a girl was to be insignificant, something she never was. She was an eye-catching peroxide blonde who believed that blondes always had the most fun. There was no doubt she had been stunning when younger and still could hold her own with the best of contemporaries. She loved to talk the talk about her life's experiences with a vast amount of men, name-dropping along the way. But I understood her language and her determination to never let passions of the heart allow herself to be pushed outside the boundaries of her own control.

She had been a model at the Lucy Clayton Agency in Manchester in the early 70s, rocking up the dance floor of the clubs while I was doing my thing in London. We were certainly similar but I found her a little bewildering. As I got to know her better, I wondered if she was trying to live out her mother's remaining years for her. I guess learning about Ruth was learning about Georgie.

It seems quite a coincidence that nearly two years after we first met in a wine bar in Altrincham, Cheshire she decided to put pen to paper and write her memoirs not unlike what I am doing now. I discovered a further coincidence in that one of her 'old friends' who gave her advice was a name I well remembered: Eddie Shah. Wherever she went, it seemed she left a trail of men in her wake but it was always George Best's presence she craved. It seems they met when he was living in a flat in Prestwich at the beginning of his acclaimed football career at Manchester United. Small world, Prestwich being then my part-time home town, too. George was, she said, the man she lost her virginity to and with whom, it seemed, became pregnant.

From *Playboy* legend Hugh Hefner to actor Richard Harris and dear old George Best, there wasn't a famous stud or super-rich male she couldn't put her name to, the super-rich and famous being what she needed around her. That, together with her love of 'bad boys', parties and clubs. Mixed in was the ever-present need to be near lots of wealth and money, but often failing to keep it around her. She had not only spent days living her life of luxury in Puerto Banus, Marbella, she had dated the son of Saudi Arabian tycoon Adnan Khashoggi (so the story goes). This girl just did not know how to play things down.

When I first met her she was living in Bowdon, Cheshire, scrimping to exist and fretting that she had lost access to her children. When I returned home from my residence in Her Majesty's Prison, we met up again. In the meantime, she had done her mother proud, using her assets to get out of the trough, and after a stint in a Didsbury massage parlour she moved quickly onto escort work, guaranteeing her excellent financial rewards from, in her words 'highly respectable men', meaning lawyers, accountants, property entrepreneurs and merchant bankers. Occasionally, she would use Exon Escorts as her base. It was her turning point and what followed was a path she took, not unlike myself, where she no longer had to undertake such work herself. Instead, she managed escort agencies and it was at this point that we shared the occasional girls and work load. If we couldn't cover the job, then maybe her team could and vice versa.

Like myself, she was an advocate for legalising prostitution, within allocated areas. We had both trod a similar path, the big difference being my family background was healthy, loving and stable, whereas for her it was a different story. Ruth Ellis, the mother from who in name she never managed to escape, consumed with jealousy had pulled the trigger and shot her lover dead and was hanged for her crime. Georgie had never quite gone that far but still she was her mother's daughter.

At Toucan, the run-up to Christmas was always special.

Patrons of the *Red Lion* would want to share a festive drink, which we did on the last day before closing for Christmas Day, that and New Year's Day being the only days we shut up shop. Ahead of time, I would be busy arranging a venue for my ladies to enjoy some party time. I hired stretch limousines, two at a time, to the delight of the men who landed the job of escorting us to our chosen nightclub, no expense spared. My ladies were spoilt and appreciated on these occasion that everything had to be the best, and rightly so. They had paid for the pleasure through making Toucan as popular as it was. The limos would be stocked with champagne on ice and we would be driven to the best nightspots in the city centre. But always their favourite was Funny Girls in Blackpool where female impersonators would take to the stage, hardly burlesque, but it wasn't meant to be.

We indulged in getting as merry on champagne as we could and had the wildest of nights on those special occasions, where the ladies forgot to act like one and let their hair down along with their clothes. I did everything to encourage their exhibitionism, and loved those moments of theatre land. No, it wasn't Broadway. Yes, it was tacky but everyone was laughing, dancing and doing their thing.

Here's a thought for you: Older men paying for sex is directly related to a lack of marital happiness. The majority of older men, and by older I mean between 60 and 70, share the following. They are well-educated, successful businessmen who have either chosen retirement or are still involved in business. They are respectful and appear very decent, displaying good manners and social skills. Forty per cent of them are either married or in long-term relationships. Another 40 per cent will be divorced and the remaining 20 per cent widowed. The power of sex delivers all sorts of men into a prostitute's web of power. Older age clients usually have issues at home, the dreaded menopause being one, and these help to line a hooker's pockets very nicely. The wife would have no interest in sex and would look at her husband as a 'pain in the arse' to even suggest it and the poor man would be sick in his desire for sexual relief.

The older man uses a prostitute's services to get fresh ideas for their bedroom activities because their wives or partners can no longer satisfy them, some not having had sex for a long time. There is an almost therapeutic aspect which is rewarded in showing that they are still sexually vigorous and able to bring a woman's pleasure out of her body with a genuine orgasm. At this stage the power of imagination works wonders and I include myself when saying orgasms are reached in full climax when riding a man who needs your body so much.

A prostitute ages alongside her clients, so catering to older men is a way for her. Although still as fit as a younger contender, but past her prime in age, she can stay in the game with older men requiring the right type of approach, with time and experience.

How would most wives think if their husband admitted to seeing a prostitute? Maybe they wouldn't care nearly as much if it was a prostitute, as opposed to a romantic relationship. Even if he were allowed to part her unwilling legs, his visiting a prostitute would mean he had no need to perform long drawn-out foreplay with no reaction, or head for a night romancing a date he may have met on line, taking all the consequences that come from that meeting. Who needs complications at any age?

Another reason, much more obvious, is that a prostitute will provide oral sex. Now there's a thing! A lot of married women either won't do it, at best just now and then, and almost none of them will swallow or let their man cum in their mouth. You would have to ask a married woman if they would care if it was a prostitute or a romantic relationship that had whet his appetite. My guess is they would be upset with either. The affair for the emotional attachment and a prostitute because in their mind's eye it exposes them to all sorts of diseases.

All my girls were guided to attend clinics on a regular basis and nearly all did it of their own accord. Anyone can catch a disease if they have unprotected sex, be it sex worker or not, so why the worry over a girl selling her body? She would be the one who protected herself the most. Her business is on the line after all.

The little wife at home is very rarely at the forefront of her man's mind when he is carried away with pleasures of the body. It is the older man who is most grateful and usually less demanding in what he requires. He is the one who knows experience is the thing you can't get free.

Chapter 32

Daddy Dearest

'Don't wonder how you do it.
Do it and wonder how you did it.'

December 27, 1999, marked the death of my beloved father as I headed towards the end of my 50th year.

His Alzheimer's had been progressing for several years and yet we had become closer than ever. He had spent so many years being protective of me, it was now my turn to step up to the plate and take care of him.

I was running myself ragged from his home to Toucan to my home and back again. Thankfully, John, who was employed as my chauffeur and protection, an amicable man in his late 50s who had the strength of someone half his age, took on the job of collecting and delivering my old man to me, and very often he would be sat in the parlour in Swinton being fussed on by the girls with lots of kisses and cuddles.

Then my father would join me for the weekend at my home, something he always looked forward to. We both loved those precious moments together. I discovered on those days more about his life and loves than ever before. Unfortunately, with Toucan commitments ever-present, there were gaps on many days when I could not have him with me and on those days a care assistant would be employed to take care of his needs. But when we were together we made the best of the day, travelling to the countryside and the seaside at St. Anne's-on-Sea, near

Blackpool, where we would dine out together, John my father and me.

We had the best of conversations sat at his dining table in Prestwich. I wanted to know so much about his life before I was born, things he had kept to himself, before his memory went from him completely. One evening while sorting his affairs, the table piled high with documents, photos and old paperwork he had clung on to, I came across an alarming discovery – his true name. Lazarus David Waxman was the name he had been given at birth but somehow along the passage of his early life the change was made. 'Why change your name from Lazarus to Leslie, Daddy?' I asked. 'Lazarus is such a beautiful name.'

With that, tears came to his eyes and I knew not to pursue the subject any further. Whatever had triggered the decision to change his name had long gone and had never been discussed but I had no need to have his answer. I figured out the reasons for myself. The name change took away his obvious Jewishness and made it easier for him to be accepted into British society those years during and after the Second World War. Those years before I was born had left their mark and here we were so many years later. The tough and resilient man that he was had disappeared along with the past and gradually it had become like looking after a child.

It's amazing how you gain strength from nowhere but somehow I did. I was struggling with depression and seemed to be battling through one trauma only to face another. I had totally lost any urge for sex or other passions in life. My energies had gone from me completely and anything I managed to muster was reserved for my father alone. My girls had become very concerned. Their boss had lost her sparkle, something unheard of. Regular clients were leaving messages wishing me well and offering their help and support.

Time came and passed and in the late summer of 1999

my father entered a nursing home. I lived each day with little else but him on my mind. Visiting my doctor for help with how I was feeling, he referred me to a psychiatrist, who in turn referred me to the Priory Clinic, renowned for curing people with drug dependency and depression. At this stage I was convinced I had every chronic illness under the sun. I only had to look at my reflection in the mirror to see my decline. Heart monitors were strapped to my chest, as I felt my heart was sure to stop beating. Electric shock treatment was suggested and immediately refused. I was as tough as the man I had been caring for and would get through this without such drastic steps.

One evening I received a phone call – a carer from the nursing home was on the other end of the phone. 'Your father has been taken to hospital with a suspected chest infection.' Her voice relayed concern. He went in and never came out, not alive anyway. When I arrived at the hospital he was on a respirator and being fed by a tube. A calmness had come over me. It's as if we both knew there was no more fight in either of us. We had come to the end of the road.

We looked into each other's eyes and, bent over the bed, I simply said, 'Please tell me what to do. Give me one blink if you want the tube taken out or two blinks if you want it to remain.' He blinked once. I had my answer.

When the tube was removed he turned his gaze towards me and said three words: 'I love you.'

His passing was as gentle and easy as he was. I had lost the love of my life once again but it's his face I see smiling at me every day, his picture the background on my mobile phone. After all these years, he is still the one I want with me every day.

Chapter 33

HRT, I Love You!

'Living in the past is like scratching a wound.
If you don't leave it alone, it will never go away.
Let it heal, accept the scar and move on with life.'

2002 was a year filled with mixed emotions. I had just celebrated my 53rd year, with a small collection of my closest friends joining me to dine out in the city. It was a calm and tranquil celebration, the way I preferred it to be.

I had once again lost my exuberant spirit. It seemed to have disappeared forever. Bouts of depression had recurred and every day was a struggle. How I managed to get through the days was a miracle in itself, arriving at my Toucan with crushing fatigue and unable to concentrate. Even when walking around from room to room, I had to support myself by holding onto furniture. I was in a bad way. My girls had seen me in states of depression before and handled it by ignoring it, knowing eventually I would rally round.

It had really started the previous December, during the Christmas period. Normally this time of year would be taken on with relish. But not that year. I spent the whole time alone with Dan my trusty dog – just him and I cuddled up on the sofa at my home in Timperley. I wished for no other company.

Boxing Day arrived with me still in the same position on the sofa. I had slept there all night, not even wanting to move to the bedroom. My phone was ringing constantly and I ignored it. Then through the letterbox, a flyer landed on the floor of my porch. A Chinese acupuncturist was advertising his skills and I took the first opportunity after the holidays to visit him. Needles were applied to my body, while I lay in his bare and cold room, praying that it would help cure my symptoms of depression.

He explained in his broken English that I had blockages that needed to be released and so he drew blood from heated glass cups that he lay on different parts of my back. 'This is a treatment called cupping,' he told me. It would get my body functioning better.

I became mesmerised with his technique and almost resident in his little clinic in Northenden, the next village to where I was living. I was convinced he had the power to cure me and every ache and pain I felt, be it in my imagination or not. He listened to my list of ailments and applied his miracle needles and cups.

While I was desperately trying anything to regain my spirit, a close friend came to my rescue. She had been experiencing some phenomenal results of sexual empowerment after having a course of HRT given directly by needle into her hip. She said it had sent her libido sky-high and sex could not have been any better once the hit had spread to stimulate her body.

'It's rocket fuel, Viv,' she insisted. Not only that but she felt on top of the world, with the energy of a woman 30 years younger. 'Shake up and regain a love life and your lust for life will improve dramatically,' she added, and with that advice an immediate appointment was made with the gynaecologist who performed this miracle service.

It's hard to explain the feeling that eventually takes over your body, but whatever it was, it was working. Energies I had not felt for a very long time returned. My brain resumed its activity, I was waking each day ready and eager to take it on. And I was smiling again. At last!

Additionally, my body came alive at the slightest touch. My nipples became large and full, my vagina was constantly juicy and I was masturbating at any given opportunity. It didn't matter where I attained my orgasm, I just didn't care. I needed to release the tension and desire from my body constantly through the day and I didn't need to have anyone to help me. Just the touch of my fingers set the spark to ignite an orgasm like I could only imagine in times past. My libido was renewed and I now longed for the biggest penis to penetrate me constantly. HRT, I love you!

How I became such a successful, in-demand madam while abstaining from sex myself, is quite some food for thought. None of my customers knew. They believed where their imagination took them. As far as they were concerned, I was a woman to desire and never would they have contemplated that the boss of Toucan had not been penetrated for days, let alone years!

That first injection was one of many to follow and before long I became addicted to the needle. But before I reached that stage there was a visual change in me on the outside as well as inside. I changed my style and hair colour from brunette to blonde and had luscious hair extensions flowing down the length of my back. I followed that with a huge breast enlargement, taking my size from a D cup to GG, expanding my skin to the max.

During this course of transformation, a friend and I took a Caribbean holiday – Jamaica, the paradise island, the land of Reggae, Bob Marley, Mount Gay Rum and black gods with bodies that knew how to fuck a woman, in every position and every way. That's what I wanted and that's exactly what I got. Jamaica – 'The land of traumatised vaginas'.

Before I begin involving you any further regarding

'men of Jamaica', I'll digress. Take a look at the active verbs used to describe the Jamaican male role in the sexual act: 'Slap', 'Dagger', 'Step inna har tings', 'Stamp', 'Jump inna it', 'Stamina Daddy', 'Draw gear inna it', 'Slam', 'Ram', 'Jam', 'Rod', 'Dig out', 'Rev out', 'Work', 'Stab it'. These are just a few words that emerged from this country of culture and you cannot forget the dance hall songs that suggest that you 'move her womb'.

Variety is the name of the sex game. Women can lie and tell each other that they want a man to make love to every square centimetre of their body and who go down on her till she cries 'stop' or 'cree' But doesn't even that get stale after a while? Which do men prefer? Do they want her to say 'make sweet and passionate love to me', or do they want her to grab the back of their neck and growl 'make me your whore' or 'it's just yours, mash it up', a phrase I soon learned in Jamaica. Do women like this caveman type of sex? Well, listening to their experiences, I have never heard them complain and, anyway, including myself among them, if we didn't like it, why would we be shouting 'harder, harder'?

I remember many a different touch during my times in Jamaica: The touch of a soft-skinned, well-built Jamaican man, with a beautiful accent and dreads, or the ones trying to drag me into a cave after travelling at exhilarating speed on the back of a jet ski. That was another touch moment.

My Jamaica adventure started as soon as we stepped off the plane. The sweet smell of jasmine immediately hit my nose and I breathed it in, taking stock of the scenery around me while sitting on the coach taking holidaymakers to their destination. I saw houses made from sheets of aluminium, abandoned houses with rotting wood. It was not immediately what I expected but then we reached amazing scenery of tall palm trees of different shapes with contrasting coloured leaves. My instinct told me that when palm trees were present, good times were ahead. White sand and the bluest of water I had ever seen. Colourful buildings of pink, yellow, green, purple and, of course, red-green-yellow, the Rasta theme to be seen everywhere.

The five-star Sandals Sport Hotel in Ochos Rios was the destination and with renewed life in my body, where else to take it than the Caribbean, where young black guys with stiff, hard cocks know how to seduce a woman. My past expertise told me that you can tell the size of a man's penis by the size of his hands and feet. If he has long fingers, he usually has a long slim cock. If he has short thick fingers, he usually has a short thick cock. And if he has big fleshy hands, he usually has etc., etc. So with this thought, and feeling like a rampant rabbit, I hit the beach in the skimpiest of bikinis – those that are held up with string at the sides. One pull and they were off! Enter Kevin on his jet ski. Enter the beginning of the end.

We met while I was lying on the jetty, my skin still wet from an early morning swim. He zoomed in on his jet ski, as close to the jetty as he could get. 'Want to take a tour on my jet ski?' he asked. I heard the voice before I saw him and when I opened my eyes there he was, rippling with muscle, black like the night sky, with the sea water glistening on his body. Who wouldn't be tempted?

He made three attempts to persuade me, in between doing his business of taking money for rides, but eager to get back where he started when he returned. I really didn't need much persuasion. The damp wet suit clinging to his body showed every curve and bump, he was well stacked for sure.

The HRT had kicked and, wet with desire, I rose, jumped into the water and climbed aboard. Off we rode, out into the depth of the ocean until we reached a cove where he rested his jet ski. I didn't hesitate to strip and swim naked in that beautiful turquoise ocean. As I climbed back on board, he spun me round, grabbing a condom from his belt and expertly laying it on an erection that was ready to burst, all with one hand! An expert at the job, I guessed.

He took me from behind without a word. There is no better feeling than having sex out in the open with the sea whipping at your body and being penetrated by a huge cock that knew its way around my vagina, pumping away with hard thrusts, the ecstasy and agony of the moment, clinging on to the rocks for dear life, the heat of the sun burning into my body. Some men have action, some men don't. This action lasted till he came with his last thrust. It was a rough and rushed experience but rough was what I wanted.

For the rest of my stay he sought me out every day, waiting on the jetty of the hotel complex. My pleasure was had outdoors and it was his body I chose to enjoy. For me it wasn't the best of sex – too much experience in knowing what best is I guess – but it did the trick in bringing my body back to life. Together with the HRT mix, it formed a powerful cocktail, the recipe to which any man would love. I was rampant.

Hedonism is a nudist beach hotel north of the island in Negril. I'd heard that *Hedonism* rocks and Kevin didn't need much coaxing to visit there. *Hedonism*, where everyone walks around naked as a bird. I love the feeling of freedom that a nudist beach gives. No-one examines your body. That doesn't come into the equation, at least it shouldn't, but you couldn't miss the men walking around with erections.

This hotel had everything. Built for pleasure and with guests being couples of the same mind we had easy access to those we could invite for some personal sex play – with my encouragement of course. Heaven was there those days, with the traditional Jamaican dish of ackee and saltfish, followed by swimming carefree in the blue ocean, or sharing the hot tub with nights spent laying under the stars, where I let Kevin devour my body.

We arrived on a Tuesday, just in time for Pyjama Night, where nudity was allowed in the disco well after midnight. Actually, we discovered that nudity was allowed anywhere at *Hedonism* after midnight.

'Wood on the beach?' Yes, wood happened. Some were proud to show it off, but the Jamaican man accompanying me had more control. For those who found the nude beach titillating and had an urgent need to hide their organ, a technique was required: Go into the water, as all penises first float but sink when the chill hits them; or lie face down on the beach chair and do not make a humping sound unless someone is underneath you; or put it to use on a raft out in the ocean, which is what Kevin did, making sure we were not too hidden, hoping we would be watched and maybe applauded.

We were not short of invites from swingers, who guessed we wanted to be lured into play, and play we did, starting in the hot tub, then taking it elsewhere.

Hedo was not really an orgy but with sex on the beach at night, where we brought our bedspread down to make our sex nest cosier, we were inevitably joined by others of the same mind. We seemed to be one of the few copulating couples, with the same people day and night doing their thing.

There were single guys around but they stayed in the distance, preferring to be voyeurs, watching but not touching. I guess kicks are achieved in many ways.

The guests were predominately white, with partners of every occupation, from doctors and lawyers to musicians and artists to secretaries and truck drivers. It was the attitude, not the look, age or money of the person as to whether or not fun was had at *Hedo*. We left after a week of spent desire, back to the hotel complex in Ochos Rios, and while I lay soaking up the rays of the sun, Kevin pursed his daily routine of earning money from tourists for the pleasure of a ride on his jet ski. I distanced myself. I'd had all I wanted from his company and indulged myself in other pursuits until the time came to say farewell.

It took some amount of discipline to leave this paradise island but I felt England calling and I returned home tanned and toned. I was happy and how good it was to return to Toucan with everything in full swing and my takings intact. I had delegated well, God bless them.

All my Toucan men had waited with baited breath for my return. They loved the new-look Viv, which did great things for my previously flagging confidence. When you are in your mid-fifties, no matter how good you feel or look, and no matter how much work you do on yourself, it's always good to hear a compliment. Words like '*You're how old? Never! I'd put you at 20 years younger,*' are music to the ears and don't we love to hear them, true or not? The new look had done the trick and guys who had never ventured through Toucan's doors were coming, literally in droves, after putting myself stripper-style on the home page of a new venture, the Toucan website.

I felt like my burlesque days were back and I was loving every moment. This exhibitionism was done purely to encourage new clients to call thinking, if the boss looks like that, what do the girls look like? Once engrossed in the website with all the girls on view in all sorts of poses, naked or nearly, and reading all the juicy details of services available in the club, no man worth his salt could resist a visit. A clever move on my part? No not really, it was just sales promotion of my business, however I could do it.

Although often asked, I had a policy of never taking part in any sex acts on my own or with my girls. First of all, my price would have been too high and also when I retired and left Aquarius all those years ago, it was never to return to business with my body, at whatever price. The sex I would indulge in would be freely given, with the people I chose to have sex with. Anyway, I had more important thoughts – expanding Toucan's premises, something that had toyed with in my mind for quite some time. Never would I have moved shop to a bigger place and while constant requests from clients to do so came in daily, I stuck to my guns. The Toucan was at 467a Chorley Road, Swinton, and that's where it would stay.

After some months away from Jamaica I was eager to return and so, after making sure all my girls were happy and clients aware I would be away for a while, I delegated again and left my receptionists and a manageress in charge. All supplies of un-perishable food, the essential baby oil, talc and tissues, room fresheners, the cupboards had been well stocked for weeks to come. A responsible person was chosen to collect and bank all the money and off I went for another HRT jab, only three days before my vacation.

Travelling home from Toucan, I had a feeling at the pit of my stomach like I was about to start a period. I brushed the thought aside but had the urgent need to inspect my panties when I arrived home. My feelings were real, there was blood everywhere, masses of it. Panic shot through my body and brain. *This can't be happening.* And my first thought as always was cancer.

After days of anxiety and waiting for a scan at the hospital, everyone was on red alert thinking the worst. My vacation was cancelled, Jamaica was the last thing on my mind. The result of the scan was something never to be rectified. Something that I thought had happened had, in fact, never happened at all. The scan showed I had a full and healthy womb and that I had never had a hysterectomy. All those years ago, before scans were invented, a mistake had been made, and what the surgical registrar had told me and what the medical records showed were different. My womb was never removed.

This meant that after Billy had died I could have chosen a different path in life. I could have, with help, had children. The HRT had stimulated my dormant womb and created a period. There were no words to describe my shock at the news.

I made a swift visit to my solicitor and was shown immediately to his office. His concern was obvious. Nick Freemen was just as shocked as I when hearing my revelation of events. 'We will sue the pants off them,' he said, and quickly got to work, planning to sue the surgeon.

Visiting his offices again sometime later I was to learn that the surgeon in question had died years before. Nick was not prepared to stop there. Suing the hospital was next on the list, his mind set on hundreds of thousands of pounds. Indeed, he was correct. The pay-out, if proved, could have been huge. The medical error had indeed affected my whole life, as I would have taken a very different path if I could have been a real mother. Instead, I took on the role of a surrogate mother to my girls and the men I chose in my life after Billy's demise were chosen because, like me, they couldn't or didn't want children.

Many women in my situation would have taken this solicitor's expert advice but my mind-set at the time was that I didn't need millions of pounds. I had no hunger for it and I certainly didn't want to face a court case where all the memories of the past were brought into focus. I had rid myself of depression and didn't want any more. Instead, I boarded a plane as planned to take me far away to Jamaica to renew the fun and happy times with carefree days of sun, sand, song and sex.

Enter Ray – The Music Master.

Chapter 34

Ray and his Reggae Rhythms

'Goals: There's no telling what you can do when you get inspired by them. There's no telling what you can do when you believe in them.

There's no telling what will happen when you act upon them.'

Ray came into my life in the winter of 2003. I intended to celebrate bringing in my 54th year in the warmth of Jamaica instead of freezing at home. If I say so myself, I was looking good, with a body a woman 20 years younger would be proud of and I left my woes of the medical mistake behind me as I ventured again to new territory, booking into the Sandals Resort in Ochos Rios, where I had stayed before.

I had become friendly with the manageress of their Italian restaurant. Jackie was a Jamaican beauty with a brain to match her looks and we got on like a house on fire. She had attached herself to me for various reasons. Firstly, I looked rich and, secondly, I had fire in my belly, the same as her. She loved my craziness, the fact that I enjoyed life and could afford to take her along on the merry-go-round. That was fine by me. I needed the extra protection from a local woman who was well-known and respected in the area. When stepping out away from the hotel complex she fended off the male interest. Being white, blonde and busty, I drew attention.

We partied on rum cocktails and danced in the reggae clubs till early morning and I woke late in the day, a little worse for wear, but eager to take advantage of exploring

Ochos Rios without the confines of the tourist entrapment.

A search for a villa where she could join me and stay till the end of my vacation was top of my to-do list, so after a swim in the pool and a very late breakfast I waited for her to arrive in the foyer and off we went in a hire car to find a spot on the beach where I could wake each morning and swim in that beautiful ocean. She knew where to take me and after enquiring from villa to villa along the coastline, an ideal home was found, right on the beach, nestled between other villas on a small complex of privately rented beach houses. It was expensive but it was perfect for what I needed, freedom to do as I wished. The villa had a housemaid who prepared all meals and was eager to attend to all my needs. This holiday was going to be bliss.

He was walking towards me. I had just left the pool of my villa and after a constant week of tanning, still wet, I let the heat of the sun dry my body. Reggae music was plugged into my ears as I was swinging my hips, treading the path down to the beach. He noticed the walk and approached me. Black and beautiful with his bare chest and muscular arms, strong neck and a toned, ripped stomach that I was tempted to punch and feel, he had stopped to introduce himself. 'I'm Ray, I'm your neighbour for the week.'

We joked together and, bold as young Jamaican guys are, he told me how he had many a hard-on watching me swim naked in my pool. 'You love to watch?' I asked.

'No, I want more than that,' was his quick reply and looking down I could only imagine what could be in store for me.

From that meeting Ray became a constant part of my life for three years. I was blown away with this young stud who also had an amazing business brain. Coming from the ghettos of Jamaica, marrying into one of the wealthiest families on the island, he took little time in telling me that his marriage had become loveless and was only maintained because of the devotion he had for his son. His determination to become one of the leading spirits of reggae music, producing and recording artists from his studio at home and breaking through into a very tough industry alongside his competitors in Kingston, was not to be taken on by the faint-hearted. But he was tough in mind and body and educated enough to realise he had the know-how to achieve his goals. I was fascinated.

Ray was and still is the best lover I have ever had. When he kissed me he ate my face off with his succulent soft lips. He knew how to suck, nibble and bite to give pleasure to every part of my body. Sex with him was a work of art that lasted for hour after hour until we fell apart exhausted. He had control of my body and knew how to get the best response. Sex with him was pleasurable to me without the use of a sex aid. None of that was needed, no dildo was going to penetrate my pussy, no paddle was going to spank my butt, nothing was going to be used to bind and restrict my body. He would have been insulted by the suggestion.

I had this huge hung man at my disposal and all sorts of things were running through my head. I was thinking, *I want him to test my limits, bend me over, spread my legs*, and any of his demands I would meet with enthusiasm. I do know with all the black pussy he had penetrated, this white pussy was the best. A master of his art at pleasuring a woman knew no bounds and I lay in bed every morning anxiously hoping for his body to take me to an orgasmic heaven.

How many times can you orgasm in one night? There weren't enough times for me but he met my demands and equalled my orgasms until the bed was soaked and we lay there drained, only for him to leave me tired and contented and then to reappear again, late into the morning, to slide next to me with kisses over my body until he reached my cherry and brought it to life again.

During that week he introduced me to his world and to his mother and sister and I became part of his life so very quickly. I was in heaven. Wanting away from the confines of his marriage, he returned to Trelawny to kiss it goodbye, with me sat in the back seat of his car while his friend sat in the front beside him and it was then that I realised what a sacrifice he would be making, leaving the comfort of his home. Rich is rich but this was enormous wealth. The house with its huge electric gates and guard dogs, with a drive that curved off into the distance, eventually to reach the house. His marriage to Simone had been set up by her father to protect her wealth, so leaving the marriage, Ray would walk out with his suitcase and nothing more.

I was leaving myself for home the following day and so we arranged to speak daily on the phone. I was hooked up to this new type of life and gushing for more and when I boarded the plane for home I knew I would help in every way so I could share his life, his body and his success. During this course of transition into the Jamaican way of life, I learnt *patois* (Jamaican slang English). I was moving towards the idea of splitting my life between England and a future home in Jamaica and the more time I spent there, within the controls of Ray's burgeoning progress in the music industry, I learned to love the lifestyle. I was accepted as Ray's 'woman' and with that title came great respect. Whenever I walked about without him I had an escort of protection and with him our protection was enormous. His skills at delegating and bringing in the best music makers to his ever-growing empire had become well-known and a risk of having his studio in Kingston blown up by gangster competition was ever-present.

Big reggae stars such as dancehall artist Vybz Cartel, Sean Paul, Morgan Heritage and Jah Cure were involved with Ray in expanding their reggae sounds. But through all of the hard living and constant watching over his shoulder, his personality was slowly changing. All the fun that I had first experienced, with his great sense of humour and passion for living, began to leave him and what remained was a sullen, miserable man.

His personal life had become non-existent as his music took control and grew and grew, while my business life became less and less in England. Whenever I had to leave him because of an expected conflict with his enemies, I would be anxious for his safety. In between all this I had decided to expand Toucan, remodelling the style into a gentlemen's club, taking it away from its seediness into a building of class and style.

I had been waiting for an opportunity to expand for some time and returning after yet another a long stay in Jamaica I was prompted into action. My girls wanted the expansion into 'glamour mixed with eroticism' and there was equal enthusiasm from our gentlemen clients. The building attached to ours had at last become available and I took the project on with relish, which did the trick to take my thoughts away from Ray Ray Ray, at least for a while.

Plans were drawn up to make Toucan into a force to be reckoned with. I had, in fact, gained this power of determination from the man himself. 'Set your sights on the highest target and make it yours,' he would say, and when I told him of my plans he was full of enthusiasm for me. Without doubt, he was visualising a joint empire together, a force to be reckoned with. I loved those thoughts he had. His idea of 'happiness' was to live with me in a villa we had spotted in Trelawny, a magnificent home, and we talked about it and decided to work towards that plan. The thought was that making Toucan into a leading gentlemen's club that would eventually be worth selling for a ton of money was the ideal plan and so the vision was put into action. Although the thought was a quick one, the project took two years to complete.

Once the plans were drawn up and the re-invention of

The Toucan began, I delegated the overseeing of the work to a trusted friend who had joined our team as a cleaner to help with her daughter's expensive education. I had known JC for some years, mixing within the same circles in Prestwich and Whitefield. She was a girl after my own heart and loved the nightlife in the city. The girls took to her warm and friendly manner immediately and although knowing nothing about the industry when she started, she soon learned to handle any problems and the girls regarded her as Viv's personal number one. She took on my workload with gusto and I left her with the challenge as I took a flight out to the island in the sun from which I had been away for too long.

I had returned to living life on the edge for a while and wrapped myself in the warmth of Ray's arms as he welcomed me back. An evening in a dance hall had been arranged for my first night's return, a simple thing to put together, you may think, but not in Ray's world. Protection had to spread themselves around our car as we stepped out and before we entered the dance hall it was scanned by Ray's men for possible problems. I was back to living the life I found thrilling. The celebrity status that Ray received took us to a VIP area where no-one, unless personally vetted by his men, were allowed to enter. How much fun can it be when you are confined to one area, not allowed to go freely on to the dance floor? Ray had me shackled to his side the whole evening and I looked on, wishing I could dance like those free to enjoy writhing their bodies to the music.

That evening we lost our driver. On our return home a gun was fired as we were stepping back into the car, hitting him in the stomach. Bleeding heavily he was quickly transferred to the back of the car where Ray's brother held him tight until we arrived at the hospital. He lay dead on his knees while we travelled and was pronounced dead on arrival. I was then whisked once again to the airport, with an anxious Ray wanting me safe in England. A war within the music industry in Jamaica had started.

One may ask what I now saw in this man who had lost his happy smile and jovial manner. Without doubt, the sex was incredible. We knew how to turn each other's bodies on like the flick of a switch. But it was more than that for me as when he occasionally took time out to fly over and join me in England, knowing that business came first, he would sit at the New Toucan bar at the end of each day ready to collect me and take me home. Never once did he show an interest in my brothel. In fact, he had never ventured into a brothel before. He had a narrow-minded view that paying for sex was nasty and he had little time for all men who participated in that game. He would sit at the bar, head down, reading the daily papers, taking no notice of the girls, other than offering an evening greeting to be polite. It was this about him that impressed me and, out of respect for their boss, impressed my girls too.

When I was at home in England I practically lived in Toucan while the refurbishments were moving to completion. Building the new brothel was like raising a child and watching it grow, and at the end of its development it would be wonderful, it was after all my baby.

It was important to keep the momentum going and keep my girls and clients happy while keeping the shop open through the days of chaos. Builders, electricians, plumbers, you name it, we had it going on while action was happening in the massage rooms. No-one was more eager get to their jobs than the happy band of labourers, listening to the moans and groans as they plastered walls and decorated.

Earning money for everyone was the number one important thing. I had to keep my girls happy. If I didn't they would be gone like streak lightening to somewhere that did. So we worked in candlelight when the electricity was switched off and in the midst of winter they walked around cuddled up in coats over their skimpy underwear when the heating was off. There could be nowhere else that had loyalty like Toucan and I had at that time.

At last the day came when The New Toucan Club opened its stylish doors. No-one doubted its future success – it was evident by the vast amount of eager men visiting to sample the vibrant new atmosphere, all exclaiming it had definitely been worth the wait. We all sailed through the grand opening without a hitch and while the men left happily with their sacs empty, my girls and I left at the end of a long day happy with bulging purses. It didn't take long before word spread far and wide: Toucan was back with a bang. This bordello was a force to be reckoned with and it would take quite a while for many brothels to step up to the plate and compete.

Being the best allowed me to be very selective in who I took on. Sometimes having to turn away a drop dead gorgeous girl if she didn't have the right attitude. Good looks alone wouldn't land the job, they had to possess personality, friendliness and offer a service at a very high level. We not only had the best facilities but the best reputation in the treatment of working girls, and most importantly for them an excellent reputation for earning money.

The girls were indeed dream makers, they fulfilled fantasies and took you to the heights you could only dream about. They role-played and pampered and in turn had a great time earning their money, and Madam dream maker felt good knowing she had a small part in creating someone's happiness.

Meanwhile, I didn't waste too much time before returning to my favourite Caribbean retreat. Leaving the care of Toucan to my trusted close confidantes, I once again boarded the plane to Jamaica for a few weeks of relaxation. My feet had hardly touched the sand when a phone call of immense urgency took away all thoughts of romance with Ray. An over-excited voice speaking loud and coherent on the other end of the phone: 'Can you hear me, Viv?' Perhaps it was the delay in my response that concerned her. Yes, I had heard every word, I was simply taking my time, making sure I gave the right instructions.

'The press are lined up outside the doors with cameras and refuse to go away. We haven't had a dog through the door for hours.' JC, by now my lieutenant, who normally took everything in her stride, had for once lost her calmness. I gathered very quickly that another famous footballer had trod the boards of a brothel, my brothel. You may think that would be good for business, great advertising, but anyone who runs a respected whore house knows that sort of advertising is not needed at all.

The name couldn't have been any bigger, nor the club he played for. What a story the press would have and, after it, mincemeat would be made of all involved. That I was sure of.

Gathering my wits, I gave an instruction that no-one should speak to the press under any circumstances. However, the precious CCTV footage of this football hero walking into Toucan and out again sometime later was worth a heap of money and the first one to jump on the bandwagon was Ray. 'Find out what it's worth and how the press picked up on the story,' was his immediate instruction to me and after a hasty call back to the UK, I discovered that one of our latest additions to Toucan, a pretty hooker with stars in her eyes, had jumped on the chance to gain exposure and money by informing a Sunday tabloid newspaper. She meanwhile had disappeared into the mist, hidden away somewhere out of sight, I am sure, hoping and praying that we in turn would add to her exposure.

Meanwhile, Ray had hastily decided to take hold of the reins and it was he who spoke to the press after getting their number from JC. Their immediate offer was £50,000 for the footage. What Ray, a novice in the industry, didn't understand was firstly that amount of money was not worth the risk of me losing my very successful business, as for sure it would have been, potentially from a raid by the police. Toucan had made headlines and they would have to be seen to act upon it. And what about the faithful fans? Could Toucan be targeted by fanatics who idolised their precious football club Respect for both considerations, and doubting the amount of money that would have eventually been put on the table, my decision didn't take long.

Returning home on the first available flight and immediately dropping off my cases at home, I arrived at the Toucan doors. Reporters and photographers were ready to pounce. The poor guys didn't last there long. By the end of the day they were gone, with tails between their legs, a whole week wasted on gaining the evidence to go to print.

It was a genuine gesture of loyalty on my behalf when I went to see my solicitor. After I explained the incident a phone call was made to the celebrated club manager. It would have been wonderful to have received a gesture of his thanks since I had saved not only one of his star players from some very bad publicity but also the club from unwanted press coverage. I doubt if the 'star' even knew of the events that followed his visit to Toucan, and if he did he certainly kept quiet about it. Hoping for a small reward, I waited and waited. If not a gesture of money perhaps a seat in the executive suite for the match of my choice. What I eventually received was a 'thank you', given not by the man himself but through my solicitor, who happened to be their solicitor, too. Disappointing indeed, still, I had done the right thing by protecting my club, as a 'canny' club manager had protected his.

In 2005, Ray asked me to sell up completely in England and join him to spend my life in Jamaica.

We had by this time made moves to invest in a property together, the beautiful area of Trelawny, where he had previously lived with his ex-wife. He wanted that lifestyle, even though his heart was in Kingston. I had been having restless nights and concerns about my future life if I permanently made the move. Even though the Caribbean was where I wanted to spend my future retirement days, I didn't want it yet. In fact, the more I thought about the transition to Jamaica, the more I didn't want it at all.

I decided to return as soon as possible and confess my feelings – bold stuff when you are dealing with the man he had become. I soon found out that he wasn't for letting me off the hook so easily. It was his way or no way. While in the midst of this dilemma, I received a phone call from a friend who was holidaying in Barbados. She knew of my situation and provided the perfect excuse I needed to leave Jamaica and island hop to Barbados. 'Fly over and join me, there's a man here that you need to meet,' she said. It sounded like the perfect escape and so, telling Ray I was urgently needed back home, I left him at the airport waving goodbye – as I knew very soon it would be.

Chapter 35

Wayne – A Master of his Art

'The truth is rarely pure and never simple.'

I remember the smell even now. Barbados has a perfume of its own and stepping off the plane from Jamaica the smell was sweeter, and I felt immediately the people were softer and sweeter by nature too. Bambas Beach Bar, what a bar! You could hear the mellow sounds of jazz music well before you reached its quaint entrance, which took you down to the terrace bar and beach. I discovered that the best of sunsets were to be viewed from that spot.

It was early evening and after a warm welcome from my friend at the airport I followed her to a little guest house at the top of a hill overlooking Paynes Bay on the west coast. I could always rely on her to pick the right spot, the west coast being where the rich and famous holidayed. Paradise Palm could never cater for anything other than fun people who liked to be as close as possible to west coast luxury without paying the price.

Pat, the larger-than-life Yorkshire owner, ran a guest house with plastic cruet sets and paper cloths on her breakfast table, ringing her bell every morning at some unearthly hour to announce that breakfast was ready. If you missed the third ring, no breakfast for you! Her beds were made with the cheapest cotton sheets but it was homely, with a little bar where guests and locals used to gather. After showering and setting my style for the evening, we headed towards Bambas Beach Bar for an evening meal.

I noticed him immediately. Well, I heard his laughter before I actually saw him, as he was lost to me in the darkness of the night. Coming closer, his broad smile showed perfect pearly teeth which lit up his angelic face. Delicately featured, with his Rastafarian locks passing his shoulders and down his back, he had a way of flicking it with a turn of his head away from his face that I found attractive. What struck me was, unlike the Third World culture in which Ray had allowed himself to remain, Wayne was different. He could drop his Bajan twang when with people who were not islanders. He was worldly and eager to learn the culture of those that he met, speaking perfectly pronounced English and Spanish if he needed. Out of beach wear he was a slick dresser and carried himself with confidence. Crucially, he had the wicked sense of humour. The first words he greeted me with when he noticed me walking in were 'I love your profile,' meaning the profile of my huge breasts. And so, I was up for taking him on immediately we met.

Within three weeks I discovered every nook and cranny of the island. He was known everywhere, riding around in his open-top Jeep, waving to everyone like he was royalty himself. We slept under the stars on pitch black nights, listening to the sound of the waves crashing against the cliffs below, only to wake listening to the sound of birds and looking at breathtaking views. In the evening we would dine at the best restaurants on the west coast. The Lone Star, The Fish Pot, The Cliff, Sandy Lane Hotel and then move into the night with 1st and 2nd Street nightlife. It took only two hours to get around the whole of the island and from west to east and north to south I discovered a different ocean and a different feel.

His guest list at Bambas was impressive. Ronnie Wood and Keith Richards of the Rolling Stones were in his address book, so was top jockey Frankie Dettori, Patti Boyd, the model and first wife of Beatle George Harrison, and the mega-rich Sangster family. Wayne loved celebrity and celebrity loved him.

His PR skills were excellent. From A-listers to Z-listers, he had it covered, especially working with the paparazzi on his select stretch of beach. Those who wanted publicity got it and for those who didn't want exposure, he made sure the press didn't come near, all for a price of course.

The way he networked was impressive. He loved the feel of money. It seems for years it had fed his own personal drug addiction, cocaine was the monkey on his back. But like the true professional that he was, he hid it well, most of the time. When I met him he had just come out of a long relationship with a tough, no-nonsense Scottish businesswoman, who took him on as her protégé, grooming him from a young man from the ghetto to what he was when I met him.

It's hard to say what he really was for, as much as he tried, he never had the ability to sustain concentration on any one thing or person for too long. Wayne was a free spirit that couldn't rest in one place for too long. He had the travel bug for sure and nothing or nobody would stop him from moving on when he felt the urge. His Scottish mentor grounded him as best she could. Being a partner in Bambas, she stayed in the background while he swaggered around front of house enrapturing everyone with his easy-flowing vibrant personality.

The difference between the man I had left behind in Jamaica and this man in Barbados was huge: Both Caribbean, both from the ghetto, but that's where it ended. Wayne was very westernised, even to his taste of music, which was extensive. From modern to traditional jazz, blues, soul, classical, country, rock, reggae, you name it, he had a collection that could fill a house. Whereas Ray, as big as he was in his industry, he was small-minded with his taste of music. They were indeed like chalk and cheese. They looked so different, too. Ray was light-skinned and loved his colour, well-built with a closely cut designer haircut. His choice of clothes had to be Armani, Dolce and Gabbana or Versace. It was a must to have their emblems on show. I guess in that Third World life in Jamaica, it showed the man's worth. His car had to be the biggest and the best, too, nothing small and insignificant for this Jamaican guy. He showed his wealth everywhere for everyone to see, with thick gold chains dangling from his neck, rings and bracelets, he strutted his stuff like a peacock.

How different to Wayne. His style was as relaxed as he was and much more tasteful. Off the beach he would wear cashmere with casual jeans, on his feet would be sandals that he had collected on his travels abroad and his collection of ethnic jewellery may not have been valuable but it was always impressive. The look was completed with his amazing locks. He was a true Rastafarian and valued his hair with his life. Out of the two, Wayne was much more aware of his stature, very confident and very cunning. Ray paled into insignificance in comparison.

I was once again moving onto new territory and thoughts of Ray had disappeared from my mind. I had by this stage switched off all my connections with Jamaica, including my cell phone. Not a good idea. It must have set off alarm bells in Ray's ears.

One evening while practising my skills at serving drinks behind the little bar at our guest house, engrossed in conversation, I took no notice of the new arrivals. It was when he sat down at the table opposite me that my breath was taken away. Ray had arrived.

Our encounter was no different to any scenario when someone wants an end to their relationship. It was upsetting to see him so sad but, needless to say, his behaviour under the circumstances was impeccable. After a private confrontation, during which where he tried his hardest to reel me back in, he kept his dignity and left the following day. It's important for me to say I always try to keep hold of a friendship after the relationship has gone and Ray and I kept in touch for a couple of years, just as friends. I hear through the grapevine that his music industry has reached great heights in Jamaica and abroad, but I had no doubt that it would.

The two weeks in Barbados had flown by and within that time I was Wayne's constant companion. When the time came for me to return to England he suggested that we meet up as he was planning to visit friends in London. 'I'll give you a call when I arrive,' he said as I went to board the plane for home.

Three weeks later he had arrived, sat on my sofa in my living room in the home I had made my castle in Timperley. 'What is it about us?' I asked him, meaning why we were here together.

'I need you and you need me,' was his quick reply. I should have studied those words instead of going into Viv mode, fantasising how it was, instead of the reality of how it really was. I always imagine the man to become something special in my life when, for whatever reason, he cannot be. In actual fact, he was being very straight with me, without flowering up his reply. He did need me. I was his much-needed escape route out of Barbados, where his cocaine addiction was taking a grip again. I needed him to boost my flagging enthusiasm for putting the Toucan on the world stage and making it a force to be reckoned with. He was prepared to support me with that goal and so it was that internal transformation at the Toucan Club took off to new heights. It was from that point that I went into overdrive and threw myself into the alteration's design.

Wayne had discussed living with me for six months of the year, while he had planned to take the opportunity offered to him in Martha's Vineyard in America for four months, taking in their summer period, working for Carly

Simon as front of house in her restaurant. Connections, connections, connections, he certainly had the best of them. The remaining two months would be spent in Barbados during Christmas and New Year when, of course, I would be joining him.

In England, living with me, he needed to establish himself not just as my lover but independently for himself and, in between, spread his wings with his social skills, those skills which were equal to mine. I guess you could say it was called 'team work' and it did work for quite a few years. But nothing lasts forever.

I had held a vision of how I wanted to transform Toucan into a sexual fantasy land since my brothel's final name change, but I had to keep that vision on hold until the right moment. This was that moment. Alone with Paul the builder and various other people, that fantasy vision became a reality. I also invited our regular clients to offer their ideas, as they would be the ones paying for the pleasure. The Toucan website was created and used to spread the word and very quickly my 'gossip page' was inundated with requests. They loved the involvement and before long they had their wish as the design and construction got underway.

Jade, an interior designer making her way in life, subsidised her income by working behind the bar at Toucan three evenings a week. A funky chic with spiked jet black hair and gothic dress, a quirky personality completed her style. There needed to be a dungeon and by the time it was completed it was given its nerve-tingling title 'Death Row'. Jade asked to construct it and her enthusiasm for the job was so evident in her work, proving to me that she didn't mind the feel of the whip herself.

The chosen room was set back at the end of the corridor. Walls were taken down, exposing brick and rough plaster. Chains were hung from the ceiling and walls, a hoist was erected for suspending the cellmate.

Hung from walls were paddles of every size, offering mild to severe spanking, whips, canes and leather belts. An authentic gas mask peered down from the wall. Ball weights and a mouth gag, a leather strapped and buckled chastity corset, thigh-high rubber stiletto spiked boots and a rubber mac. The piece de resistance was a very realistic mock-up electric chair, which took centre stage. This chair sent shivers down the spine of men who had been bad enough to be punished on it.

The cell door was made of iron with a viewing window to watch the punishment being administered. There was, of course, a charge for this, where the voyeur was willing to pay. There were those who gained erections just knowing they were being watched, the erection quickly disappearing with a little administered pain. Proof that pain and pleasure go together.

The Dressing Room was displayed with uniforms, lingerie, a secretary's outfit, evening gowns, baby wear, including a glass display cabinet containing nappies, feeding bottles, dummies, baby bonnets, wigs and make-up, slap for the face for those who wanted to become a woman, costume jewellery, large size stilettos and boots and lots of PVC. We had outfits to suit every occasion. Nurses were the most popular uniform chosen and this included a real stethoscope. Naturally, the medical problems were usually in the nether regions, around cock and balls and this, indeed, was a real sickness, more mental than physical.

The bedrooms were huge, with lots of pillows and cushions piled comfortably on the massive beds. I always stressed to my girls that dressing the bed was very important. 'Illusion is the first of all pleasures' was one of my mottos. The theme rooms included a genuine invalid room with wheelchair access and a bed that could be made higher or lower to suit the needs of clients. These clients were often brought to the club by a friend or relative and quite often by their wife. That gesture proved true love. Why not provide sexual stimulation to the man in your life, after tiring of sex when too much care has taken over from those desires?

I loved the job that became so much more to me than being just the 'Madam of a brothel', and memories come flooding back of how it used to be when these poor souls, desperate for some sexual satisfaction, were hurled from the wheelchair at the bottom of the steep stairs and dragged up them by a strong-armed girl who was always exhausted by the time she lay him on the bed before getting into action.

The reception lounge was wonderful, with its relaxing atmosphere. It was a huge room with three doorways leading into it. There was a doorway at the end of the hallway from the main entrance and another leading from the reception, which was handy for the launderette ladies to delivery fresh towels daily from their base next door. An internal door led from the reception into the girls' changing room, where dressing tables and illuminated mirrors were installed for them to perfect their make-up and seats to relax in while waiting for their paying guests. Leading from the girls' room was the kitchen and restroom. This was planned so that they could arrive incognito from a side entrance off the street, straight into their changing room without being seen. My thoughts were that a man coming for business doesn't want to see his fantasy girl in her daily attire. Fantasy versus Reality, the rules always remained.

The reception very quickly became known as the Club Room as Toucan became recognised as a gentlemen's club, not a brothel. Silly, I know, but in my mind's eye a brothel was Toucan before the refurbishment and a gentlemen's club was the correct title, lifting the image from seediness to a more select feel. My judgment proved to be wrong in some cases. The truth is, men love being 'punters' and creeping into a seedy brothel, collar up and head down to hide their identity, is part of the thrill for some.

The Club Room colours were chosen to relax the mind and body, with subdued lighting to set the mood. A massive plasma screen playing constant porn movies, soft black leather sofas and a long illuminated bar stretched almost the length of the room. A glass wine cabinet for refreshments and alcohol, all freely provided. Along the top of the bar, a huge glass vase filled with fresh flowers and bowls of snacks and fresh fruit. Magazine racks, displaying very readable porn among the daily newspapers, were on hand. Across the room from the sofas a large fish tank and every girl had a name for her favourite fish. Watching fish can be so relaxing, especially after finishing a working day. Toucan's customers were spoiled to the extreme.

Pictures of the girls were constantly updated on the Toucan website and also displayed around the walls of the Club Room. In the original Toucan their pictures were never discreet, displaying many girls naked and in erotic poses. I made a decision that the new Toucan should have a different vision and more tasteful pictures were required. Professional photographers were hired and were on hand at the shortest of notice whenever they heard the call for 'lights, props and camera, a new recruit has joined the team.' Such photography sessions were available for the waiting clientele to watch and often they spent time ogling the girls and suggesting different poses. It was team work that included customer participation and they loved it.

Sex was evident everywhere. There was a glass display stand, packed with sex toys to either buy for home or use in-house. Viagra, poppers, condoms, everything was for sale. Loyalty cards were placed inside display boxes to tick off after each visit. Whenever the card became full a reward of a free half hour session with the girl of their choice would be their prize, everything free except her personal services, of course. Everywhere, there were notices showing the 'extra charges' for sexual services in the room. No excuses for not paying up at the end of their fun time. Music was constantly piped around the rooms and internal phones connected the rooms to the bar so that contact for whatever reason was readily available. It might be trouble with an over-anxious client or the need for another girl for a two-woman experience, or if the receptionist's company was required to watch the action, for which she would receive a tip.

Did this huge operation take some running? Yes, it became an enormous project and responsibility but the rumour that we had reached a time when the Labour Government, with their leader and Prime Minister Tony Blair, had thoughts on relaxing the laws on prostitution encouraged my enthusiasm. Unfortunately, those rumours never came to fruition but at the time we were living in hope.

Chapter 36

Making a Man Feel Like a King

'Rise to the challenge of bringing your dreams to life.
Do not be discouraged by resistance, be nourished by it.
Success is the experience of rising to the level of your true
greatness.'

No-one quibbled about the price they had to pay and I am sure if I had demanded it, they would have paid much more, but I wasn't the type to get my hands on a man's wallet and squeeze it dry. My gentlemen would much rather spend money on a bunch of prostitutes who were honest, than on most wives and girlfriends. And at least they got their money's worth.

A brothel must be many things to many people and for many reasons, and it's obvious what it means for most – a pay-then-play parlour. Clients come because they are needy, it's a supply situation, strictly catering to a demand, and as long as there is such a thing as a male libido there will always be a demand for a brothel. But take my word for it: There were some who used to visit Toucan and didn't want to get laid at all. Others visited because a discreet prostitute was the only person to whom they dared expose their sexual hang-ups and avoid a scandal.

Don't be surprised to learn that there was a high percentage of so-called eligible bachelors who loved to visit Toucan, even though there was so much free fluff around. It wasn't hard to guess when the doorbell rang late in the night why he was visiting. He'd been on a date with a girl, wined and dined her, been turned down and failed to complete the procedure, and with his appetite to lay a woman not dimmed, he phoned his favourite club. For less money than the cost of his evening out, he discharged himself into a prostitute's pussy without any hassle.

The highest percentage of clientele was the married, out-of-town businessman who had recently split up from a relationship, all wanting the exotic and unusual that their woman at home didn't provide. Dead in bed, just lying there on her back waiting for the inevitable penetration. Who would not want to break away from such boring bed activity?

I had discovered that Jewish men were the most frequent and most favourite customer. Having a wonderful sense of humour, they behaved themselves and treated the girls with consideration. Their main focus and appreciation being a well performed blow job, perhaps because their fastidious wives would not stoop to smear their lipstick. When they came to call it was a breath of fresh air because of their appreciative and understanding attitude. It's amazing how a Jew immediately recognises one of their own. There is a certain style and mannerism that distinguishes us from others. Quite often a slight feeling of embarrassment would prevail regarding the situation we had found ourselves in. But it was a temporary blip that quickly moved on to respectful friendship.

Whatever a man is looking for, a good madam should be able to provide. A successful brothel has a plentiful selection of girls on hand to entertain customers. Toucan was an international house of pleasure, full of birds of different feathers. Blondes, brunettes, redheads, Russians, Asians, black and mixed race and South Americans, who were famous for their love of sex and big boobs.

The girls chose professional names for themselves to separate their double life. My girls were required to obey house rules and expected to look immaculate at all times.

These rules were not hard to follow as they were all intelligent working girls who knew they had to dress to impress and show off their best assets, from a seductive and elegant Lycra clinging evening dress plunged to the waist to a dangerously dominant leather basque and thigh-high stiletto boots and everything in between. I trusted their judgement. I in turn set an example of the perfect madam, not to attract too much attention, wearing the lightest of make-up, my hair always shiny clean, and a smart but seductive suit. I tried to make the atmosphere warm through my personality and not through my looks. The personality of a madam is what counts and distinguishes one house of pleasure from another.

If a client had a problem choosing a girl, either through shyness or because they were overwhelmed with the choice, I'd step in and stand near him at the bar, chat him up for a while as I served him a drink, then gently put my hand on his thigh to put him at his ease and quietly say, 'Would you like to make your choice or would you care for me to do it for you?' Either way, he was ready for action and on his way up the stairs to heaven.

An important understanding between myself and my girls – and which gave them confidence in trusting me – was a simple acknowledgement that they paid their rent, so they had priority over the visiting customer. They could reject a man if he seemed too drunk or badly behaved. On the other hand, I never wanted my customers to be referred to as a 'punter'. Forbidden, too, was talking about money, as sometimes the girls could get carried away with the amount of money they were making and compared notes within hearing distance of ears that didn't need to hear their calculating conversation. A cute babe could become money-hungry, rushing men in and out of their bedroom with her brain clicking away like a cash register.

One girl I hired, called Crystal, had a huge appetite for earning. I overheard her tempting a young guy waiting for a vacant room. 'I'll give you a quick blow job in the girls' room.' Of course, she didn't achieve her goal. In fact, she didn't get the opportunity to work at Toucan again as I quietly dismissed her from the premises by calling her into the girls' room for a little chat.

I liked my girls to act like ladies out of their bedrooms and whores when they were in them. Anyway, she should have known a man always prefers more for his money. Did I ever have to handle an irate girl after a dismissal? Yes, but it was part of the package and a toughness naturally came over me, protecting my brothel's reputation before any thought for myself.

A prostitute is excellent at making a man feel like a king, even if he is under-endowed, a lousy lover, or with a face only a mother could love. It's so easy to fake it and let him enjoy what he pays for. You have to be a good actress and give as well as take. If a girl came to me unskilled I would put her in Fay's expert hands. There wasn't an area of a man's body that this woman didn't know how to titillate. Cleanliness is next to Godliness, so it was vital that everyone regularly showered, including sharing a shower after the heat of the moment was over and he had released his sperm over her body or in a condom. Sharing a shower had a double purpose – to keep clean and soaping up and washing down his body so that the pleasure was continued after his load had been shot. Of course, if it was a simple hand job not so much care was needed and a girl then enjoyed freshening up on her own.

As the new Toucan's reputation grew, it became well-known for clients with special needs and my girls were up for the job. As every stroke of fantasy is considered a perversion, we came into contact with them all. Fetishists, masochists, golden shower lovers, who enjoyed the taste of her water and desired nothing more than to be urinated in or on, and a willing worker would be asked to hold her urges for the toilet until he arrived.

John, who was a humble slave, used to pop in after he finished his day job to slip on an apron and with a broom and duster he fannied around naked, except for his precious pinny. He was one of the most faithful slaves. Coming from an aristocratic family who was sent to a famous public school, he was regularly beaten and flogged. As he was cultured and endowed with an upper-class scorn of work, with me he could play his favourite role, that of a submissive slave. With the opportunity to serve the madam of the house he jumped to orders when being told, 'Go and see the madam now, she is furious with you,' and off he would go, trembling on his way for another hour of domination and domestic chores.

Larry used to call every daytime in between his business appointments. He couldn't get through the day without penetrating two or three girls, one after the other without taking time to catch his breath. Strutting around as proud as a peacock, declaring to all that cared to listen, just how many times he had managed to release his sperm. Larry had gained a male following, too, befriending clients, and before they knew it he had them desiring his penis. They would arrive sheepish and wait in the Club Room for him to make his grand entrance, where after time at the bar drinking and chatting he would choose a girl or two to join him in pleasuring his punter. Larry became a trusted friend and a permanent presence at Toucan. He came to every party event and helped to set the atmosphere, while encouraging our party punters to throw all cares to the wind, let loose and join in an orgy or gang bang. His tempting technique never failed and before long everyone was up for trying anything.

Party Time was something else! The anticipation and excitement of the forthcoming event consumed the conversation in the Girls' Room weeks before the day actually arrived. They just loved to party and when one party finished and they left exhausted after a hard day working their body, the Toucan cash queens were eager for the next event.

Most of the girls who attended you could say were my stock in trade and out of a choice of eight to ten girls for each party, I introduced only two or three new faces to the team, preferring to rely on those who could stand the pace and, most importantly, those who loved to party.

Enter Cassandra, professional in every way, from the way she managed each time to present herself with glamour and style in the most seductively erotic outfits, each one selected to emphasise her wonderful body. She was the most mature of all the party girls with an estimated age of early forties. It had to be a guess as she kept her true age strictly under wraps. Her only desire was to prove to everyone she was the best in the business. Her long platinum blonde hair was always immaculately coiffured, her make-up perfectly applied. It amazed me how she managed to keep it in place after having every man at the party take her apart in every position they could possibly get her body into.

The adoration from each man she took on encouraged her to be more adventurous and before long her perfectly siliconed large breasts would be out, her G-string would be off and anything from water sports to taking on as many men in the club room in an exhibition of sex that had everyone mesmerised, allowed her to believe she was the star turn.

My next choice was always Flame, a tall and very slender light-skinned mixed race beauty in her very early twenties. If bodies were given a vote she would win hands down. Her huge breasts stood out against a tiny size six figure, every inch of her genuine. No man or girl could resist nuzzling up in between her cleavage and sucking on her milk-producing nipples, a speciality that she kept producing even many months after giving birth. How those men loved the taste of her milk. She loved to tangle with the girls, too, and eagerly awaited a two-girl booking where she could languorously lay exposing her nakedness, legs adrift and yearning for that special touch to bring her to orgasm. 'It takes a girl to know what another girl craves for.'

Another party girl who wasn't shy of showing her expertise at body-trembling orgasms was Marnie, a bubbly fun-loving blonde, only she had an extra speciality of ejaculating from her pussy nearly as much as men could produce sperm. She soaked the bed with her pussy fluid. How those men loved to watch her squirt!

Phryne was as unusual as the name she chose for herself. A black beauty with a body that rippled with toned muscle, when she entered a room men took notice. She demanded it. Total anal penetration was just one of her specialities but what exceeded that was her ability to swallow a man's penis right up to his balls, his shaft disappearing with great ease slowly into her mouth. It was said she had a sucking power like no other. The only problem with Phryne was that she really wasn't a party-type girl, preferring to stay in the 'Only Two Can Tango Room' rather than step out and mingle. But the fact that men always requested her company at a party kept her on the team. These four helped others to lead the way in making our parties a huge success.

I chose different hostesses to help me behind the bar, welcoming party people as they arrived. The night before a party I was either on my own, rushing after midnight to a supermarket after working hours on reception, then home with the goodies to prep for the following day. If Wayne was in residence he would take control of the catering and I could relax and prepare myself for the onslaught to come.

Deposits were taken weeks in advance as the party guys wanted to guarantee their admittance. By the time the party was due we had a rough idea of how many we would be catering for and that decided just how many girls I would need in attendance. Advertising was done through the website and a large poster was placed on the wall in the Club Room advertising the forthcoming event. These pleasure parties had a theme that were advertised in a fashion no-one could resist.

'Rumble in the Jungle Party', 'Come Get Wet Party', 'Rubber Cult Party' (wear rubber and latex only), 'The Big Bang Party' (play and watch as we bend the laws of physics), 'Doctors and Nurses Ball' (book your appointment in the electric chair, if you dare!), 'Classy Swingers Party' (ladies with their partner or singles welcome) and 'Tokyo Delight Party' (a celebration of all that is sexy, kinky, or just plain beautiful).

There was always a really funny and odd variety of food to arouse my guests, who found the desire to be around the buffet bar as orgasmic as the sex being fed to them. Home-made chilli, where Wayne's culinary skills came into practice and far exceeded mine. There was something about the Caribbean spice mix that got everyone going. Sausages and buns to eat with the chilli was a must. Potato crisps with sour cream and dips of all flavours for the girls to dip their sausages in and munch very temptingly. My mixed salad drizzled with herbs and olive oil was temptingly good but centre stage and pride of place stood the home-baked cherry soufflé, with its mouth-watering consistency, the cherries full and succulent, like eating from a cherry tree.

To finish off this array of edible delights were little fancy foods to get the taste buds going and to wash it down, wine, whisky, brandy, beers and, of course, the much-needed Viagra. The whole presentation was always time-consuming but pleasurable and it went without saying the food and atmosphere alone were worth every penny of the entrance fee. As quoted in the book *The Threepenny Opera* by Berthold Brecht: 'Food comes first, then morals'.

It would be hard for any man to resist the advertising out there in large letters: *SEDUCE AND SEE BEFORE YOUR EYES REAL ACTS OF DESIRE – INDULGE YOURSELF IN GROUP SEX AND LIVE YOUR FANTASY – THE PLACE WHERE ANYTHING GOES.*

Each bedroom had meaningful names: 'The Exhibition Room', 'The Fetish Play Room', 'Only Two Can Tango Room'. The girls were always scantily dressed in costumes to suit the theme but once everyone settled in, naked was the only way to be and our gentlemen, too, apart from a few shy guys who preferred to keep their meat and two veg under wraps while in the Club Room. Perhaps for some it might have been a little daunting watching me viewing their goods in between stashing the cash in a money belt I wore around my waist and below a plunging neckline dress showing masses of cleavage, which drew their attention to more desirable objects.

Sex was openly available in the whole of the building, including the Club Room, and while I served drinks and plates of food I did as voyeurs do and watched as my girls straddled their men on the sofas, jumping up and down on an erect penis while simultaneously sucking off another. The madam of the house watching added to their prowess, while many men preferred to display their erections, hoping the view would be appealing to me.

At a sex party the exhibitionist was always welcome and very popular. There's nothing quite like a surprise, impromptu exhibition and my girls were always on the lookout for a 'show off' who rose to the occasion and had no problem performing before an appreciative audience. There was one particular couple that everyone looked forward to joining us at party time. A sugar daddy past his prime and his lovely girlfriend. His idea of pleasure was to watch her squealing with delight while being humped by every man in the building. Be it on the floor, in the hall, staircase or bedroom it didn't matter. She was such a brilliant performer with amazing stamina who provided an exhibition for free. While her sugar daddy's only role in this spectacle was to follow her around like a panting puppy dog, his tongue dribbling with excitement, a handkerchief at the ready to catch the juice from his dribbling penis. It takes all types to make 'party time' a guaranteed success.

Finally, before the party was through the ever-ready camera came into action as either a girl or hostess was asked to take some erotic shots of the party action so that they could be displayed on the Toucan website, all done with face shots out of view, of course. Hell would have been let loose if that hadn't happened.

Toucan held two parties each month on the same day. The first from 1pm till 5pm and the second from 7pm till midnight, with different girls working each party, the theme being the same for the evening as the day. When everything was done and my well-drained gentlemen had kissed and waved goodbye, 'till the next time' was always their goodbye message.

Chapter 37

Cuba – An Unbroken Spirit

'I'd rather have a day of something wonderful than a lifetime of nothing special.'

While all this entertainment was reaching great heights, I could never have imagined it still was not financially a good time to see my future retirement date. Don't be shocked, it was inevitable. Too many takers, too many bad investments in property and men. Right from the death of Billy my financial decline had started to happen and at the end, as my long-standing male friend told me, 'The only mistake you continue to make is the choice of men in your life...' But did I listen?

With Toucan riding on the crest of a wave and my 60th birthday looming, I was still shelling out shed loads of money to the present man in my life. I had come to know no different but my thoughts were to sell and be dammed I was tiring physically and mentally of keeping control of a business that now was running me, not I running it.

Wayne convinced me otherwise: 'Give it another five years and you will be able to retire in wealth and comfort with me.' He relayed his vision of sitting with his woman on the porch of a beautiful villa in Barbados. I thought that woman was me and so I listened to this man I had become obsessed with and it wasn't long before he convinced me again to make a business investment in an apartment project within a resort complex in Barbados, to be completed by December 2012, just in time for my retirement. I was happy again and I was sure he was right when he said those few words years back that we needed each other.

I discovered that the main thing I needed him for were the escapes from the confines of Toucan with his ability to take me on a magic carpet ride into another world.

He taught me how to fish for salmon in Scotland, he took me on long country hikes up hills and down dales, he taught me how to catch fish and skin them ready to barbecue on the beach in Barbados, he took me to the spas in Bath, he taught me how to meditate in India, he took me to Miami, to the Jewish quarter. While in Miami we stayed on Collins Avenue, South Beach and partied till dawn every night. He took me to Thailand, where we welcomed in the New Year on an island lying on cushions on the powder puff beach drinking from buckets of champagne, watching fire eaters and listening to the music with some great company and then waking on New Year's day in a hammock to rise and hire a motor bike and discover the island. He took me to Dominica to explore the rainforest. He took me to heaven, at my expense.

He was my lover, although a very average one. A very selfish lover who really thought the huge size of his penis was enough to satisfy any woman and that he had little else to do than penetrate you as deep as he could, believing that the moans were of desire.

He lacked imagination and so I found myself having to use my flair for making sex more adventurous. While he lay back, I bestowed my skills of devouring him and giving him oral sex that drove him crazy. Did he return the gesture? No. It seems it's forbidden within the Rasta religion to go down on a woman and he never broke that rule. What was I thinking, to continue with a lover that only loved himself? Only a shrink could figure it out but for me at the time the adventure he gave me out of bed outweighed the adventure between the sheets.

Approaching my 60th birthday, Cuba was beckoning and I couldn't wait. I didn't know it then but it was our final escape together. The decay in our relationship was already evident but I brushed those thoughts aside and looked forward to flying over to Barbados and spending a week there before a short flight to the Caribbean island of Cuba. A very different adventure there was to begin.

Maybe Wayne had never loved me at all and I was just a stepping stone until he moved on in the direction that had been planned for many years.

He had returned from America after spending the summer working again at Martha's Vineyard. On his return he declared he was done with America. I have never been a possessive lover and when away the mice can play, as long as no-one gets hurt along the way. He used to be amazed at my lack of interest regarding his life when away from me but truly I had no interest. My whole life had become Toucan, with the occasional choice of a young stud to rumble in the sheets with. It didn't take him long before he got what was on his mind off his chest.

Curled up on the sofa together while he played with my hair and gently stroked my face and neck, I was purring like a contented kitten. And then it came, the revelation that shook my world. 'I am 45 years old and need a child, Vivien,' he said.

The caring nurturing Aquarian nature came out in me and I immediately sat up, spread my legs across his knees, looked straight into his eyes and asked what he was feeling. Of course, it was much too late for me to conceive and he knew all the reasons why I was childless, but he didn't want a mixed race child anyway from anyone. It had to be pure black blood and not only that, it had to be the best blood and that required a black girl with good genes. But that was all taken care of.

It seems he had chosen the girl to have his child many

years before, when she was still a young schoolgirl, after visiting East Africa and discovering her hidden away in a tin hut in the Tanzanian ghetto. There was more to his tale. He had been subsidising her through school for many years to get her to the point where she was ready for a child. He continued with his story: he only wanted to fertilise his sperm in her vagina and after she conceived, this designer baby would be kept in Africa, where we would visit on a regular basis.

I was unsure of my hearing. Had he really believed I could be involved in this farce? No, not me, not ever! And so we continued with the planned Cuba trip without a mention of it again and I buried all my thoughts of his baby plans deep away inside me and continued burying my head in the sand, too.

We boarded the plane to take us to Cuba after a short visit to Barbados. I had joined him there after delegating the running of Toucan while I was away, once again leaving with a wish from everyone to have a good vacation. While joining Wayne in Barbados, I took the opportunity of checking over the building site where eventually my apartment would be built. There was no sign of anything happening, except for a cordoning off and pegging of the land, but I had no worries.

The old Havana is where we based ourselves and found a little house among the cobbled streets with a young friendly family that were pleased to welcome us into their humble home and where we would dine in their kitchen most days, getting to know them and their culture and view on life in Cuba. Everyone seemed happy to live within the confines of this communist country with little desire to leave it, even if they could.

We hired two horses and jumped on the back of these old boys, travelling through the towns and streets until we reached the beautiful city of Trinidad. It was like entering a time warp, the colonial architecture a treasure trove of ancient wonder. Everything was unchanged from the days when it was a major centre for sugar and slaves 200 years before and after finding another local house to rest in, we changed from horseback to bicycles and rode the streets passing the crumbling buildings on our way. Classic American sedan cars, dating back to the 1950s, were the only mechanical car transport. The cobbled streets and terracotta roof-topped pastel coloured houses had to be explored. A time warp it surely was.

Later through the day we reached the Plaza San Francisco Church and stopped to enter its idyllic atmosphere. Then, when light was turning into night, we found the sunset in Trinidad breathtaking. Valadero was Cuba's top beach destination, with its soft sands lapped by the waters of the Kawama Channel. Al Capone, the American celebrity gangster, discovered it in the 1920s. I sipped mojitos in the bars after baking myself on the beach, while Wayne spent time walking and talking in his broken Spanish to the locals. Here we rented scooters to see more of this stunning spot, where the caves and forest added to its magical allure.

Havana was a city trapped in time with faded glamour. Walking the boardwalk along the ocean and visiting the Cathedral de San Cristobel in the daytime and in the evening listening and dancing to the salsa music in the open air bazaars with parties that lasted all through the night.

The old Havana was what took my breath away the most. Surely, it has to be one of the most atmospheric places in the world. The people, the buildings, the music, the history. The La Casa Del Son is a beautiful place where we took up private dance lessons. It was a must to learn the salsa, to join in the fun of the evening, dancing with the local people in the open air squares. The Tropicano nightclub was truly fabulous. It made you feel like you had transcended back into the Cuba of the 1950s, listening and watching the original artistes that put salsa music on the world map.

Before we left for home we had to visit Che Guevara's home and see how he lived and had left it before he died. Seeing his handsomeness looking down on me from huge posters, he was a man after my own heart, a rebel with a cause. I was in love with this man that became a legend.

Boarding the plane back to Barbados and by the time I had left for home, I had realised in all the time we had spent in Cuba, sharing the experience of this amazing Caribbean island our bodies had hardly touched.

Chapter 38

Harsh Measures

'What counts is not necessarily the size of the dog in the fight – it's the size of the fight in the dog.' – Dwight D. Eisenhower

February 2009 Manchester was stricken, as the rest of the country, by heavy snowfall. There was a sharp frost in the air, which hit my face as soon as I stepped off the plane from Barbados after two months away living in a completely different world.

I have always had the ability to store thoughts of anything past in a compartment in my head until I want to bring it out and remember it, and I immediately snapped back into thoughts of Toucan. After collecting my luggage from the arrivals terminal, my first thought was to phone my club and see how the land lay. The news was good, everything was hunky dory without disasters of any kind. Well, nothing too bad that I couldn't put right immediately. Larry, who had virtually lived in the club, had been allocated to bank the takings and had done his job. How trusting was I? How honest was he?

Settling in at home, I received a phone call from a friend of Wayne. Goosey needed to see me as soon as possible and so I suggested he came for dinner. While we sat around the dining table drinking wine he put it to me. 'Has Wayne given you any money to pass to me?' Not quite understanding what he meant, I asked him to repeat the question. My negative reply didn't please him. His face turned from brown to red and with eyes glaring he said,

'You know he is abusing your relationship and has no respect for you at all?' I looked at him in amazement, what abuse? 'Catch your breath,' was his reply.

His African baby bank had given birth in December and while he was celebrating my birthday with me in Cuba he had phoned Goosey and asked him to Western Union money to her, with an understanding that on my return from Barbados I would repay him.

Within a day, all his possessions, everything, was bin bagged with the help of two of my closest girls and delivered to a charity shop dealing with Third World countries. I figured eventually if he searched hard and long enough, he might find them somewhere in Africa, eventually. At the same time I also allocated them to blow him up on a world-famous networking site as I didn't use it myself. Us women have to stick together and warning signs needed to be registered with every woman who fell under his spell. 'Hell hath no fury like a woman scorned'.

This message was on the social networking site without being spotted by him for a few weeks, the reason being he had boarded a plane from Barbados to Tanzania immediately after I had left for the UK. While there, in the back of beyond, he didn't have internet access. When he did there was a very troubled man on the other end of the phone.

He had no shame, at first denying his baby, then breaking down and asking me not to end the relationship. 'I love you Viv.' No woman likes to hear a man beg unless it is part of a sex game.

His pleading cut no ice with me and there was no possibility of misinterpreting my response by ending the relationship completely, a cut and dried situation.

When the going gets tough, the tough get going. This knock was a drop in the ocean to others I had felt before and really, if you focus on the good parts, and there were many, then the bad parts don't feel so bad. Some weeks later, with instructions to my receptionists to ignore his calls, I had changed all my personal phone numbers and had moved on.

Never being a girl to sit and mope, I dusted myself down and took time to be pleasured by an array of suitable studs. This man was out of my head, my body and brain. We had a big party ahead to arrange and look forward to. The date was set for May 11 (2009) and I needed to be back on form for it. The party that had been long-awaited by my girls and guys never materialised. The Toucan Club was raided by the police on May 9, two days before the party.

In the chaos that followed, with 20 cops with sniffer dogs and cameras ready to photograph evidence, one policeman noticed the poster glaring down from the Club Room wall advertising the forthcoming party event and declared his obvious disappointment that they had got their timing wrong. If they had held back for two days they would have come across more than they had bargained for.

The proceedings that followed took two years to conclude in court, but before that day in August 2011 I had a heavy task on hand.

My immediate reaction when they came to arrest me was, why now? Meaning why now 25 years after 467 Chorley Road, Swinton, opened its doors as a brothel, with the police station not five minutes down the road and with full co-operation from the local constabulary, while at the same time accepting our police charity donations year after year. Why after all that time?

There was no answer to my question. I was handcuffed along with my girls and also clients sitting and waiting for a service. Four guys that were getting their rocks off in the bedrooms upstairs were taken out of action with the appearance of cops with dogs at their bedroom door: A young cocky guy who gave them plenty of lip, a sheepish grey-haired first-timer, a regular client who consoled me while trying to fasten his flies as he was being led away, and a regular rabbi, God bless him. Talk about being caught with your pants down!

I had to pass my house keys over, too, and I was warned if I didn't they would break my front door down. All the money was taken from the business safe, which was extremely unfortunate as I had transferred all my money and valuables from my home, just in case I had an unwelcome visit from Wayne. Because I didn't trust that situation, a whole heap of money and all my jewellery was transferred into police funds.

I had a policy that had to be adhered to, being the fair but firm madam that I was. No drugs, no illegal immigrants and no underage girls. I ran a clean house.

My first thought was that Wayne had set me up in payment for my actions towards him. Would he have gone that far to destroy me and my business? No, I didn't believe it, although many were pointing their finger in that direction. As time went by and my appearance after appearance in court progressed, the mystery was solved. A new chief constable, who wanted to gain more stripes on his shoulder, raided Toucan. But how was he and all his men going to prove they had no knowledge it was there? They would not have been able to and I proceeded to countersue and take 41 cops to court with an 'abuse of process' charge.

Larry had missed the raid by 30 minutes. He was ringing the doorbell as we were being taken away down the road, his trusted friendship continuing well after Toucan's doors were closed. I had been interrogated for hours like a murderer. Was I a money launderer? Did I have a partner? How many bank accounts did I have? Question after question. My answers to all questions: 'No comment.' Not that I was hiding anything but I had always been taught it was a standard necessary answer to give until my solicitor arrived to rescue me. When I was eventually released on police bail and sent into the cold midnight air, my loyal girls were waiting there for me. We had been locked up in police cells for nine hours.

In the weeks and months that followed, business after business offer came my way. So many people over the years had dreamed of the chance to be in business with me and they thought this was their opportunity. From syndicates to single businessmen, all looking for their main chance, it seems everyone was grieving the loss of Toucan. It was like a death in the family for all my many loyal customers and my girls were finding it hard to settle anywhere else. Missing our little family unit, they waited with baited breath for the resurrection of Toucan 2. That wish never came to life. The end of Toucan was the end of my life in the sex industry, it was time to go and retire gracefully, even though my retirement was brought forward without the financial security a few more years would have given me.

I focused my time on winning my court case and nearly every waking moment consisted of working towards that goal. Those bastards were not going to get away with it and they were certainly not going to beat me. They would regret entering Toucan that day. My solicitor constantly kept reminding me to take it easy. 'Keep a lid on it Vivien.' What did she mean? How could I do that? I had been robbed and wronged. Instead, I demanded to see the pocket notebooks of all the visits the police had made over the years, a challenge for them indeed, which would nicely add to their working day. I was determined to show them I was up for the fight and they had chosen the wrong girl if they thought they would have an easy time getting a guilty verdict.

For me the loss of 467 Chorley Road was felt very deeply. It wasn't just the loss of income, although that was major, it was the loss of a massive part of my life. I had lost my baby and I missed it dreadfully.

Six months down the line and with Christmas approaching and the courts closing down until the New Year, I decided to take the stress away by planning a trip back to Barbados and while there checking once again on the progress of my apartment.

Within those six months Craig had entered my life. He had actually made me aware he existed while the last party event was in full swing by phoning, asking my hostess if he could speak to me. When I took his call, he explained that he had left the party a little time before having overheard a conversation between two of my girls, discussing their dissatisfaction with the amount of money they would be receiving for the amount of bodies they had to pleasure. I was grateful for his information and asked for his cell phone number. The party was still rocking and I didn't care then to take my attention away from it. It will be no surprise to learn that once phoning him and gaining his information regarding just what he heard and the circumstances he had heard it in, the two culprits were never allowed to work at Toucan again. They had broken a very important rule: don't discuss money issues in the company of clients. Never!

After the raid, Craig texted me. It seemed he had called for some girly fun and found to his dismay we had left the premises. When I explained the circumstances, he offered his help. After he had further investigated my arrest his comment, 'I'm checking on the checkers,' aroused my curiosity. Who was this man?

I took the chance to invite him to tell me more about himself and how he managed to gain information about me. I was not alone when he called. Lydia, who I was intending to spend time with in Barbados, had called to discuss our plans over lunch. I opened the door to this guy I had never seen before. It seems he had been a regular visitor to Toucan but would never have stood out in the crowd, with quite insignificant looks, pale skin, red hair and average body, nothing to turn your attention to. His questions made me realise immediately that he was a man with an important position. I was right with my assumption, as he declared quite casually, 'I work for SOCA.' Not knowing what it meant, he explained, Serious Organised Crime Agency and from that little information I gathered he had strings he could pull.

His advice leading up to my court case helped me gain what I needed to hopefully win my case, so I thought. But, unfortunately, his mind was set on other things as his lust for me grew with every meeting, to such an extent that he was creeping around everywhere in my daily life, kissing me with soppy kisses at any opportunity. But like a true professional I put up with it. I needed his advice whenever a situation arose and with his help I was instructing my solicitor and barrister in the way to run my case.

Christmas 2009 was fast approaching and nothing was due to happen in court till the spring of 2010 and so Lydia and I met up with others we knew and with the same plan and took off on that big bird heading once again for Barbados for some well-deserved rest and relaxation. Well, that was the plan.

Chapter 39

Bajan Breeze and Coconut Trees

'To whip across the coral reef in Barbados where the blue sea turns to green.'

We had some fun, Lydia and I on that island I adored. She was a girl after my own heart, eager to accept any party invitation and capable of getting where gas couldn't. She was also free of any inhibitions, as she joined me sunning herself in the nude, which could only be done around the poolside of the villa, Barbados unfortunately having strict rules about showing too much flesh on the beach.

I had made a wise choice when selecting the Sands Villa in Holetown, St James. Ten minutes from all the night time action in 1st and 2nd Street with some of the best beaches on the coast. The position was idyllic, being a distance from the main road. It was secluded and away from preying eyes and we were pleasantly pleased with its quite luxurious decoration.

During the lazy, hazy days we drove in our hired car or jumped on a reggae bus with music blasting in our ears to rediscover our favourite beaches. Mullins Bay was the closest to our rented villa and most times not a wise choice as the tide would engulf the beach, wrecking beach beds and all that lay on them.

We chose instead to travel to Crane Beach on the south east coast, which had great breakers for surfing and breathtaking views alongside its sandy beach, with the blue waters, cliffs and coconut trees. I loved the seclusion of Ju

Ju's on the west coast, a little beach rum shop that feeds you the best grilled fish and fries ever.

We would change our style a little and lay out on Sandy Lane Beach, where we mingled among famous celebrities sipping cocktails on the terrace at sundown. Totally different was Bathsheba, riding the waves with Bajan and holiday surfers, this picturesque little fishing village was where we would end up drinking Banks beer at Smokey's and enjoying the local chat around the bar.

Then finally Bottom Bay, protected by jagged cliffs on an isolated beach lined with coconut palms, it had a true Robinson Crusoe feel to it and where I would take a picnic and bathe in the crystal waters. It was my chosen place to take a lover. Bottom Bay was by far my favourite and also the closest beach to the apartment resort I had invested in. Simply heaven!

One thing is for sure. After spending nearly every waking moment in the company of businessmen, eligible or not, sorting out their sexual problems, listening to their perversions and seeing every cranny of their bodies, erect or not, I needed different company.

It wasn't long into the first week before I met up with a guy called Henry, who was running a string of Russian prostitutes in Sandy Lane Hotel. He had the run of the place and George, the manager, under his spell. Henry knew about my connections to the industry through Wayne's loose lips. Why do some people find the need to discuss other people's business without permission? But that indiscretion soon passed to the back of my mind as more important things took over.

Henry wined and dined me at the hotel, ordering champagne with the click of his fingers, and I was prepared to listen to his sales pitch. Sandy Lane is expensive so I took advantage of evenings spent in his company, while pretending to show interest in helping control his harem of Russian beauties that were arriving weekly at the airport terminal. These poor souls didn't have a clue who he was and, most importantly, if he could protect them. On studying the man, I didn't fancy their chances and so I spent two weeks of my vacation playing mother hen. At some meetings Lydia would assist me and, like a true professional, she acted as my secretary, pretending to take notes that I would never refer to. We used the situation and lasted out until we got fed up with his big talk and bullshit and it wasn't long before we moved on to play elsewhere.

Walking the beaches in my itsy bitsy bikini, my body held up to the best of them 20 years younger. I don't brag, it was those good genes again. Shaun, a cute Bajan guy, caught my eye for a while and so I indulged in giving him what he loved to do the most, suck and tongue my cherry while I screamed with delight. He could spend a whole heap of time indulging in the art of cunnilingus, only occasionally coming up for air. Apart from penetration there is no better pleasure than having your cherry sucked and nibbled. Shaun knew his stuff.

It only took a day before Wayne found out I was on the island. News travels fast in Barbados and he had received confirmation of where I was living from Henry and so kept popping up the hill to the villa to visit and check on me, usually finding me naked by the pool. How we ended up even talking again now amazes me but life is too short to bare malice. Or maybe it was the good disposition that everyone seemed to think I possessed that had risen to the surface again. When I looked at him I wondered what I had ever seen in him and I was thankful for the feeling.

Lydia left the island in early February after joining me in celebrating my birthday. I had no desire to return to the UK just yet. There was nothing to rush back for and I was still in holiday mood. It only took a day before I gained another interest. Lying on a remote beach, enjoying the tranquillity, Johnnie entered my life. He was coming out of the ocean like James Bond in Speedos, bronzed and muscled with a hairy chest I would have loved to nuzzle into. While exercising on the beach, he spotted me, came over for a chat and before long we were sipping brandies on ice and enjoying the light conversation.

I guess it was the body massage rubbed in with sun tan oil that did the trick and encouraged me to meet up with him on 2nd Street that evening and there I discovered that Johnnie was a lover of the arts. Ballet and dance and opera were his passion. An American opera lover, I was impressed and after two weeks of constant experimental sex, we agreed to keep in touch as he left for his flight back to Boston. His offer of joining him on a cruise taking in Miami and the Bahamas I, of course, accepted, especially as it was at his expense, which made a very welcome change. Johnnie had been in the haulage business and had recently retired and was intending to make the most of his retirement years travelling and discovering the world outside of America. I had decided I would certainly help him a little along the way with that desire. After he had said his goodbyes and left the island it wasn't long before I decided to do the same and return home and back to the real world.

February in the UK is the only month that can pass by without a full moon. That's a fact. It is also a fact that it has to be the worst month in the calendar. New Year celebrations are by now a distant memory and we search for something, anything, to lift our spirits. For most it's Valentine's Day when Cupid fires his bow. But for me there were no bows heading in my direction, not near enough to reach me, anyway.

Nothing new was happening when I eventually returned home from Barbados. I usually have a great knack of being able to adjust from one environment to another at the drop of a hat, but now I was restless, with no business to keep me occupied except the business of making sure I kept myself out of prison. I had at last a date for my court appearance. The summing up and verdict was set for the beginning of August and here I was, stuck in the gloom of February, with little but lawyers' meetings to keep my spirits up. Nothing except for Johnnie and his constant sweet messages in emails that kept our sparkle alive.

Craig was still in the picture in more ways than one. He had kept communication going while I was holidaying in Barbados, not in a good way, though. Finding an email message from him with an attachment, I opened it and there he was in full glory, displaying his pink skinned penis dangling down to his knee caps, not a pretty sight. But, unfortunately, I needed him and he played on that need and so I tried hard to swallow my disgust when he arrived at my door, with an excuse of coming with more advice; being in SOCA he surely could give it. One thing was for sure. He would never get his wish of releasing his sperm, in or out of my body, never in a million years.

Johnnie's invitation to take a cruise out of Miami to the Bahamas was hugely tempting and as he whet my appetite with colourful descriptions of the fun we would have together, it was easy for me to yield to the temptation. The thought of being held close upon his hairy, muscular chest and wrapped within his powerful arms had me working Mr Rabbit in overdrive. In between messages of his desire to taste my body again, were sweet poems and verse. He certainly knew how to woo a woman.

He was equally anxious to see me as soon as possible and a date was set in June. When the day arrived I easily left all my troubles behind and boarded a plane to head towards Miami and Mr Wonderful.

Johnnie had some pedigree, an Italian American brought up in the Bronx, where the Italian and Jewish mafia were kicking ass (his words). Making it big in haulage, I guess you could say he was quite a catch. Arriving early, I booked into the airport hotel to freshen up and have some rest before meeting him. I was as excited as a girl on her first date.

When he came towards me in the arrivals lounge he was sweaty and stressed. I had taken the initiative of keeping my room on for him to shower but he refused the offer and wanted to make his way to the ship as it had already docked. OK, no problem.

The *Norwegian Sky* was huge, for sure, but nothing compared to the size and elegance of the *QE2*. Still, what would compare to the magnificence of her? It seems he had travelled many times with this company and had a special invite on board and after an introduction buffet we were shown to a tiny cabin below deck. This was surely not the *QE2*. He did his best to spoil me in bed and out of it. Everything was all-inclusive and I was sailing free so I made the best of the time on board.

There was certainly no glamour. Everyone was walking around with bright yellow badges with their names displayed for all to see, like they were on a school trip. Not my style at all.

Thankfully, the bars were free, so I spent as much time as possible knocking back rum and Coke, a taste he enjoyed too. We got tipsy together often and I discovered he might have a drink problem, although he denied it. He woke each morning needing a drink before breakfast, so you could say he was well on his way to it. We danced the hours away in the evening and the rest was sex, sex and more sex, in between his exercise routine of running the length of the deck back and forth for hours. After that, all he wanted to do was sit somewhere with me away from the rest, sampling the wine and any other alcoholic drink he could get his hands on. I was glad to get my feet on dry land. Thank God for Miami!

We arrived at our hotel on South Beach but once again it was second rate compared with what I had been used to. He would get up at the crack of dawn, go down for breakfast and bring me what was on offer on a tray and proceed to feed me in bed. Sex was necessary for him as often as possible and a good tip was needed for the chambermaid who had to face a bed wreck every day. The poor woman would have to strip the sheets and clean the bathroom. He had to share a shower with me and have sex in there, too.

Not that I was complaining. The sex was good and he loved to experiment. Well, he had a very willing partner. We dined out each evening but unlike me he didn't mix with others well. He hated my attention to other guests, which caused him to fret and on occasion lose his temper, sulking in his bed until I arrived back there to join him, for more sex! I realised he was getting his sexual experience through my body. He was a man who obviously had lived his life with women who were not as adventurous as I and he took every opportunity of drawing that adventure out of me. It wasn't hard as I enjoyed playing the teacher and took control of his body completely. In sex he became submissive and did as I asked. He would get as dirty as I wished him to be and vice versa but, unfortunately, all his complexes got in the way of having enjoyment any other way but in the bedroom.

We eventually came to the end of our holiday with our friendship intact, just. In return for his generosity – after all, I didn't have to put my hand in my pocket for anything, an experience I hadn't had for quite some time – I invited him to spend time with me in England, a country he had never visited.

Within weeks Johnnie had arrived and I made sure that he returned home with fond feelings for my country: London, Scotland, Wales and, of course, the wonderful county I live in, Cheshire. Surrounded with world-famous footballers, maybe, but it's the countryside around me that I love and I now have the freedom to enjoy walking in it. It is only now that I can truly appreciate its beauty. I see the world differently now. I am at last free.

Johnnie turned out to be suffering with some form of compulsive disorder, something I hadn't noticed before. Everything had to have a place and there was a place for everything. Before time he was running my home and before time he was gone without an invitation to return.

Chapter 40

Free at Last

'The greatest revenge is to accomplish what others say you cannot do.'

It was the beginning of July and just six weeks to go before my court appearance and I was relishing the thought. Apart from my brief respite with Johnnie, I had been constantly working towards attaining the perfect solution, that being the judge throwing the case out of court as an abuse of process.

Nothing was going to distract me from spending time focused on gaining the perfect result, insisting on attending court dates even though I was not ordered to. I had to make sure that the judge noticed my attention to detail and my keenness to be there at any opportunity. I also made sure my barrister sympathised and was doing all he could to win my case. Forty-one policemen that knew me needed to answer to why, after all those years, they raided Toucan that day. The whole thing consumed my every moment. I was focused and very bitter.

How could it be that a legally run brothel, although in law be deemed illegal, be finished, ended, over, kaput! I was devastated and the only thing that kept me going was having my day in court. The judge had to listen to me.

Striving for more help in promoting my dilemma, I contacted Max Clifford, the renowned publicist. He didn't reply to my call. I thought of all the men I had known, pillars of society present and past who had been charged with sexual offences, which had been regarded all those decades ago as not unusual activities, but now were being accused and convicted of a crime.

I thought of my many years in the sex industry, mothering my girls and caring for my clients. I loved the industry I had been in. It helped to bring happiness to many men and protection and care for my girls. It was harmless and so very necessary. I thought of Her Majesty's taxman that had been taking their quarter of money, legalising the industry even more. They knew exactly what the business entailed. Should they be hauled up in front of a judge for pimping?

I detached myself from all other thoughts with great help from my friends around me. People who had known of my industry, well-connected and successful in their own right, they were inspired by my honesty and boldness.

Finally, the day I had been waiting for arrived and I made my way to the city courtroom alone. Dressed appropriately for the occasion in a black suit and white blouse, with my hair tied neatly back off my face, and the lightest of make-up. Walking up the court steps, noticing the press interest with cameras at the ready, waiting for the verdict, I was greeted by my barrister, who relayed the news. The judge, while looking over my case, had made a decision not to give me a custodial sentence, as things stood, but if his verdict went against me and I lost the abuse of process case, that decision might change. Added to that, the prosecution had put a deal on the table that morning. Here was the deal. Drop my case against the police and they would return all my assets except my money. This meant my jewellery would be safe and they would not be interested in attaining my property here or abroad. Very decent of them!

Sat in the courtroom cafe, solicitor and barrister either side of me, deliberating my decision while they pressed for me to take the offer, a woman approached our table and politely asked if we would like a top-up of coffee. Looking up I recognised the smiling face, as she had recognised me too. 'How are you Viv? It's Anita,' she said, and with that gave me the biggest hug.

It was Anita, who all those years ago, while we were sat opposite each other on the sofa thinking of a name to christen my brothel, christened it Toucan. Now she was working in the court cafe and serving lunch to the judges. 'Keep your head down when you walk outside. There is a lot of press interest,' she said. And so I took everyone's advice and did as my barrister suggested and succumbed to the prosecution's request. But was I pleased with the outcome? No. I felt unfulfilled and a failure. But I didn't go to prison and I could have done. We cannot stop the waves but we can learn to surf.

Judge Jefferies, on his deliberation, called me out from behind the glass screen in the dock and directed me to sit close to him while the charge was read. My feeling was he felt no need for me to be there with two court officers either side and wanted me in a more natural environment. That pleased me. Asking if I had anything to say and with my mother's words ringing in my ears, 'Sparkle Vivien,' I rose and presented him with my thoughts of how prostitution needed to be legalised within delegated 'red light' areas in brothels that, like my own, took great interest in the welfare of clients and girls.

After all, Scotland was not a long distance away and it was legal there. England needed to follow in its footsteps, take prostitution off the streets and put it where it belongs: in safe houses. The courtrooms would be less busy with a reduction of rape charges as those that needed sexual gratification could step into brothels legally.

Judge Jefferies sat intently, looking at me straight in the eye. 'I understand all you have said to me and I am sure many people share your beliefs. But what is written here in front of me and the way the law stands at this moment, you are guilty of running a brothel that is illegal.' And with that, he handed me a gentle four-month suspended sentence with no fine. 'It would not please me to see you here again in front of me,' were his final words. I knew what he meant. He wished me to move on with my life.

Things sometimes are just not fair. There's a saying: 'Take risks. If you win you will be happy, if you lose you will be wise.'

FOOTNOTE: Autumn 2014. At their conference in Glasgow the Liberal Democrats overwhelmingly reaffirmed their call to decriminalise prostitution within designated brothels. They are leading the way on this important issue. Other parties now need to take note.

Chapter 41

Stepping into the Future with a Blast from the Past

'After all these years, I am still involved in the process of self-discovery.

It's better to explore life and make mistakes than to play it safe.

Mistakes are part of the dues one pays for a full life.' – Sophia Loren

Being a lover of quotes that inspire me, it seems the great actress and beauty Sophia Loren is a girl after my own heart.

Although the court judgement wasn't the best result it proved to be the turning point in life that I needed. At the age of 62 I was indeed free from the restraints of an industry that had consumed me mentally and physically. Until my forced retirement I hadn't realised just how much but there were still a few loose ends that needed to be tied up, the first on the list being my assets. The only one that I hoped would elevate me back into being financially safe again was my investment in Barbados.

Daniel from Harlequin Properties wasn't playing ball with me when I discovered that the project had come to a standstill. Every excuse under the sun was given for its delay but news travels fast, certainly from Barbados, and the news there was not good. I detected a sniff of a scam in the air and sought advice from a solicitor.

Perhaps I had chosen the wrong career, as I seemed to be spending most of my time studying law. The lack of response convinced me my gut feeling was right – the Harlequin project was indeed a dead duck. I had a battle on my hands once again. When you pay out a vast amount as a deposit and the conditions of the contract have not come to fruition, you expect that deposit back. I am still waiting. I guess you must know me well enough by now to appreciate I have tried every which way to get my hands on the money that would help secure my future and give me the freedom not to seek a man to take care of me financially. Looking back through my life, I have never chosen that road out of business hours, always preferring the freedom that earning your own money brings.

This wasn't the time to sit and brood and think about what I had previously but what I could do with what I had now. My first move was to open my own website, my thoughts being that with all the knowledge I had collected over the years there wasn't a thing I didn't know about the art of sex in all its different forms. This was knowledge I intended to share. All my new prospective clients had to do was click the mouse to pay and become a member, giving them access to me personally.

My website took off to such a great extent that my computer was attached to me like an umbilical cord. There was not a moment in the day when I wasn't blogging away to all my members. That wasn't enough, as I progressed to pick out just a few of my titillating personal sexual experiences and audio them for people to hear my voice. I had to stop there though, as no money in the world could have made me take any steps further. Many requests, some desperate to speak to me personally, came in daily but knowing I would have to transcend into fantasy land, bringing men to an orgasm, the thought sent me cold.

I guess the image of me in full view had them champing at the bit, as I have to profess this chick looks amazing for her age. It's all down to those genes again and as the compliments were coming in as fast as their membership payment I was content for a while. But it didn't last for very long. I threw the towel in and had to confess to myself that this was just not the occupation for a gal hitting mid-60s. Not for this gal anyway.

The easiest thing to be in the world is yourself; the most difficult thing to be is what other people want you to be. I couldn't put myself back into the past and I couldn't change back to that person that I was then. I was this person now, a happier person, although poorer in monetary terms, wealthy in spirit and I discovered there were no truer words said than those of Oscar Wilde: *'Taking joy in life is a woman's best cosmetic'*. The simplest things in life make me happy and I wake looking forward to the day, without stress, without need of sexual stimulation. I have become asexual again, just for the moment. I have no need for a lover in my life, I am free from the hassle of those desires. I have a wish to learn more about my religion and discovering all there is to know about being a good Jew.

Pursuing this desire of spiritual education, I was introduced to a rabbi who invited me to his home to take part in the Friday night Sabbath dinner, which was an education in itself. Welcomed warmly by his wife and nine children, I couldn't catch my breath as each one kept appearing to introduce themselves to me. It seemed to me that the lady of the house had spent most of her time in the bedroom creating these gorgeous children, who were polite and helpful. It was a happy family atmosphere and as I joined the dinner table with other guests while prayers were being said, my deepest wish was to understand the ritual that lay before me.

Aware of my ignorance, the rabbi took me under his wing and, along with his sweet wife, explained that this was the time for a transition from everyday life to a more spiritual one. The table was set with a white tablecloth, candles, wine and what I learnt to be challah bread, all there to start the religious rituals. There was mouth-watering gefilte fish, chopped and boiled, chicken soup, glazed chicken and potatoes, roast asparagus and a delicious mousse cake. How generous this family were to welcome guests to join them at their table and I watched and learned as they blessed the candles, blessed the wine, blessed the children and blessed the bread. When I made my excuses to leave later that evening – although I was invited to stay till the Sabbath end – I departed fulfilled in stomach and mind.

A few days later and still filled with the happy memory of the occasion, I explained the experience of the evening to a friend who knew the family well. The story goes that my spiritual rabbi had been spirited off, arrested in a brothel raid some months before our meeting. It seems when God created 'man' he underestimated his ability.

My last attempt at finding 'love' came in the autumn of 2012. I had met an Italian/Israeli Jew called Marchello. He was different and, as you know, I love different. Born in the city of love, a Venetian sculptor, a craft he had inherited, he was also a very successful businessman, owning a large real estate company in Tel Aviv. And so I took up his offer and travelled to the Jewish homeland, Israel.

There was no mistaking his large muscular stature as I took an anxious look around after tumbling into the arrivals lounge, laden with bags. How many items does a girl need on a four-day holiday?

Rushing forward, his face hidden behind the largest pair of Aviator sunglasses, he gallantly lightened my load, at the same time handing me a huge bouquet of flowers, while waiting for us outside was an enormous American Jeep. Was everything going to be large in his life?

There was no time to discover, as he whisked me away

at full speed to refresh myself at his apartment, which was designed and furnished to perfection and, of course, sumptuously huge. This guy certainly had lots of style and knew how to treat a lady. I was impressed.

After a hasty shower and a moment to titivate myself, he swept me off for an al fresco meal. His style was certainly different, if not a little strange, as he caught the attention of the head waiter and reserved and paid for the tables either side of us so no-one would disrupt his attention to me.

I slept like a baby that evening, totally exhausted from the journey and the alarming high intensity of the security at both airports. It seems entering Israel is not for the fainthearted: interrogation after interrogation as to who, why, what I was, eventually to pass through the immigration controls somewhat brow beaten and exhausted.

Night had turned into day and within the silky sheets of his enormous bed our bodies hadn't touched. There was no-one there to cuddle and caress me when I woke the following morning. He was up and out, packing the cases into the car. No worry, I thought, I had another three nights to enjoy him.

His wish was for me to experience floating in the Dead Sea's salty waters, a holistic experience that he was sure I would enjoy. A five-star spa hotel had been booked for the occasion and while sunning myself on the beach after a professional masseuse had rubbed a whole heap of Dead Sea mud on my body, I lay baking as fighter jets flew low above my head, making their way to Gaza, a serious confrontation once again had erupted between Arab and Jew. Could anything be normal in my life?

There was no question as to why we had got together. It was evident from the instant rise in temperature I felt in my panties that I would have him. He was my idea of pure sexual desire. The toast to my spa holiday found us celebrating the occasion among other revellers at an open air nightclub. The heady atmosphere had brought our lips together as well as our bodies and I felt the heat of what surely was a semi hard-on pressed into my mound as we moved to the music. I was holding the back of his head, my fingers grabbing his hair as I crushed my lips to his, loving how full they felt. Oh, how I wanted to drop to my knees and unzip his trousers and unleash his manhood so I would see for the first time the stiffness the atmosphere had produced, and thoughts of animal lust were evident as I grabbed his firm butt, pulling his hips to mine.

There really is nothing better than feel and touch and at last what I longed for I had in the grip of my hands. Was this the beginning of the most erotic holiday I could ever imagine and were we about to play out every fantasy of sexual desire?

Well, that was then and this was now. I had let my imagination run away with me on the dance floor but reality struck in the bedroom as I was brought face to face with the very distant past. Of times spent with Mike, who my dear mother had desired for her future son in-law.

For what I discovered when Marchello stepped out of the shower, exposing his naked body to me for the first time, was to my shock and horror he had the penis the size of my little finger. Which just goes to prove that lightening CAN strike twice.

19365146R00165

Printed in Poland
by Amazon Fulfillment
Poland Sp. z o.o., Wrocław